Reagan'

Reagan's Cowboys

*Inside the 1984 Reelection
Campaign's Secret Operation
Against Geraldine Ferraro*

JOHN B. ROBERTS II

McFarland & Company, Inc., Publishers
Jefferson, North Carolina

LIBRARY OF CONGRESS CATALOGUING-IN-PUBLICATION DATA

Names: Roberts, John B., II, author.
Title: Reagan's cowboys : inside the 1984 reelection campaign's secret
operation against Geraldine Ferraro / John B. Roberts II.
Other titles: Inside the 1984 reelection campaign's secret
operation against Geraldine Ferraro
Description: Jefferson, North Carolina : McFarland & Company, Inc.
Publishers, 2020 | Includes index.
Identifiers: LCCN 2020024026 | ISBN 9781476678122 (paperback : acid free paper) ∞
ISBN 9781476641249 (ebook)
Subjects: LCSH: Roberts, John B., II. | Reagan, Ronald. | Presidents—United
States—Election—1984. | Political campaigns—United States—History—20th
century. | Political candidates—Research—United States. | United
States—Politics and government—1981-1989. | Ferraro, Geraldine. |
Vice-Presidential candidates—United States.
Classification: LCC E879 .R63 2020 | DDC 3243.973/0927—dc23
LC record available at https://lccn.loc.gov/2020024026

BRITISH LIBRARY CATALOGUING DATA ARE AVAILABLE

ISBN (print) 978-1-4766-7812-2
ISBN (ebook) 978-1-4766-4124-9

On the cover: President Reagan at the debate
in Kansas City, Missouri, 1984 (Ronald Reagan Presidential Library);
inset Geraldine Ferraro as a member of the U.S. House of Representatives

Printed in the United States of America

McFarland & Company, Inc., Publishers
Box 611, Jefferson, North Carolina 28640
www.mcfarlandpub.com

For Mary Pauline Porath
&
Lt. Col. Robert Benjamin Roberts

Acknowledgments

Without my wife Elizabeth's love, encouragement and assistance, I could not have written this book. She is my partner, my co-author on previous works, and my constant supporter in so many ways. She not only helped me make the time to write this manuscript, but she once again bore the sacrifice of becoming a "writer's widow" for the many months it took to complete the book. She was invaluable in reading and critiquing each draft. Her many helpful suggestions have made it a better book.

Without Lyn Nofziger's prodding, I would never have accumulated the notes and anecdotes that went into the making of this book. When I first went to work for former governor Reagan in the late 1970s, Lyn told me to keep a journal and repeated that advice when I joined Reagan-Bush '84. Thanks to him, the material I needed to chronicle this aspect of the 1984 presidential race exists.

My agent and former editor, Bob Shuman of Marit Literary Agency, has my gratitude for his faith in my writing career. Bob's support made this book possible.

I would also like to thank Michael Pinckney at the Ronald Reagan Presidential Library for his help in curating the photographs. The Reagan Library has a remarkable collection of more than one million photographs and generously makes them available to authors at a nominal cost.

Liz Guerra assisted me as I exhumed the past and threw light on the dark intersection of politics and organized crime. I am grateful to her for her help.

Finally, I want to acknowledge the contribution of our Border Collie, Sasha, whose walks were considerably shorter during the days spent writing the book as she loyally kept me company in my office. Her patience will be rewarded with longer hikes in the near future.

Table of Contents

Acknowledgments   vi

Preface   1

1. "Who did I piss off in this town?"   7
2. Out of the Rose Garden   12
3. A Field of White Crosses   24
4. Ferraro Enters the Fray   42
5. Promise and Peril   58
6. Just Because You're Paranoid…   64
7. Yours, Mine and Ours   73
8. Frenemies   84
9. Implausible Deniability   92
10. Watergate Redux   99
11. Our Man on the Hill   110
12. Failure Is an Orphan   121
13. Inquiring Minds   133
14. Under the Microscope   138
15. Mobbed Up?   146
16. Debate Disaster   159
17. The Heartland Special   171
18. Arrested and Booked   187
19. Eddie Chan, the Inside Man   198
20. The Verdict   213

Epilogue   220

Index   237

Preface

During the 1984 presidential campaign, I and a colleague were put in charge of a secret investigation of Geraldine Ferraro, the Democratic Party's vice-presidential candidate. The election pitted incumbent Republican president Ronald Reagan against former vice president Walter Mondale, who made history when he chose Geraldine Ferraro as his running mate. Until 1984, no major political party had a woman on its national ticket.

This book is my political memoir of how the White House and Reagan-Bush '84, the president's reelection committee, handled the unprecedented challenge posed by a female vice-presidential contender. The details of how our opposition research operation was run and why it was so effective have been kept secret for decades. Our efforts resulted in a congressional investigation into Ferraro's compliance with the Ethics in Government Act and the exposure of numerous connections between Geraldine Ferraro and organized crime figures.

In 1984 Ash Green, an editor at Alfred A. Knopf, encouraged me to write this story. I pursued it seriously until one of President Reagan's closest advisors, Stuart K. Spencer, asked me not to write the book. He felt it would embarrass the Reagans, particularly First Lady Nancy Reagan. Edward J. Rollins, Jr., Reagan's former campaign manager, seconded Stu's opinion.

I have decided to tell this story now because of the misuse of an opposition research dossier compiled by Christopher Steele, a former British intelligence officer, during the 2016 presidential election. Although Fusion GPS hired Steele to investigate President Donald Trump's business activities in Russia, the work was funded through a law firm which in turn was paid by Hillary Clinton's presidential campaign and the Democratic National Committee. The Steele dossier is more appropriately thought of as a product of the Clinton campaign.

Negative campaigning and maligning political opponents is as old as the Republic. There is ample precedent in American history for Hillary Clinton's disparagement of Trump supporters as belonging in a "basket of deplorables." Martha Washington called Thomas Jefferson a vile dema-

1

gogue. Federalist newspapers attacked Jefferson constantly and published the first charges that he fathered a child with Sally Hemings, his slave. John Quincy Adams was accused of procuring his family servant to provide sexual favors to the czar of Russia. The second time Andrew Jackson ran against Adams for president, Jackson's wife Rachel was smeared as a "convicted adulteress." As my book *Rating the First Ladies: The Women Who Influenced the Presidency* (Citadel Press, 2003) documents, such tactics are ordinary in American politics.

What is extraordinary about the 2016 presidential campaign is the involvement of a British ex-spy and his solicitation of Russian sources, who may well have been under the influence of the Russian government, to compile negative information about then-candidate Donald J. Trump. While foreign interference in American elections is not unusual—in 1984 one of my tasks on the Reagan campaign was to identify the ways that the Soviet Union would attempt to influence the election—it is unusual for a presidential candidate to not only invite, but pay for, such foreign involvement.

My aim in publishing this book is three-fold: to better inform the voters about the inner workings of presidential campaigns; to cast light on the need for candidates and their political operatives to adhere to certain norms and avoid actions that could undermine the integrity of our elections; and to complete the historical record of the 1984 presidential contest.

This is not a comprehensive history of the 1984 campaign. It features the 100 days between Representative Geraldine Ferraro's selection as Walter Mondale's running mate and Election Day and the tactics used by the Reagan campaign in discovering and exposing Ferraro's links to organized crime. I have chosen to tell the story as it unfolded in 1984, rather than from the perspective of hindsight. Because it is a first-person account, I do not attempt to go beyond the confines of what I knew as it was happening. For example, the book does not give any perspective on how the same events were viewed inside the Mondale-Ferraro campaign. Nor is it a comprehensive account of the Reagan-Bush presidential campaign. It is my inside account of the substantial risk to President Reagan's reelection posed by Geraldine Ferraro's candidacy and our subsequent investigations into her finances, her associates, and her background.

Other than in this preface, I do not discuss the use of opposition research in the 2016 presidential election. By revealing the tradecraft and illustrating the self-imposed constraints under which we operated during the 1984 presidential race, it is my hope that readers will be able to see for themselves the contrasts between the 1984 and the 2016 presidential races and appreciate why it is important for presidential campaigns to be judicious in how they gather and use opposition research about political opponents.

As I write this preface, U.S. attorney John Durham's criminal probe into the origins of Crossfire Hurricane, the FBI's counter-intelligence investigation of President Trump's 2016 election campaign, is still underway. Durham's task is to determine whether the FBI had sufficient justification to launch its investigation of a presidential candidate during an election or whether it exceeded and abused its authority.

The Clinton campaign's opposition research dossier played an important role in the FBI's investigation. It was used to obtain Foreign Intelligence Surveillance Act (FISA) court warrants to eavesdrop on Trump campaign official Carter Page, even though the CIA and FBI could not verify many of the allegations in the dossier. Additional Clinton campaign opposition research information was funneled to the FBI through a Justice Department official, Bruce Ohr, whose wife Nellie was employed by Fusion GPS to search for damaging information about Donald J. Trump.

The Justice Department's inspector general, Michael Horowitz, has already concluded that the FBI committed 17 serious errors or omissions in its applications to the FISA court for warrants to listen to the telephone calls and monitor the communications of Trump campaign staffer Carter Page. Horowitz also discovered that an FBI official altered an email to conceal the fact that Mr. Page had already reported his contacts with Russians to the Central Intelligence Agency.

Horowitz was particularly damning with regard to the dossier. His report states:

> The FBI concluded, among other things, that although consistent with known efforts by Russia to interfere in the 2016 U.S. elections, much of the material in the Steele election reports, including allegations about Donald Trump and members of the Trump campaign relied upon in the Carter Page FISA applications, could not be corroborated; that certain allegations were inaccurate or inconsistent with information gathered by the Crossfire Hurricane team; and that the limited information that was corroborated related to time, location, and title information, much of which was publicly available.

Attorney General William Barr went one step further. "The Inspector General's report now makes clear," he said, "that the FBI launched an intrusive investigation of a U.S. presidential campaign on the thinnest of suspicions that, in my view, were insufficient to justify the steps taken."

In late January 2020, the Justice Department concluded that in at least two of the FISA court applications to continue surveillance of Carter Page the FBI lacked "probable cause to believe that Page was acting as an agent of a foreign power."

Despite the lack of corroboration of its meatiest allegations, the dossier was freely shared with news organizations. None of them could sufficiently substantiate its claims to warrant publication. Shortly before Donald J. Trump was sworn into office, BuzzFeed published the dossier's allegations without verifying their authenticity. By writing news reports about BuzzFeed's action, the same media organizations that had been unable to verify the dossier's allegations were now able to justify publishing them as a story-about-the-story. What followed next were more baseless allegations about collusion between the Trump campaign and the Russian government, followed by Independent Counsel Robert Mueller's investigation.

In short, the Clinton campaign succeeded in using dubiously-sourced, uncorroborated information to damage a political rival, cast doubt on the legitimacy of a presidential election, tarnish the reputation of the FBI, and indirectly cause an impeachment crisis. During President Trump's first term in office, the dossier and many of the events it helped set in motion have convulsed American politics. Spreading unverified rumors about the opposition isn't research. It's slander, pure poison in the body politic.

The standards we established in 1984 are a model for future presidential campaigns to follow.

In contrast to 2016, the opposition research effort we undertook during the 1984 presidential race deliberately excluded the FBI and any other Executive Branch agency or department. The dossier we compiled on Geraldine Ferraro and her husband, John Zaccaro, was in depth and verified before any information was shared with Congress or the press. Partially as a result of the information we developed, an official investigation into Ferraro's compliance with congressional ethics rules was launched. Unlike in 2016, the results of that official investigation confirmed the majority of the charges against her.

Conversations in the book have been reconstructed from notes I made during the campaign, recollections written down in the years following, and my memory of events. While I have taken care to faithfully report the gist of these conversations, they are generally not verbatim accounts and others may recall details differently. In some instances, such as the briefings on Ferraro by the campaign's director of survey research Chuck Rund and the campaign strategy conference calls, the quotes are taken verbatim from my contemporaneous notes and memos.

For decades original documents from our investigations of Ferraro have remained in my custody. These include property records, Federal Election Commission files, documents sent by anonymous tipsters, notes of meetings, contemporaneous press clippings, copies of Reagan-Bush '84 memoranda and reports, and the dossier we compiled on Geraldine Ferraro and John Zaccaro's business dealings. These records amount to thousands of pages of documents. Even so, not everything we did in the course of probing Ferraro's candidacy was written down. Some information was considered so sensitive that it was not committed to paper. Often, the pace of the campaign made it impossible to stop and take time to write down the events of the day.

This is the first book ever published about the Reagan campaign's secret opposition research into Geraldine Ferraro. While numerous books have been published about the 1984 presidential election, only a few mention the opposition research effort and the details they contain are generally both scant and inaccurate. Those wanting an account of Geraldine Ferraro's reaction to the scrutiny her candidacy underwent will find it in *Ferraro: My Story* by Geraldine A. Ferraro with Linda Bird Francke (Bantam, 1985).

1

"Who did I piss off in this town?"

Miami Herald *Newspaper*
One Herald Plaza
Miami, Florida
July 27, 2005

Ignoring the "No Firearms" sign on the glass doors, Art Teele strolled across the *Miami Herald's* polished terrazzo floor to the lobby reception desk. Wearing his trademark tortoise shell-rimmed glasses and dressed in a sky-blue shirt and dark pin-striped suit with a burgundy handkerchief tucked into his breast pocket, he had the look and bearing of the prominent south Florida politician he was. At 59, with the tight waves of his hair graying, he was almost patrician.

Art had been in public service for decades. After graduating from college, he enlisted in the military. He fought in Vietnam and later served as a judge advocate general for the 18th Airborne at Ft. Bragg, North Carolina. In the 1980 presidential campaign he was national chairman of Blacks for Reagan-Bush.

During President Reagan's first term Teele headed the Department of Transportation's Urban Mass Transit Administration, where he was responsible for a budget of almost $800 million. In Reagan's 1984 reelection campaign, Art played a pivotal but unsung role in running a secret opposition research effort against Democratic vice-presidential nominee Geraldine Ferraro. That is how we met. Neither of us knew when we met that July in 1984 that our secret project would be the beginning of a professional relationship that turned into a personal friendship spanning decades.

After Reagan's reelection, Art returned to Miami and entered private law practice. He became a rising star in Republican politics when he was elected Dade County commissioner in 1990. In 1996, he made a bid to be Miami metro mayor. I helped him on that campaign. Art ran a good campaign but was defeated in a run-off by Alex Penelas.

7

Undeterred, Art ran to represent the city's downtrodden Overtown neighborhood as city commissioner and won. During the era of Jim Crow, Overtown was called Colored Town. Teele was a popular commissioner who didn't hesitate to throw himself into controversy if he thought it was in the interest of his constituents. As chairman of the Community Redevelopment Agency overseeing the neighborhood's revitalization, Teele made political enemies among developers less interested in building up local businesses than in getting hold of real estate with development potential.

Art paused in the *Herald*'s lobby and called Jim DeFede for the second time that day. DeFede was the only newspaper columnist in town Art trusted.

DeFede was surprised that Teele was in the building. The ex-city commissioner had called him just an hour earlier, sounding distraught and defeated. At one point, DeFede thought Art might cry. They had spoken for about 20 minutes.

"Who did I piss off in this town?" Art had begun the conversation. He recapped the avalanche of problems he faced, beginning with an incident the previous August. Teele, a former Army Ranger and Vietnam War veteran who had been awarded the Bronze Star and Purple Heart, had gotten into a car chase through the streets of Miami with a man he thought was stalking his wife. When Teele confronted the man, several other cars pulled over. A squad of detectives from the state attorney's public corruption unit had been tailing Art and his wife. Before the officers identified themselves, Teele warned them that he carried a gun and would defend his family. A few days later he was arrested and charged with "corruption by threat" and battery with a car.

Citing the arrest, Governor Jeb Bush severed Teele's political lifelines by suspending him from his job as a city commissioner. The suspension wasn't mandatory; with the charges unproven it was within Bush's discretionary power to let Art keep working until the charges against him were proven in court. Bush called Art "a good friend" and "a good public servant" but suspended him anyway.

DeFede knew the problems Art faced but listened sympathetically.

In December, Teele was arrested a second time and charged with taking kickbacks from contractors. Miami-Dade State Attorney Katherine F. Rundle held a news conference to spotlight the charges against Miami's only African American city commissioner. The following May, Teele lost his trial on charges stemming from the run-in with the detectives and was sentenced to attend an anger management course, two years of probation, and 200 hours of community service. In July he was indicted on federal charges of money laundering and wire fraud in connection with an 8-A minority contract, a category of federal contract for businesses headed by women or minorities.

"They've got a deal out on the streets," Art told DeFede. "If anyone comes forward with damaging information about me, they can get a get-out-of-jail free card."

Art told the columnist that prosecutors were offering deals to individuals charged or convicted of unrelated crimes in exchange for implicating him in their corruption probe. Art said he was being set up and was confident he would lose if he took his chances in court.

The latest outrage was that day's cover story in *Miami New Times*, an alternative newspaper. The headline was "Tales of Teele: Sleaze Stories." The piece was written by a journalist named Francisco Alvarado. The article was accompanied by cover art and illustrations that gave it the appearance of a graphic novel. It was based on redacted police informant files deliberately released far in advance of Teele's trial on corruption charges. It was prosecutorial hardball.

One source, Fredrick Davis, told a lurid tale of having oral and anal sex with Teele when Art was high on cocaine. Davis, a self-described transsexual prostitute in jail awaiting trial on charges of assaulting a police officer, claimed that Teele was a client of his. The alternative weekly printed excerpts from his informant reports verbatim, without reaching out to Art or his attorney for comment or independently verifying the allegations despite multiple inconsistencies in Davis' account to the police. It was a gross violation of basic journalistic standards.

Teele told DeFede he was sure prosecutors had disclosed the investigative dossier in order to undermine his credibility with the African American ministry. Black preachers had always been a pillar of Teele's strength with his constituents. Prosecutors knew that many African American ministers took Biblical admonitions against homosexuality literally. Any hint that Art might be gay would undercut his support in the community when he needed it most.

"You know what happens when you Google my name?" Art asked DeFede. "The transvestite allegations come up. The transvestite allegations come up! That's the way everyone's going to remember me."

Art was distraught that this was the way his decades in public life were ending, but he was more worried about the impact on his wife and son than on his legacy. He denied wrongdoing to DeFede, knocked down the latest charges and allegations, protested his innocence.

DeFede told him to have faith in his lawyers and asked if Art wanted him to write a column about how prosecutors were trying to destroy him with the black ministers. Teele told him no.

"Jim, I thank you for your kindness," Art wrapped up the conversation. "You are one of the only reporters I trust. You are one of the few people I trust."

When the first phone call was finished, DeFede felt that Teele was calmer, more stable. DeFede pushed the button and stopped recording the call. He hadn't asked Art for permission or told him he was being taped.

The second phone call was short. Art told DeFede he was leaving a package for him in the lobby. The columnist said he could come down in 20 minutes and get it.

Art told him not to worry. It could wait until morning.

Jim said thanks. Art thanked him in return and said goodbye.

Felix Nazco was working at the reception desk that afternoon. After Art hung up the phone, he asked Nazco for a favor. He wanted Nasco to ask DeFede to please tell Art's wife, Stephanie, that Art loved her. It was an odd request, but Feliz Nasco wrote it down and had Teele look it over to make sure it was right.

Then Art took a Sig Sauer semi-automatic pistol out of a green canvas bag he carried and walked toward the center of the lobby. Alarmed, Nasco alerted security to put the building on lockdown. The police were alerted. Several cruisers raced to One Herald Plaza. As word spread throughout the building that the former commissioner was about to shoot himself, journalists hurried from their desks with cameras and recorders to cover the story.

When the police arrived, Art calmly put the gun to his head.

He fired into his right temple and fell to the floor, face up. He lay in full view of the press as blood streamed from the exit wounds in the back of his head. The spectacle was broadcast live on the 6 o'clock evening news. When paramedics arrived, Art was conscious and could blink his eyes in answer to their questions. He was still alive when he was taken to Jackson Memorial Medical Center.

There, at 7:50 p.m., Arthur E. Teele, Jr., was pronounced dead.

I'd just moved from Florida to Colorado when I heard the news through the political grapevine that connects veterans of Ronald Reagan's political career from his earliest days as governor of California to the glory years in the White House. I couldn't believe that Art was gone. When I read the press coverage and especially the *Miami New Times*, I didn't recognize the politician being profiled as the Art Teele I knew. The more I read the more I doubted the veracity of the allegations being made and the basis for the legal charges against him. It looked to me as if Art was being set up, through dubiously-sourced and sensationalized leaks and deals for leniency made with convicted criminals in exchange for incriminating evidence against him.

I was furious. I thought about going to Miami and devoting the time and resources it would take to uncover what looked to me like a plot against Art. I had no illusions about the clannishness of the town and the strong divisions between the Cuban-American, African American and Anglo communities. The polling and focus group research we did for Art's 1996 mayoral campaign clearly showed Miami's racial and ethnic polarization. I was sure the answers I sought lay in Miami's murky cauldron of clashing cultures and political rivalries.

Whoever was behind this hit job on Art's character and career was more interested in destroying him than in exposing wrongdoing. It looked to me like someone in a position of authority was abusing their power. In the process, they'd driven a good man, my good friend, to kill himself.

Twenty-one years earlier, in the 1984 Reagan-Bush campaign, we carried out our job in a completely different way. When Art and I were charged with investigating allegations of Mafia ties made about Congresswoman Geraldine Ferraro, the Democratic nominee for vice president, we rejected the unethical and probably illegal tactics employed by Art's current adversaries. We didn't leak government files or give journalists unverified news tips from doubtful sources.

Where we found evidence that Ferraro had broken the rules, we encouraged the appropriate officials to investigate. But we never urged an investigation that wasn't warranted just to embarrass the opponent. Without powers of subpoena, without authority to use search warrants, without the ability to cut plea bargains with witnesses or accomplices, we nonetheless unearthed compelling evidence of connections between Geraldine Ferraro and organized crime figures.

Art Teele and I didn't know one another in 1984 when we were thrust together in an intense, risky investigation of Geraldine Ferraro that lasted from late July until the first week in November. In a little more than 100 days, we progressed from learning to work together to forging mutual trust and sharing deep secrets to genuine appreciation and admiration of each other's skills and ethics. We started out as strangers but ended up as buddies. It was a friendship that endures today.

This is the story of how that collaboration converted Geraldine Ferraro's candidacy for vice president from a serious threat to Ronald Reagan's reelection into a net plus for the president when the final votes were tallied.

2

Out of the Rose Garden

Office of Planning and Evaluation
Room 375 Old Executive Office Building
The White House
February 1984

Whether I wanted it or not, change was in the air in the winter of 1984. Over the past several weeks, Edward J. Rollins, Jr., had called several times to ask me to join the Reagan-Bush '84 reelection campaign. After several years as assistant to the president for political affairs, Ed had been named the campaign manager.

To complicate matters further, between Ed's calls the State Department offered me a place in its upcoming Foreign Service Class, a post I'd applied for back in 1979.

When I left London in the summer of 1980, I had no intention of staying in the United States. An Oxford buddy and I had just launched a magazine when I was notified by the State Department that I'd passed the written Foreign Service test and needed to appear for interviews and an oral assessment. They were only administered in the United States, so I flew from London to Los Angeles on what I thought was a trip home for a few weeks. My plan was to visit family in Orange County, meet with a publisher and a former employer in Los Angeles, then go to San Francisco for the Foreign Service interviews and oral exam, meet with more family in Nevada, and then fly back to London.

In Los Angeles I dropped by Reagan's campaign headquarters to meet with my old boss, Franklyn C. Nofziger. Lyn had hired me in the late 1970s as an editorial assistant at Citizens for the Republic, former governor Ronald Reagan's Santa Monica–based political action committee.

I gave Lyn a copy of our magazine and some articles I'd written about Reagan for British publications. He looked them over, and to my surprise offered me a job in the campaign press office at national headquarters. He wanted me to start right after the GOP convention.

I accepted, thinking that I would work to the end of the campaign and then return to England. But one thing led to another. When Reagan won, I took a job as director of news and information for the presidential inauguration. Next came a stint in the White House Speechwriter's Office. Then I moved to the Republican National Committee as deputy director of communications, where I was put in charge of special projects supporting Reagan's legislative agenda during the Administration's first year in office.

By 1983, I was back in the White House as associate director of the Office of Planning and Evaluation (OPE), a job that involved tracking the progress of Reagan's top policy priorities and alerting the president to developing trends. OPE was often described as the White House think-tank. It gave me access to all of the White House polling and experts in government, academia, and non-profit organizations. We set up briefings for the president on foreign and domestic policy priorities and emerging issues.

In early 1984, I was still working at the Office of Planning and Evaluation. I liked the policy job. It encompassed a broad range of domestic and foreign affairs issues and gave me great latitude. I was thrilled to be in the Cabinet Room with Ronald Reagan. The work was interesting and varied, and I had no intention of leaving when Rollins began asking me to work on the 1984 reelection campaign.

Then Nofziger intervened.

One day at work he called my direct line.

"Your White House job doesn't mean a damned thing," he said. "You think you'll still have it if we lose this election? The only thing that matters now is getting this man reelected. You have friends over here, and your friends need you. So when are you coming?"

Nofziger was one of Reagan's longest-serving advisors. He'd been a reporter for Copley News Service until Reagan ran for governor of California in 1966, when Lyn was drafted into the job of press secretary. When Reagan won, Lyn became the governor's communications director in Sacramento. He was a major player in Reagan's failed 1976 presidential bid, after which he managed Reagan's political action committee, Citizens for the Republic (CFTR).

CFTR's offices were in Santa Monica, California, and I was paid just enough to afford a studio apartment on West Channel Drive across from the beach. It was a sweet set-up that allowed me to walk under the Pacific Coast Highway in the morning through a tunnel, body surf for 20 minutes, shower, shave, eat and make a five-minute commute up the bluff to Santa Monica. Life in Los Angeles in your early 20s doesn't get any better.

I told Lyn I would give him an answer by the end of the week, hung up the phone, and lit a Marlboro Light.

My choice was between a career in the Foreign Service and a second presidential term for Ronald Reagan. My then-wife was opposed to the idea, but I was seriously interested in the diplomatic corps. Some of the kids I went to middle school with in Spain came from diplomatic families, and I was fascinated by their stories about different countries and cultures. In London I was invited to a reception given by the U.S. ambassador for visiting state legislators where I made friends with a Foreign Service officer who was a Russian specialist. The more I learned about the life of an FSO, the more I wanted to have a career that took me overseas and gave me the opportunity to learn more foreign languages.

One of the perks of my current job was that my best friend, Tony Blankley, worked in the same office. We carpooled together and often stopped at a restaurant off the George Washington Parkway called Potowmack Landing for cocktails on our way home.

I told Tony about my dilemma. We got away from work a few minutes earlier than usual to have time to discuss matters freely outside of the office. The sun had already set and the lights shining on the Washington Monument and Jefferson Memorial gave the stone a warm glow. Our view from the bar included the Capitol Dome and the city's lights shimmering on the Potomac.

"What specifically do they want you to do on the campaign?" Tony asked.

"Lyn wants me in all the strategy meetings," I said, "The title is senior advisor."

He asked me about the Foreign Service offer.

"It's in the political cone," I said. "That's very rare. Most junior FSOs start out in the consular cone."

"Would it still be open after the campaign ends?"

I shook my head.

"If I decline this opportunity, I go back on the waiting list until another equivalent need opens up. It could be months, or it could be years. It took three years from when I completed processing until this offer came up."

Tony walked me through the pros and cons and in the end encouraged me to go with my heart. I knew Tony well and could see that he was excited about the offer to work on the campaign in a senior capacity, but I also knew he'd never push his own preference on me. As we walked through the parking lot to his car, I felt no closer to a decision.

"One choice could mean a 40-year career," I said. "The other won't last any longer than four years, and that's only if we win."

Tony nodded sagely. We both read the White House polls prepared by Richard B. Wirthlin's firm, Decision Making Information (DMI). Dick Wirthlin had been Reagan's pollster since 1968. Our office was one of the handful in the White House that received a copy of every one of DMI's polls as soon as they were available. They were as thick as phone books. The information in the cross-tabulations, which broke down poll results by rich economic and demographic detail, fascinated us. We both devoured them.

In hypothetical head-to-head polling Wirthlin did in late 1983, the former astronaut and U.S. senator John Glenn beat Ronald Reagan. A number of other Democrats were equally formidable. At this stage, it was impossible to tell who would win the Democratic nomination or how strong a candidate they would be against Reagan. But one thing was clear from the polling: Reagan was not a shoo-in. He was vulnerable to the right candidate and might be yet one more in a string of one-term presidencies that began with Richard Nixon and continued through Gerald Ford and Jimmy Carter.

That night I had one more discussion about the Foreign Service with my wife. Our son was barely a year old, and she was reticent to agree to a life overseas in what might be a series of postings in the Third World. There was no way I could leave my son, so I made one of the toughest decisions in my career.

The next morning I called the State Department and turned down their offer. Then I called Lyn Nofziger and told him I would come onboard as soon as I could. My boss, Bruce Chapman, was disappointed but understanding. He thought my talents were better applied to policymaking than political campaigns but made it easy for me to wrap up my work at the White House and start on the campaign.

From left to right, Mike Deaver, Lyn Nofziger, Ronald Reagan, Frank Donatelli and Jim Baker in the White House, May 9, 1984 (courtesy Ronald Reagan Presidential Library).

Because the Office of Planning and Evaluation fell under the purview of Counselor to the President Edwin Meese III, I met with him to explain my departure. He had interviewed me before I was hired at OPE and given me my first tasks. A colleague of Reagan's since his Sacramento days, Meese was one of the "troika" who ran the White House. The other two were White House Deputy Chief of Staff and Assistant to the President Michael K. Deaver and Chief of Staff James A. Baker III. Baker was the only member of the troika who had not been a longtime Reagan confidant. Meese supported my decision to join the campaign and said he'd welcome me back when the election was over.

*   *   *

After viewing several sites for the Reagan-Bush '84 headquarters, including one that overlooked a cemetery, Ed Rollins leased several floors in the National Association of Counties Building (NACO). The location was close to Congress and a short drive down Pennsylvania Avenue to the White House. My new office was on the fourth floor, one door away from Rollins' corner office on one end and down the hallway from deputy campaign manager Lee Atwater's office at the other end.

The campaign headquarters was near the Hyatt Hotel and Mitch Snyder's homeless shelter. Snyder was an activist and ardent critic of the Reagan Administration. The shelter drew frequent attention from the D.C. police, who cleared dozens of arrest warrants on each visit. Its presence made some of the women walking to their cars after dark nervous, but most of the homeless who hung around the neighborhood were harmless. The neighborhood had some good Irish pubs and a restaurant called the LBJ Bar and Grill just across the street that might have been hot in the mid-'60s but was definitely past its zenith.

My first impression of the headquarters was that it was relatively plush for a political campaign. By comparison, Reagan's 1980 headquarters across the Potomac in Arlington, Virginia, were downright gritty. The NACO building was clean and spacious, the elevators were modern and free of the musty smells that seem to sprout from their shafts in older buildings, the carpeting was thick and new. Most offices had windows and glass partitions that made the entire working space airy and bright. There were plenty of conference rooms for large and small working groups, and there were just enough offices with no windows or glass partitions for those behind-closed-door meetings that politics requires.

Nofziger wanted me included in all the campaign strategy sessions, a weekly senior staff conference call on Saturday mornings to coordinate action for the coming week, and a daily morning "Attack Meeting" Lyn chaired on how to respond to attacks the Democratic candidates were making on Reagan.

Lyn created a network of surrogates—former Republican officials, members of Congress, celebrities, all outside the campaign—to launch daily attacks on the Democrats. The purpose of the Attack Meetings was to develop the messages for the surrogates to use, identify who should deliver the attack and when and where it should happen, and then coordinate with the surrogates to make sure they carried out the attack. Early in the campaign, it was the only meeting in the building that resulted in daily political engagement with the Democrats.

Throughout the winter and spring of 1984, Reagan used the advantages of incumbency to run a Rose Garden reelection strategy. Its essence was for Reagan to remain presidential, seemingly above politics, throughout the Democratic presidential primaries while his opponents flayed one another in their quest to win the nomination. The Rose Garden strategy meant that most of the action still centered on the White House.

On the campaign, we busied ourselves with building the state organizations, preparing opposition research on the leading Democratic presidential contenders and potential vice presidents, and developing the advertising strategy.

Throughout the Democratic primaries Dick Wirthlin gave Walter Mondale no more than a 55 percent chance of winning the nomination. Beginning with a surprise victory in New Hampshire, Colorado senator Gary Hart had run a formidable campaign against Jimmy Carter's former vice president. But in a late May conference call, Wirthlin raised Mondale's odds of beating Hart to 70 percent.

The "confidence coefficient" was one of the metrics Wirthlin used to gauge the turning points in a political campaign. It measured the number of attacks candidates made on their primary campaign opponents to the number they made on the opposition party's candidate. By comparing the number of Mondale's attacks on Hart to his attacks on Reagan, it showed that by late spring Mondale's confidence he would beat Hart had risen to 66 percent.

Mondale was certain to emphasize the war and peace theme.

The image of Reagan as a war-monger was a critical weakness that had yet to be dispelled. It had dogged him since the 1980 campaign, when Jimmy Carter, the incumbent president, depicted Reagan as a B-grade movie actor with a nostalgic vision of America who couldn't be trusted to have his hands on the nuclear launch codes.

Carter also attacked Reagan as racist. The lowest blow, authorized by Carter, came from Patricia Roberts Harris, Cabinet Secretary for Health, Education and Welfare. Harris delivered a hard-hitting speech saying Reagan would "divide black and white, rich and poor, Christian and Jew." She finished her race-baiting diatribe by saying that whenever she heard Reagan speak she was "reminded of the specter of the Ku Klux Klan."

Carter's negative attacks backfired when the two candidates met in the 1980 presidential debate. In front of a nationwide television audience of millions, Carter invoked his daughter Amy's fears of nuclear war to make his challenger seem dangerous.

Responding to a charge that he opposed Medicare, Reagan defused the attacks with a devastating one-line retort.

"There you go again," he said, and he went on to correct the record. Polls showed audiences interpreted Reagan's response as a rebuke to all of Carter's attacks.

By 1984, the public knew that Reagan wasn't racist. But the jury was still out on whether his defense build-up and assertive foreign policy would result in a war.

When the Soviet Union deployed SS-20 medium-range nuclear missiles capable of hitting any city in Europe from deep inside Russian territory, tensions between Washington and Moscow reached levels unseen since the 1962 Cuban Missile Crisis.

NATO, the North Atlantic Treaty Organization, lacked a comparable deterrent to the Russian SS-20s, which threatened the stability of the fragile nuclear balance between the United States and U.S.S.R. Reagan's response was to move thousands of Pershing II missiles and ground-launched cruise missiles into Europe, where they could easily strike Moscow if the Russians used SS-20s against Europe.

The deployment of these intermediate- and short-range nuclear weapons was immensely controversial and spawned widespread demonstrations that came to be known as the Nuclear Freeze Movement. Millions of Europeans marched through the streets of major cities in protest, and almost a million Americans joined them in a demonstration in New York City. The U.S. entertainment media quickly got in on the act. In 1983, ABC television broadcast a nuclear holocaust film, *The Day After*, about a fictional war between NATO and the Warsaw Pact that escalates into a nuclear exchange. More than 100 million Americans viewed the movie, which starred JoBeth Williams, Jason Robards, and John Lithgow.

Between the protests, the entertainment industry, and a steady barrage of Russian propaganda, a sizeable portion of the European and U.S. population viewed Reagan as a dangerous ideologue whose defense build-up could lead to nuclear war with the Soviet Union.

*   *   *

One of my tasks on the reelection campaign was to analyze the ways in which the Russians would try to influence the 1984 presidential election. Tensions between the United States and the Soviet Union had already resulted in the Russians boycotting the 1984 Summer Olympics, scheduled to be held in Los Angeles in July. I came up with a five-page memo outlining actions the Russians could take, ranging from launching a "peace offensive" public diplomacy campaign to staging an incident in Nicaragua (where the United States was backing a Contra rebellion against the ruling Marxist government) to using a terrorist proxy to disrupt the Summer Olympics.

The minimum the Soviet Union would do to interfere in the election would be to foster fears of a confrontation between the United States and Russia through official statements and actions. They would also use front groups to introduce propaganda into the news cycle.

The Russians exploited the Nuclear Freeze Movement, providing covert funding to pro–Soviet groups to participate in the protests. We assumed that the Russians would escalate their efforts to turn U.S. and European public opinion against Reagan. They were also actively exploiting political divisions inside NATO, including attempts to influence foreign elections. Soviet diplomats had recently been expelled from several European countries after being caught meddling in their elections, and there was every reason to believe it would happen in America.

Among his close staff, Reagan used humor in talking about the Cold War competition between the nuclear arch-rivals. A favorite joke he liked to tell involved a Russian and an American boasting about whose country was the freest.

It started with the American boasting.

"We're so free we can say anything we want about the president and the government can't do anything about it."

"Oh yeah?" says the Russian. "We're so free we can stand right outside the Kremlin and criticize Chairman Chernenko until we're hoarse."

"I can beat that. I once took a leak on the presidential limousine."

"That's nothing," the Russian says. "I once took a dump right in the middle of Red Square while Chernenko was giving a speech."

"That's pretty impressive," the American concedes. "I guess I have a confession to make about the limousine. The president wasn't in it when I pissed on it."

"I've got a confession to make too," the Russian shrugs. "I had my pants on when I took that dump."

But there was nothing funny about the high stakes in the U.S.-Soviet confrontation. Healing the rift in U.S. and European public opinion wasn't just important to Reagan's reelection. It was crucial to attaining his policy objective of deterring war with the Soviet Union and bringing its leaders to the bargaining table on nuclear arms control.

Reagan had an abhorrence of nuclear weapons and genuinely feared an atomic apocalypse. It was what made him embrace the idea of a Strategic Defense Initiative to create a shield against incoming nuclear missiles. There

Lyn Nofziger and Ronald Reagan sharing a laugh, December 12, 1981 (courtesy Ronald Reagan Presidential Library).

was nothing he wanted more than to reduce the number of nuclear weapons in the world in order to prevent the collapse of civilization.

It was a message we were determined to get across to the voters. By late May, Doug Watts, the national advertising director for the campaign, had finalized plans for the first batch of Reagan's television ads. Doug was still in his 30s and hadn't worked on a national campaign, but his track record in California's ultra-expensive political campaigns and advertising markets more than qualified him. He had been communications director for California governor George Deukmejian and coordinated the advertising during Deukmejian's successful 1982 campaign.

Watts worked directly with Michael K. Deaver's deputy, Michael A. Mc-Manus, on the campaign advertising. Deaver's title was White House deputy chief of staff and assistant to the president. He had worked with Reagan since he was governor of California and had a close personal relationship with the president. More than any other senior White House aide, he was responsible for Reagan's image. Working closely with First Lady Nancy Reagan, Deaver came up with the idea of using Madison Avenue advertising agency professionals instead of political campaign advertising experts.

Instead of hiring a single advertising agency, Deaver began recruiting talented advertising executives. Phil Dusenberry of BBDO, Hal Riney of Ogilvy & Mather, Tom Messner of Ally & Gargano, Jim Travis of Della Femina Traviano, and Sig Rogich of R&R Partners were among the group that Deaver and Travis dubbed the "Tuesday Team." They were named for Election Day, the first Tuesday in November.

The group's introduction to political campaigns came in the latter half of March, when Dick Wirthlin, Robert M. Teeter (another pollster on contract to the campaign), television producer Roger E. Ailes, and Doug Watts met with them in New York.

Wirthlin gave a sobering briefing on the polls and outlook in the Electoral College vote. The ad agency executives quickly grasped that the outcome of the election was up for grabs. In that first meeting, the outline of the ad campaign that came to be called "Morning in America" was sketched out.

At a subsequent meeting in the Old Executive Office Building, the Tuesday Team made their formal pitch to senior White House and campaign officials. The meeting had barely begun when Ronald Reagan popped in.

"I figured if you're going to sell soap," he said, "you ought to see the bar."

He invited questions about his policies, but the group was hushed.

"Well, I'm going now," Reagan said, "before I destroy the illusion!"

Watts invited me to join some of the strategy sessions for the ads. My task was to synthesize the key points our pollsters and strategists made about what the ads needed to accomplish politically as a guide for the Tuesday Team in applying their creative skills. Through the meetings I quickly got to know Watts. Doug was smart, organized, good at coaxing out insights and able to keep a meeting on track. He also had a wicked sense of humor.

Roger Ailes attended some of the meetings. Ailes had won several Emmys for his work as executive producer of *The Michael Douglas Show* and gone on to become a political consultant. Mike McManus was a constant presence.

A consensus developed that the advertising campaign needed to reinforce the renewal of hope taking place in America after the bruising 1970s, with its steep recession, an oil embargo, and the humiliating fall of Vietnam and seizure of the U.S. embassy in Iran. "Prouder, Stronger, Better" was one of the television spots in production. It began with the opening line "It's morning in America."

One of the TV spots Doug and Hal Riney produced was called "Bear." It featured a man alone in the woods. A voice-over narration that said there was a bear in the woods that might or might not be dangerous. The ad ended with the tag line "If there is a bear in the woods, isn't it good to be at least as strong as the bear?"

For political advertising, it was unique. Most political ads were straightforward to the point of being blunt. This one was based on ambiguity. It was the equivalent of abstract art compared to realism. It never mentioned de-

fense, or the Russians, or peace. It relied on the viewer to intuitively understand that the subject was Reagan's defense policy.

In mid–May Watts previewed the commercials for the campaign's senior
staff and key White House officials. White House Staff Secretary Richard G.
Darman disliked the ad campaign and wrote a detailed memo critiquing the
approach. He thought the ads, particularly those focusing on the heartland of
America, would seem old-fashioned and too nostalgic. He proposed advertising featuring high-technology that would associate Reagan with the future
as a way to blunt the age issue and also generate a sense of excitement about
a second term in office.

Wisely, Watts arranged a showing for the president and Mrs. Reagan
before skeptics like Darman had a chance to rally opposition. The president
and First Lady were enthused by all the ads, but Reagan was most impressed
by the Bear commercial. He felt it communicated his policy toward the Soviet
Union perfectly.

"I'd like a copy of that to take up to Capitol Hill and show those guys
right now," he told Doug and Rollins when the preview ended.

One of Reagan's last high-profile events in the Rose Garden strategy
was to commemorate the 40th anniversary of the D-Day invasion at Normandy on June 6. The trip to Normandy was to be preceded by state trips
to Ireland and England, replete with all the pomp and ceremony of a Buckingham Palace visit. The D-Day commemoration coincided with the California Democratic primary, a crucial contest where former vice president
Walter Mondale was expected to finally win enough delegates to clinch the
nomination.

The goal was to get television and press coverage contrasting Reagan
as a vigorous and thoughtful world leader against a haggard-looking Mondale; the bags under his eyes had grown steadily darker throughout the
hard-fought primary contests with Gary Hart. The contrast between a tired
politician claiming his party's nomination and an incumbent president pro-
claiming his policy of peace through strength in order to deter future world
wars was calculated to make a powerful political statement.

Reagan's press coverage was important to our policy objectives. As
much as we wanted to have an impact on American voters, we also wanted to
change European attitudes. In Europe public opinion about Reagan was still
highly negative due to Reagan's installation of short- and intermediate-range
nuclear weapons in western Europe.

The White House Office of Presidential Advance wanted me in Normandy because of my experience with the press and structuring of presidential events. Deaver had identified an event at the American military cemetery
at Omaha Beach as the "trip photo," the photo opportunity with the president
and First Lady most likely to summarize the theme of the visit and appeal to

newspaper and magazine photo editors as well as television producers. I was given responsibility for handling the site.

Deaver's theory about presidential events was that the pictures, whether video or photography, mattered more than the words reporters and television news correspondents used to describe the event. The visual image was what communicated best to people. Veteran speechwriters like James Hume described it this way: the ear is one-tenth the organ that the eye is. Memories are visual more often than verbal, and getting good pictures of Reagan at a presidential event would convey the right message even if the press coverage itself was critical.

My new assignment was a welcome break from my desk job at Reagan-Bush '84 reelection headquarters, but it was no vacation. In less than two weeks President Ronald Reagan would meet in Normandy with allied leaders of the G-7 to commemorate the D-Day landings and invasion of Nazi-occupied Europe. Mike Deaver expected the Normandy media coverage to boost Reagan's reelection effort. There were literally thousands of details that had to be planned to achieve the results Deaver anticipated. It was in the planning and execution of events like this that political strategies succeeded or failed. A mediocre strategy well executed would beat a brilliant but poorly-executed strategy any day of the week.

In the late 1970s when I was a graduate student at Oxford University, I jotted an entry in my journal about the Normandy anniversary commemorations. "D-Day was thirty-three years ago tomorrow," I noted. "Maybe I'll go to Normandy to mark the event." Seven years later I was on my way, along with the president of the United States.

3

A Field of White Crosses

Colleville-Sur-Mer
Normandy, France
May 26, 1984

The U.S. embassy vans sped us from Charles de Gaulle airport in Paris through the fields and hedgerows of Normandy, verdant in the late spring-time. I'd flown overnight with several other members of the White House advance team from Dulles Airport in Washington, D.C., where we'd talked the TWA gate agent into bumping up our government-rate coach class tickets into first-class seats.

The French countryside was stunning, a lush green expanse that stood in stark contrast to the urban sprawl outside Paris. This was my first visit to the country since 1980, when I lived in London and an English girlfriend and I spent a weekend in Paris. We crossed the English Channel on a hovercraft and took an express train straight to the metropolis. My views of the country-side were confined to what could be glimpsed through the train's windows. I looked forward to a few weeks in Normandy and a chance to get acquainted with rural France.

My briefing materials said thousands of World War II vets were ex-pected to come to Normandy for the 40th anniversary of D-Day. My father was a World War II veteran who flew in the 8th Army Air Force Bomber Command. He piloted a B-17 bomber on 50 combat missions, mainly over Germany. The casualties suffered by the 8th were the highest of any combat unit in World War II. For the first few years that the United States was in the war, the 8th carried the brunt of fighting against the Axis powers when they were at their peak.

When my brother and I pestered him enough, my dad told war stories about Messerschmitt fighters and German anti-aircraft batteries as bedtime stories. One weekend at Oxford I rented a car and made a trip to Bury St. Edmunds to try to find the location of his airfield. After querying some locals in a pub, I drove out to a farmer's field they thought might be the place. Some old Quonset huts, semi-circular metal pre-fab buildings used as barracks during the war, were still standing. The locals said the farmer used them to grow mushrooms. I tried to imagine the place filled with B-17s, the scene of his thrilling adventures as a 19-year-old bomber pilot.

My father spent 32 years in the Air Force and went on to fight in two more wars, Korea and Vietnam, earning a Bronze Star and numerous air combat awards and citations. In August 1982, he shot himself in the heart.

A few months after his suicide, the Vietnam War Memorial was unveiled in Washington. I wandered to the Mall to witness the thousands of veterans who marched that day. For the first time since the war's end Vietnam vets were allowed to publicly demonstrate pride without being reviled by protestors. After a decade of bearing humiliation they were reclaiming their honor. You could see it in their walk, sense it in the air as if it oozed from their pores. There was no swagger, just men standing tall.

I wondered what my father would have thought of the newfound reverence for the veterans' sacrifices. Would it have made any difference if he had lived to see this rebirth of national pride?

The French countryside showed no traces of the fighting, at least from what I'd seen so far. The farmhouses were tidy, the villages intact, the fertile fields splendidly lush. Unlike when my family lived in Spain in the 1960s, where bomb-split buildings and bullet-pocked facades from the Spanish civil war were common. During vacations to England and Germany in the late '60s, I'd seen entire blocks of devastated cities that remained as they'd been left in 1945, patiently waiting to be rebuilt. Those experiences, and growing up on a Minuteman missile base during the Cuban Missile Crisis and the height of Cold War nuclear tensions, made me keenly aware of the need to avoid wars.

As we approached the medieval city of Bayeux our pace slowed. The town's cathedral had a majestic spire. The vans wound their way through narrow streets to 9 Rue Tardif, where we had rooms in a three-star hotel called Le Bayeux. I grabbed my luggage and headed to Room 12 to change from the casual clothes I'd worn on the flight into khakis and a blue blazer, and then I had a quick bite to eat before we headed out to see our sites.

My first impression of the American cemetery was its immensity. It covered 176 acres on the bluffs overlooking Omaha Beach and included a visitors' center, a small chapel, and a memorial. What struck me most were the fields of white crosses, some with Stars of David, marking the graves of U.S. soldiers who died in the invasion. Beyond the edge of the bluffs, the English Channel shone brilliant blue.

As part of the D-Day ceremonies, French president François Mitterrand and President Ronald Reagan would jointly place a wreath in honor of the 9,387 American soldiers buried at the cemetery. The president and First Lady also wanted to spend a few moments of solitude to pray in a small chapel on the cemetery grounds.

Phillip Rivers was the superintendent of the cemetery. He worked for the American Battle Monuments Commission. We shook hands and one of the advance team who had gotten in a few days earlier walked me through the preliminary plan for the site.

"No press coverage at the chapel?" I said.

"No coverage. The press can cover the president and First Lady during the greeting and the drive to the chapel, but not inside."

I made a note.

From the chapel, the Reagans planned to walk to the grave of Theodore Roosevelt, Jr., and place a bouquet of flowers. I walked down to look at the site. This was where Mike Deaver thought the money shot was. He had identified Nancy's flower-laying moment as the single D-Day event that would be the most photogenic. The ground sloped away from the chapel in such a way that anyone walking in the rows of crosses would appear to be surrounded by them. It would be a powerful image of sacrifice and remembrance.

The wreath-laying with President Mitterrand was decidedly more formal. It called for national anthems to be played, an order of arms ceremony, and brief speeches. Following the remarks, the two presidents and their wives would proceed to view the Garden of the Missing. Reagan and Mitterrand would then walk past a joint U.S. and French military cordon to the visitors' center. The Mitterrands would depart by helicopter for Utah Beach, and the Reagans would follow a few minutes later on Marine One.

At Utah Beach numerous heads of state and royalty would be gathered, including Queen Elizabeth and Prince Philip, the Duke of Edinburgh. A 21-gun naval salute was planned, along with a fly-over by vintage British military aircraft. After color ceremonies, President Mitterrand was to speak.

Reagan's major speeches were to be delivered at Pointe du Hoc, where Army Rangers made a heroic assault on German artillery positions by scaling a cliff, and at Omaha Beach, scene of the fiercest fighting on June 6, 1944. These speeches were our opportunities to get the message across to the American and European public.

That was the plan. It was our job to make it happen.

CBS wanted live coverage of the D-Day commemoration. Nine months earlier, I'd worked with CBS producer Susan Zirinsky when Ronald and Nancy Reagan attended the memorial service at Camp Lejeune, North Carolina, for the 241 U.S. servicemen killed when terrorists drove a truck bomb into their barracks in Beirut. CBS covered that memorial service live, but it didn't happen without some heavy persuasion.

I was working in the White House Office of Planning and Evaluation at the time. When the Reagans decided to attend the service, I took the first available plane from Andrews Air Force Base to Camp LeJeune to start making preparations. It was a noisy military cargo plane with web seating. I felt incongruous in my blue blazer. The flight crew handed me earplugs to muffle the roar of the engines.

The request by Zirinsky's television network to cover the memorial service live was controversial. The White House supported the request, but Major General Alfred M. Gray, Jr., commander of the Second Marine Division at Camp Lejeune, and later the commandant of the Marine Corps, opposed the idea when I presented it. CBS wanted extra phone lines at his headquarters for live coverage. At the time, General Gray was responsible not only for troops in Lebanon but also those who had just invaded Grenada. He reminded me sharply that CBS's request for extra phone lines if the coverage went live came second to his duty to run the command center for Marine operations.

I didn't want to draw Deaver into the issue. Something told me the general's concerns were more about propriety than logistics.

In a tense meeting, I made my pitch. If coverage was limited to the network news, I said, we would be lucky to get five minutes of broadcast time. Millions of households would be able to watch the unedited memorial service if coverage was live. It would allow the nation to share not only the grief but also the dignity of the service commemorating the fallen soldiers.

Finally, I said that Americans had been shocked by the attack. It would restore national pride if they could share in the full memorial service. The general not only relented but also invited me to accompany him to meet wounded Marines who had just been evacuated from Grenada.

I hoped I'd be working with Susan Zirinsky again. We were about the same age, and her working style meshed well with my own. While Zirinsky was thoroughly professional and detail-oriented, she was like me in the sense that we both knew trip schedules evolve through bargaining and mutual accommodation. Susan understood that nobody from the president to the Secret Service to the White House staff to the event host or the press gets everything on their wish list, and she wouldn't drive me nuts trying to get everything CBS wanted. Conversely, I understood the importance of good press coverage, and I was going to do everything I could to make sure CBS got what it needed.

Ideally, a campaign's press strategy and advertising strategy complement each other. In reality, the advertising is within the control of the campaign but the press strategy often ends up driven by external events beyond the control of the campaign.

That was not the case in Normandy. If we handled the press advance competently, the message coming out of Normandy and the campaign advertising would be perfectly synched. D-Day and the liberation of Europe was something Americans could take pride in, and the president's speeches would emphasize the need to deter future wars through strength. They would make explicit the message that was implicit in our campaign advertising, especially the Bear spot.

Once I'd gotten familiar with the site, I went to the staff office to check on messages and then to the White House Communications Agency room to get my radio, earpiece and hand-microphone. It was connected to the radio by a wire that ran inside my jacket sleeve, with the radio itself worn on my belt. Aside from the earpiece, it was relatively inconspicuous, except when I talked into the mike. It looked like I was taking a furtive bite from a candy bar clenched in my fist.

There was a countdown meeting at the Hotel Bayeux scheduled for 5 o'clock that afternoon. In countdown meetings, all the elements of the advance team—White House staff advance, Secret Service, the military, the White House Communications Agency, Air Force One advance, the presidential helicopter advance, and sometimes a host organization representative—sit down together and go through the trip scenario and movements minute by minute.

The meetings could take hours and sometimes involved heated disagreements. When a disagreement couldn't be resolved in the countdown meetings, it got kicked upstairs to the relevant senior officials at the White House. Because it was considered bad form to push our problems up the chain of command, we tried as hard as possible to resolve any differences among ourselves during the countdown meetings.

At that first countdown meeting, I saw familiar faces around the room, guys I knew well and had worked with before. Jim Kuhn, who worked on the 1976 and 1980 Reagan campaigns, was in charge of the Normandy advance team. Steve Hart was in charge of press advance. They were both friends as well as colleagues and I was happy to join them for this adventure in France.

I was paired with some new people at Omaha Beach. Mark Rosenker was a volunteer press advance man who worked in the Electronics Industry Association's Washington, D.C., office. A Californian named Tim Coyle was responsible for the president and staff entourage at the cemetery site while I minded the press arrangements. But this division of responsibilities wasn't neat and tidy. What the press needed often had the potential to impinge on what the staff needed and vice versa. It was up to Tim and me to work together to reconcile conflicts.

By the end of the meeting I sensed it might be tough working with Tim. He was not one of those laid-back Californians I'd worked with previously. His personality was more intense than mine, and he was eager to get definitive answers from me about the press arrangements.

The problem was, I didn't have many answers yet. Live TV is unlike edited television coverage. The story can't be told with footage from several vantage points, put together later in the editing suite. It has to follow the action as it is happening. Until I met with the CBS producers and we did a walk-through together of the president's movements I wouldn't be able to give him any answers. Further complicating matters, every time the staff advance team changed elements of the plan for the cemetery, such as where the color guard would stand or where the president would enter or leave an area, the television planning would have to change. That meant Tim and I might be making adjustments right down to June 6.

The next morning Charlie Bakaly II gave me a preliminary run-down on what Reagan and Mitterrand would do at the cemetery. Charlie was another good friend, and he seemed to have a handle on things right down to where CBS could position its cameras. When I ran into Tim Coyle, he wanted to walk through the site together. After we finished, we went to the transportation office to get a car so we could check out the ruins of a small church nearby that had been destroyed on D-Day and was never rebuilt.

The U.S. embassy in Paris had hired cars and drivers so that the advance teams could easily move back and forth between their hotels and the multiple sites involved in the D-Day commemorations and go out to local restaurants.

A supervisor assigned us Patrice and called him out of a smoke-filled room where the drivers were clustered around a TV set watching porn movies.

Patrice was a young Parisian who spoke fluent English. He introduced himself as Patrick. We jumped into a new Mercedes 190E and took off on our first sightseeing adventure. There wasn't much to see in the small stone church. Artillery had done a pretty good job demolishing the building's interest. Only its shell remained. We stopped at a café for lunch. Tim seemed relaxed. I thought he might not be difficult to work with after all.

That afternoon I went to the cemetery to look over the site again. The schedule called for the president to arrive at 3:15 p.m., and I wanted to check the sun angles throughout the hour and 45 minutes that he and Nancy would be there. There were lots of places to check: the visitors' center, the chapel, the route the presidential limousine would take to the chapel, the route Ronald and Nancy Reagan would walk through the cemetery, the memorial, the Garden of the Missing, the visitors' center again for the departure coverage.

As I sauntered over the grounds, a couple who appeared to be in their 50s or 60s watched me closely. I noticed them following at a distance as I walked from the visitors' center to the chapel and on to the Roosevelt grave. When I got to the Omaha Beach overlook, I paused for a minute to take in the view and heard a voice from behind.

"Excuse me, are you here from the White House?"

I turned and saw the couple. They seemed almost embarrassed to be interrupting me.

"Yes," I nodded. "I'm John Roberts. Nice to meet you."

"I told you so!" the woman said, as they both smiled at me.

"We've seen a few of you guys with the blazers and khakis," the husband said. "We figured that's what it was. Are you with the Secret Service?"

"No, I'm with the White House planning team." His eyes lit up.

"Can you tell us what the president's going to do here?" They looked at me like they thought they shouldn't ask.

"Sure, I can give you an idea."

I sketched the outlines of the event, staying away from any details we wouldn't make public in the routine press announcement that is issued before a presidential visit. I pointed out where the main events would occur.

"We should go see those," the woman said. She turned to me. "He was here, on D-Day. Ask him to tell you about it."

The man looked slightly uncomfortable.

"My dad flew B-17s in the war," I said. "Were you in the army?"

She gave him a nudge. As he poured out his story, he gestured to the beach below, as if the crumpled bodies and machine gun fire were still present. After a few moments he stopped, unable or unwilling to go further.

"I guess we should let you get on with your work," he said after the pause.

"Thanks for sharing your story with me." I gripped his hand. "Sometimes we get so caught up in the details of the events we're planning we don't take time to stop and think about why we're really here."

We walked together to the memorial. I told them I needed to watch the sun angle for about 20 minutes. We said good-bye and they wandered off.

Charlie's scenario was solid, but I had a hunch things were going to get a lot more complicated. I made notes about which angles would work and wouldn't if we needed to move the camera positions.

At our next countdown meeting, on the 28th, the problems became apparent. The proposed position for the French military color guard blocked the view of the two presidents from the press platform. To carry out security screening of the audience and media, the Secret Service and French security wanted the press positioned on the platform by 2:50 in the afternoon. That meant they would have to stand around for almost two hours. The cordon of troops would have to make their initial movement five minutes before the presidential entourage left the Pointe du Hoc site en route to the cemetery or their movement would block the CBS live camera from getting a head-on shot of President Reagan walking to the memorial. There were a lot of moving parts to the Omaha Beach events, and so far they weren't in synch.

The next morning I met with two CBS producers. We did a walk-through—I was getting to know the cemetery pretty well—and they pointed out additional issues. They wanted dedicated positions for live cameras at the arrival point, an additional live camera at the memorial on stage right, an additional camera platform, and a location for a microwave tower.

When I talked this over with Tim Coyle his jaw clenched.

The following day, Steve Hart and I did another walk-through with a team of CBS producers. I briefed them on Reagan's movements in detail, and they identified a number of additional locations where they wanted to position cameras and platforms to get the best shots.

The requests grew and grew. The CBS team were story-boarding their coverage like this was a Hollywood movie. Their enthusiasm for telling a great story about the anniversary was contagious to me and Steve, but I doubted it would spread to the other parts of our advance team.

While we talked and gesticulated, men in their late 50 and 60s, sometimes with wives and sometimes alone, would stop to watch us. After the walk-through, I sat by myself on a bench jotting notes on my map of the cemetery. Some of the watchers approached, either singly or in small groups, to ask if I was from the White House. Like the couple before, they wanted to know what the president would do at the cemetery.

Invariably, they turned out to be either D-Day veterans or their relatives. Many were attending reunions of the military units they belonged to in the war. Most were American, but there were also Brits, Canadians, and even Germans who had come to Normandy for a separate anniversary event. It chagrined Reagan that German chancellor Helmut Kohl was excluded from the Normandy commemoration. He promised Kohl he would visit a German military cemetery during the 1985 summit in Europe.

When I asked, most veterans were willing to share their D-Day experiences. Many became emotional. I really regretted I hadn't brought along my microcassette tape recorder to capture their memories. I was getting an oral history of the turning point of World War II from men and women who lived it.

* * *

After checking the construction work on the press and camera platforms, I reached a point where there was little I could accomplish for a few hours. With a few exceptions, my every daytime minute had been tightly scheduled since our arrival. I took advantage of the free time by grabbing Patrice for some sightseeing, starting at the museum that housed the Bayeux Tapestry. I was fascinated by the 900-year-old, 225-foot-long textile chronicling William the Conqueror's invasion of England in 1066. I'd first read about it in *National Geographic* in 1966 at the age of 11 and dreamed of seeing it in person.

The museum was no disappointment, but what I really wanted was to get my hands on the wheel and drive around aimlessly. Patrice protested that it was strictly against embassy regulations, but I persuaded him I'd be careful. The little 190E handled beautifully on the narrow French roads that spanned the countryside. Here and there I pulled off at an antique shop or scenic vista, but mainly I just turned up the music and drove.

Patrice watched me vigilantly, clearly nervous about losing his job if I wrecked the car. It took him a while to relax. I offered him a cigarette, and he offered me one of his. I liked the Mercedes so much I thought about importing one. The dollar was very strong against the French franc and some of the guys were buying a Mercedes and shipping it home for only $12,000 total. But it was financially beyond my reach. I had a 16-month-old son at home, and a mortgage, and it would stretch my budget just to buy the set of French copper cookware I wanted to take back to the States.

I asked Patrice how far it was to Mont-Saint-Michel. I wanted to see the quaint medieval town which turned into an island during high tide.

"About a hundred kilometers, more or less."

"How long does it take to get there?"

"Two hours for you. An hour-and-a-half if I drive."

I ignored the jab.

"Not enough time to make it today," I said. "Maybe tomorrow."

When Patrice and I got back we bumped into Tim Coyle. It turned out he wanted to see Mont-Saint-Michel and was after some copper cookware too. He already had the address of a shop that sold it.

We were scheduled for a day off on Sunday, so I suggested we go together. Tim quickly agreed. Hoping to smooth over the bumps in our working relationship, I decided to draw him out a little.

"I know you're from California," I said. "Did you go to school there too?"

"I went to San Diego State University. How about you?"

"UC–Irvine. I had a high-school friend who went to San Diego. Alice Stein. She liked it there."

"You went to high school with Alice Stein?" he looked at me with sudden interest.

"Yeah, for a while. Do you know her?"

"We had some classes together," Tim said. "I tried to get her to go out with me a couple of times, but she said she had some boyfriend back home…"

His voice trailed off. Great, I thought, I'm just trying to make small talk and now you think I'm the reason she wouldn't date you.

"Not me," I said quickly. "That was another guy, a surfer. Alice and I were just friends."

It was a lie. Alice had alternated between dating me and the surfer, but Tim didn't need to know that. He looked at me like he wasn't buying it. We set a time to meet on Sunday and parted ways.

On Sunday morning Steve Hart woke me up with a phone call.

"I'm going into a meeting with the press and I'd like you with me," he said. The tone in his voice was resigned.

"I made plans to go to Mont-Saint-Michel with Coyle. What's up? Has something changed?"

I couldn't think of any reason why we'd need to do another walk-through or meet with producers unless there'd been a major change in the schedule.

"It's about Walter Cronkite," Steve said. "The president's going to do a unilateral interview with him. I'll tell you about it over breakfast."

Walter Cronkite was a legendary reporter and anchorman for *CBS Evening News* until 1981. He was known as the "most trusted man in America" because of a public opinion poll in which he topped the charts. He had been with the *CBS Evening News* since its launch in 1962 and reported on all the major events of the 1960s and '70s: the Kennedy and King assassinations, the Vietnam War, the moon landing, and the U.S. embassy seizure in Iran.Cronkite got his start as a journalist in radio and had been a sports announcer, like Reagan. During World War II, as a war correspondent for United Press, Cronkite was among the first reporters to fly combat missions on B-17s. In one bombing raid, he took over a .50 caliber machine gun from a crewman and fired at Luftwaffe pilots until he was waist-deep in empty shells. On D-Day, Cronkite flew along on a plane assigned to bomb German artillery emplacements above Omaha Beach. He landed at Omaha Beach several days later to report on the Allied invasion.

When we met, Steve explained that the White House press office had given CBS network an exclusive one-on-one interview with Reagan. When the other media organizations found out, they were furious at being scooped and wanted access to the interview.

"What's the purpose of the meeting?" I asked.

"All we can do is listen to them," Steve said apologetically. "They need to vent. The decision isn't going to change. Cronkite gets an exclusive. I'd like you to be there."

I poured a cup of coffee and lit a cigarette. Steve was my superior on this trip, and he could easily have ordered me to join him in what was going to be a very uncomfortable meeting. Instead he put it to me as if I had a choice. I really wanted to see Mont-Saint-Michel, but Steve needed back-up. It was better if the journalists saw a united front from us.

"What's our justification for denying them access?" I asked.

"CBS was the only news organization to request a unilateral interview, and they did it months ago," Steve said matter-of-factly. "If other organizations had made a request then, it would have been considered. Now it's too late."

Our rationale might have the virtue of truth, but cynics would dismiss it outright, and the only professionals more cynical than journalists are parole officers. No matter what we said, the interview with Cronkite would appear to be favoritism, special treatment because the network was covering the anniversary live and thereby guaranteeing Reagan a huge audience.

I raised Coyle on the radio and told him to go without me.

"How long's this meeting going to take?" he said. "We can leave a little later."

"I have no idea. Could be one, could be two hours, maybe longer."

"Do you want me to pick you up a set of pans?" he volunteered.

I couldn't afford a whole set and had planned to pick three or four of the most useful sizes, but I didn't want Tim to have to make that choice for me.

"Thanks, but no, I may get out shopping yet. Have a good time."

About an hour later Steve and I met with several dozen journalists in a crowded hotel conference room. The mood was cantankerous. They immediately began pummeling us with questions. Steve patiently explained that Cronkite was the only one to request an interview. And the schedule was now set.

Next they asked for access to the event, which would have turned it into a news conference. We turned them down. We didn't have facilities at that location to accommodate all the press and at this stage weren't going to try to find another venue.

Then they negotiated for press pool coverage, in which a small number of reporters representing the group gets access, but we had to turn that down too. It still would have been a news conference.

They let their exasperation show, but in a way, it was like Kabuki Theater. Their editors and news executives didn't want Cronkite to have an exclusive, and the ritual called for them to explore all avenues and push as hard as they could in order to satisfy their bosses that they had tried their best. Our role was to calmly absorb their anger and professionally explain, explain, and explain again the reasons why we couldn't change the president's schedule at this late date.

After about an hour of venting, it blew over. More than once during the ordeal all I could think was that I'd just lost my one chance during the trip to enjoy a day off and see Mont-Saint-Michel. It was uncomfortable on both sides, but a good test of our ability to maintain our composure, weather criticism, and still be able to work professionally with the people in this room to obtain the best results for all sides: the press, the public, and the presidency. Whenever I felt my irritation growing, I reminded myself that they were just like me, trying to get a demanding job done well, and that the White House had tossed them a ringer with the Cronkite interview.

When it was over Steve and I were drained. We found a café in Bayeux and ordered beer.

* * *

On D-Day minus one, I was back on Omaha Beach when another middle-aged American couple approached the bluffs. The man was balding and had a black goatee streaked with grey. He was accompanied by a short woman. As they neared, I did a double-take. It was Lyn and Bonnie Nofziger.

Lyn and his wife stopped on the cliffs overlooking Omaha Beach, gazing out toward the English Channel. I had two colleagues with me, Mark Rosenker and Grey Terry from the White House Advance Office. I went to say hello and introduced the others.

Lyn had never talked to me about World War II before, but he did now. I knew he'd been in combat and he lost parts of two fingers in an explosion. What I didn't know was that he was a veteran of the fighting in Normandy, or that Bonnie had enlisted in the Women's Army Corp during the war.

Lyn landed on the third day of the invasion. As his platoon passed a captured squad of German SS troopers, Lyn said he stared slack-jawed at the six-foot-tall blond warriors. It was his first face-to-face encounter with German soldiers, and he told us he was afraid they'd have to fight these guys all the way to Berlin. He didn't realize they were an elite unit.

Lyn did fight his way through the Normandy hedgerows, until he was wounded. His eyes filled with tears as he reminisced about the invasion and his comrades. Lyn said that not all the French welcomed their liberators. Concerned about damage to their farms and villages if they became centers of fierce fighting, some Normans set the Americans up in ambushes. Knowing that German troops were lying in wait, the French would wave the Americans on as if there was no danger and then scatter when the ambush began.

We gave Lyn and Bonnie a quick tour of the site and showed them what the president would be doing. They were invited to a formal dinner with the Reagans and other dignitaries gathered for the 40th anniversary, but instead Lyn suggested we all meet for dinner in Caen.

I was surprised that the Nofzigers would forego the presidential invitation to dine with us, but Lyn said that it "beat the hell out of being with the president."

He didn't mean this as a reflection on Reagan. Lyn was one of the very few White House staff who was personally close to Reagan. He and Reagan got along extremely well. The Reagans had Lyn and Bonnie over for private dinners at their residence in the White House. It was the pomp and ceremony of formal events that Lyn preferred to skip.

We ate at a good restaurant and capped off the meal with a dessert of profiteroles and shots of Calvados, Normandy's famous apple brandy.

"I don't suppose you've seen this week's *Time* magazine, have you?" Lyn asked.

"I haven't," I said.

Mark and Grey shook their heads.

"The cover has San Francisco mayor Diane Feinstein and a congress-woman named Geraldine Ferraro on it," Lyn said. "the headline is 'And for Vice President … WHY NOT A WOMAN?' all in capital letters."

"Is there a push on to name a woman?" I asked.

"Looks like it," Lyn said, chuckling.

In less than 24 hours the California primary would be over and Mondale's attention would shift to selecting a running mate.

"Who's Ferraro?"

"Beats me," Lyn said. "Nobody's ever heard of her. She's in her third term in Congress and apparently a favorite of Tip O'Neill. We should put her on our radar screen."

"Do you really think they'll nominate a woman for vice president?"

"Gary Hart makes more sense," Lyn said.

I agreed. One of the advantages of picking a running mate who's been through the primary campaign is that any dirty laundry has already been aired. If the press didn't find it, their opponents would, and their candidacy either weathered the exposure or cratered under it. It was an axiom of presidential politics that you never picked an unvetted candidate for a running mate and there was no better way to vet a contender than to see them run the primary gauntlet.

We wrapped up dinner early. The next morning was June 6, time to see if our well-laid plans would work.

*   *   *

I showed up at the cemetery early. Small French and American flags fluttered on every grave. Volunteers had put them there the day before. It was a sunny day and the thousands of red, white and blue flags against the white crosses and green grass were stunning.

Everything looked in order. It would be mid-afternoon before there was any real work for me to do, but on an advance I always hung around the site, just in case somebody got the bright idea to change something and in the process undid two weeks of my efforts. Protecting the integrity of the site from last-minute changes was important, even if it meant a lot of uneventful watching and waiting.

The press who'd been with the president since morning would be hungry by the time they arrived at Omaha Beach, so I'd arranged for sandwiches and refreshments to be delivered to the cemetery. I planned to move them from storage shortly before the events began, during an interval when they could grab a bite to eat without missing anything.

When I heard the sound of Marine One's rotors as the presidential helicopter arrived, I went to check on the sandwiches. Security at the site was now jointly managed by the Americans and the French. Young French soldiers manned some checkpoints, including one I needed to pass through. When I got there, a soldier challenged my credentials. I showed him my White House advance identification and started to walk past the barrier when he leveled his machine gun at my stomach.

"Only the Secret Service may pass," he said to me in French. Next to me was Larry Cunningham, one of the Secret Service agents assigned to the press for the trip.

"What did he say?" Larry asked.

I explained. The agent whipped open his coat, flashing his badge and gun.

"I'm the Secret Service," he said, and we walked through without further translation.

With the sandwiches safely delivered, he and I walked down to the Roosevelt grave. The press platform was packed with photographers. CBS had its own reserved position. Just to be sure nothing had been disturbed by the arrival of the media, I did a quick walk along the path Ronald and Nancy Reagan would use to go from the chapel to the Roosevelt grave.

For a short distance, they were to walk between rows of grave markers. We wanted them walking among the crosses because it made a far better photograph, but Nancy Reagan dreaded stepping on a grave. She thought it was extremely disrespectful. The advance staff found out from Phil Rivers exactly how much space there was between graves, and then put small holes in the turf. Inside each hole was an arrow marking the pathway the Reagans should take to avoid stepping on a grave. The arrows themselves were slightly below ground level. They couldn't be seen unless you were right on top of them.

Everything was intact. On my way back to the platform, I found a key ring with several small keys on it. I showed them to Cunningham.

"Has anyone reported missing keys?" I said.

"I wonder who they belong to," he shook his head.

"Could be anybody."

My guess was one of the photographers on the platform or maybe one of the volunteers who placed the flags might have dropped the keys. I put them in my pocket, intending to hand them over to Phil Rivers when I ran into him.

There were only a few minutes to go before the president and First Lady arrived when I started hearing snippets of conversation on the radio. Because I was in a low spot in the cemetery, the coverage was poor and the conversation was broken up. For some reason there was a delay in the president's movement from the visitors' center to the chapel, but I couldn't get why.

My imagination conjured the worst possibilities. The Secret Service had been concerned about the cemetery's exposure to the English Channel and the potential for terrorists to use a small boat and rocket to fire at the president. To offset the vulnerability, a French naval vessel was offshore ready to intercept any boat traffic. It was possible something was happening right now.

Several friends of mine were with Reagan at the Washington Hilton when John Hinckley, Jr., attempted to assassinate him. Rick Ahearn, an affable but thoroughly professional advance man whose nickname was "Ambassador Ahearn," was right beside the president. Hugh O'Neill, a former Capitol Hill policeman who got into presidential advance in the Ford Administration, was also in the line of fire. O'Neill wasn't with us on the Normandy trip. During an earlier presidential visit to France Hugh was declared *persona non grata* and expelled from the country after he let French officials know what he thought about the sub-standard treatment they were planning to give Reagan.

Jim Brady, Reagan's press secretary, was grievously wounded along with the president, Metropolitan police officer Thomas Delahanty, and Secret Service agent Timothy McCarthy. McCarthy put himself in the line of fire to shield Reagan.

I wasn't friends with Brady but we were on a first-name basis. When he was released from the hospital O'Neill threw a small party for him at his townhouse in Old Town Alexandria, Virginia. When I arrived Brady was seated in a wheelchair in the living room. I knew how serious his brain injury was, yet to my amazement Jim recognized me immediately and greeted me by my first name.

While I didn't consciously dwell on the dangers of being in close proximity to the president, my body was aware of it. The physical sensation was a heightened sensitivity of my senses and the surface of my skin. I felt it now. My vision was sharper, my hearing more acute, my skin tingling.

"Do you know what's going on?" I asked Larry.

The Secret Service had its own radio frequency and sometimes the agents knew about a security issue before the White House staff did.

"It's not on our end," Larry said.

A radio call came advising me the president would be late arriving at the Roosevelt site. I asked what the problem was but didn't get an answer. Briefly, I considered leaving the site and wandering to a point where I could get better radio reception. But CBS cameras had either already gone live or were about to, and I didn't want to blunder into the shot or risk being away from my post if the president and First Lady suddenly began coming my way.

After a delay that seemed to last half an hour but was actually less than 10 minutes, a clear radio call came through.

"Roberts, Roberts, Kuhn," the voice said.

It was Jim Kuhn, the lead advance man. He would be right by the president. Presumably, the radio call was clearer because they were moving closer to us.

"Kuhn, Roberts, go," I answered.

"Rawhide is 77 your location."

I'd made the right decision. I turned around and told the waiting photographers that the Reagans were on their way. There was a brief bustle on the platform and then hushed stillness.

A cluster of officials came into view, including Chief of Staff James A. Baker III and Mike Deaver, the president's personal aide Dave Fischer and physician Dr. Daniel Ruge, Director of Presidential Advance Bill Henkel and Press Secretary Larry Speakes. They had all been briefed, along with the president's Secret Service detail, to stay away from the Reagans as they walked through the graves. If all worked according to plan, we would get a clear photo of the two of them.

Baker was deep in conversation. I held my breath until at the last moment he and several others stopped and then moved out of the picture. Behind me there was a long staccato burst of automatic winders on 35mm cameras as the photographers shot the duo walking to the gravesite. The burst subsided and then resumed once more as Nancy knelt to place the flowers.

It was perfectly choreographed. We had the shot. As the Reagans left I moved ahead to the memorial, escorting the pool of journalists who would cover the president during speeches and wreath-laying with Mitterrand.

When it was over I tracked down Tim Coyle.

"What happened?"

"Someone lost track of the keys to the chapel," he said. "They couldn't get in."

Security protocol required the Secret Service and military to sweep the chapel for bombs and eavesdropping devices, after which it was securely locked with a guard posted until the president's arrival.

I fished the keys out of my pocket.

"Is this the set?"

Coyle looked at me in a mixture of surprise and concern.

"Let's go ask."

We went to Jim Kuhn and gave him the keys. He showed them to Phil Rivers, who looked shaken and chagrined.

"Where did you find them?" Rivers asked.

"Down by the Roosevelt site," I said. "We didn't know what they were."

"Didn't you hear any of the radio traffic about the chapel?" Jim said.

"We had broken reception down there. I knew there was a problem, but I didn't know what. Nobody responded when I tried to find out what was behind the delay."

The Secret Service agent I'd worked alongside confirmed it.

"I didn't get anything on my end either about the church or missing keys," Larry said. "We had them the whole time."

Judging by Phil Rivers' ashen face, I had the sinking feeling we had a big problem on our hands.

"What was the president's reaction?" I said. "Is he mad at being locked out?"

"The only thing he said was 'I would really have liked to have seen that chapel,'" Jim said.

"So it's okay?"

"They're not upset," he said. "They just wanted a few minutes to pray."

The following morning we stopped briefly at the American embassy in Paris on our way to the airport. I purchased several bottles of 1976 Taittinger Blanc de Blanc champagne to take home. After checking in for my flight at Charles de Gaulle, I went straight to a newsstand. The cover of every European paper had the photograph of Ronald and Nancy Reagan among the rows of crosses.

Deaver had been right. It was the trip photo. Reagan's speeches at Normandy were stirring, but in the end they were just words on the wind. It was the imagery that told the story and stayed in the mind.

President Reagan and First Lady Nancy Reagan, American Military Cemetery, Normandy, France, June 6, 1984 (courtesy Ronald Reagan Presidential Library).

The First Lady had a particularly emotional expression on her face. We were probably the only ones who knew it was because she was concentrating very hard on avoiding stepping on a serviceman's final resting place.

I bought one of each paper and caught my flight home.

4

Ferraro Enters the Fray

Reagan-Bush Headquarters
Washington, D.C.
June 30–July 14, 1984

Walter Mondale was taking his time deciding who he wanted as his vice-presidential running mate, but inside Reagan-Bush headquarters our attention was on other matters. Now that the Rose Garden phase of our strategy was over, it was time to start campaigning. To do that, we needed to develop the strategy for July through November.

"Ronald Reagan is carrying the campaign, just as he has in every Reagan campaign," Stu Spencer began. "Research shows that his personal attributes are strong, so negative attacks won't stick."

The most important political advisor on the Reagan campaign didn't have an impressive title. Stuart K. Spencer was an unassuming man in his late 50s, with a full head of gray hair and pale blue eyes, who liked wearing bolo ties and dressing in cowboy boots. To look at him you would never know he was one of the country's top political strategists or that his home was Newport Beach, California, not Cody, Wyoming. Spencer was the one advisor Ronald and Nancy Reagan trusted the most. He had managed every one of Reagan's campaigns since the 1966 race for governor of California.

Spencer had tapped me to draft the campaign strategy. At 9 o'clock on Saturday morning I joined a small group in a windowless conference room on the fourth floor of campaign headquarters. The others were pollster Bob Teeter; speechwriter Ken Khachigian; his aide Kevin Hopkins; and Doug Elmets. I'd worked with all of them before except for Teeter and Spencer. Hopkins had been at Citizens for the Republic and on the 1980 campaign. We'd worked closely together. I knew Doug Elmets from the White House. Both Kevin and Doug were contemporaries, in their late 20s or early 30s.

At the start of Reagan's first term, I worked for Ken Khachigian in the Office of Presidential Speechwriting. Khachigian was smart, thorough,

Ronald Reagan and Stu Spencer in the Oval Office, October 4, 1984 (courtesy Ronald Reagan Presidential Library).

and diligent. He was a veteran of the Nixon White House. He instilled a high level of professionalism in Reagan's speechwriting staff. I helped him on some of Reagan's key early speeches, notably the remarks for Margaret Thatcher's state visit in 1981 and Reagan's addresses on his economic recovery plan.

Khachigian was no longer on the White House staff, although he continued to work on Reagan's major speeches. He left the White House in May 1981 and returned to California to begin building his reputation as a political consultant. He joined Reagan-Bush '84 to manage the opposition research into Walter Mondale and devise an attack strategy against Carter's former vice president.

My job was to synthesize the findings and distill the conclusions into a well-organized document that would go to the president and the White House staff. This wasn't just a strategy for the campaign to follow—it was *the* strategy for Ronald Reagan's reelection.

I placed a tape recorder in the center of the table and started taking notes. The discussion ranged from polling data to policy issues to Reagan's strengths and vulnerabilities as well as angles of attack against Mondale. By the end of the day I had 13 pages of handwritten notes and the tape just so I didn't miss anything.

By July 1, my first draft was ready for Stu's review. The overarching theme of the campaign, which we termed the "umbrella theme," was Reagan's leadership. The strategy document included the sub-themes and campaign issues and included a week-by-week outline of events and actions so that the campaign could stay on the offensive. It identified "issue cycles," or periods of time in which specific issues would dominate the news. Some would be created by the White House and campaign, while others, like the Summer Olympics in Los Angeles and the September 18 opening of the United Nations General Assembly in New York, were already fixed on the calendar.

It did not include a section on Mondale. Khachigian was developing that separately and didn't expect it to be ready until mid–July. The document was silent on the question of Mondale's running mate. A day earlier, the National Organization for Women had wrapped up their convention in Miami Beach by calling on Mondale to select a woman for vice president. But conventional wisdom was that voters cast their ballot for the top of the ticket, not the person in second place. The plan was for Reagan to run against Mondale. His vice-presidential pick was inconsequential.

Lyn Nofziger ran the morning Attack Meeting I routinely attended, along with daily campaign strategy meetings and senior staff meetings. Lyn's meeting on July 2 featured Mondale's vice-presidential selection process.

"I hope the Democrats don't nominate a woman," he said, "because if they do I'll spend the rest of the campaign trying to figure out how to make her cry in public."

Mondale's decision about a running mate was dragging on inconclusively. Lyn called it a "public relations personality parade" in which Mondale seemed to be calling on every politician who had a constituency in the Democratic coalition. It looked as if Mondale didn't want to offend any bloc of Democratic voters by failing to interview their preferred candidate. Lyn wanted our surrogates to draw a contrast between Mondale's leadership style and Reagan's, saying that Reagan would simply interview the contenders and pick the one who was most qualified.

After Lyn's meeting concluded, Spencer's strategy group reconvened. By the July 2 meeting, I'd collected comments on my first draft, incorporated the useful changes, and revised the campaign strategy document.

It was a short meeting.

The decision was made that the campaign strategy should focus on central, national issues rather than regional ones. Reagan's blue-collar voter coalition was intact, except for some minor movement of lower-income blue-collar workers away from us. Even if Gary Hart was on the ticket as Mondale's running mate, it looked likely that Reagan could expand his support among suburban voters. But key Electoral College states like Ohio, Illinois, Texas and New Jersey were in play.

At the end of the meeting, deputy campaign manager Lee Atwater's aide, Jim Pinkerton, dropped off a copy of my first draft with Lee's comments scrawled on it. There was so much red ink, it looked like it had been used to wipe up a crime scene. Bob Teeter intercepted the copy and took it. When the meeting broke up I saw Teeter headed toward Atwater's office. It was the last I saw or heard of the marked-up document. Teeter gave it back to Atwater and told him that the group had already reached a consensus. Atwater's comments were too late.

Dick Darman had used a similar tactic in trying to change the campaign advertising strategy. He too submitted a heavily marked-up critique of the campaign memo outlining the advertising plan. His criticisms also went nowhere.

I had noticed that Darman came frequently to Atwater's office. They clearly shared a different vision of how the campaign should be run, one that was out of sync with the rest of the team.

Stu Spencer reviewed my second draft. He asked me to make a few minor changes and then sent the plan to the White House. The Rose Garden phase was definitely over. We were ready for the contest to see who would be the next president of the United States.

* * *

Stu Spencer (left), Ronald Reagan, and Lee Atwater onboard Air Force One on the way to Alabama, October 5, 1984 (courtesy Ronald Reagan Presidential Library).

On Saturday, July 7, my phone rang at 9:45 a.m. The campaign's weekly strategy conference call was about to start. In alphabetical order, Lee Atwater, Vic Gold, Bill Greener, Ken Khachigian, Jim Lake, Eddie Mahe, Dan Morris, Dick Wirthlin and I were on the phone. The purpose of the weekly call was to share information and coordinate actions for the coming week. The topic turned quickly to Mondale's vice-presidential choice.

"The free media is really turning bad on Mondale over this veepstakes," Atwater said. "Ferraro really hurt herself. The Mondale people are mad at Hart so it won't be him. I think they're heading toward Dale Bumpers or Cardiss Collins."

Atwater had picked up on rumors circulating through the Washington press corps that Ferraro had failed to distinguish herself in a series of interviews with Mondale. Dale Bumpers was a U.S. senator and former governor of Arkansas. Cardiss Collins was an African American congresswoman from Illinois.

"Any speculation on Bradley?" Greener asked. Bill Bradley was a former professional basketball player and served in the Senate.

"Cuomo didn't give Mondale an opportunity to ask him about being veep," Wirthlin said. The governor of New York had taken himself out of the running.

Eddie Mahe wondered if Mondale would announce a running mate just to bring the negative press coverage to an end.

"Will Mondale get out from under it this week," he said, "to get out from under this negative media on the veep selection process?"

"Yes, but it's a mistake to announce it in advance," Atwater said. "It gives groups time to mobilize against it from the convention. Broder told me yesterday that Mondale simply got out too fast, without thinking, on the veepstakes."

Dave Broder was a veteran *Washington Post* columnist who was nicknamed "the Dean of the Washington Press Corps." His balanced, insightful columns were "must-reading" inside the Beltway.

Nofziger's idea to attack Mondale's vice-presidential selection process was paying off. The media had seized it and made it their own.

Atwater wanted to go on the attack by going after Jesse Jackson. He was the only African American in the Democratic presidential primaries and had run third behind Mondale and Hart. Jackson's foreign policy proposals were out of the mainstream, and Atwater wanted to press Mondale to either support or disavow them.

"This Jackson thing needs to be played right down to the end," Atwater said.

Jim Lake quickly shot the idea down. Lake was a veteran media strategist in Reagan's 1976 and 1980 presidential campaigns.

"Our greatest risk is screwing up what they are doing to themselves," Lake said. "We don't want to do something that detracts from their own great ability to fuck themselves."

Wirthlin agreed. He thought we should keep the focus on Mondale and highlight the "leadership dimension."

"We should not do anything apparent or overt," Lake said. "We can implant this in the press analysis through background comments ... we have to do very little. They are, the press, already there."

Because the media were already critical of Mondale's vacillating over his vice-presidential pick, Lake argued for subtlety on our part.

Wirthlin gave a quick assessment of the campaign outlook.

"Reagan is up 22 points over Mondale, in a poll taken about a month ago, but our real lead is probably only 13–14 points."

"Why?" Eddie Mahe wanted to know.

"We had a good month, with the Normandy speech, good economic news, and the intensity of the Democratic infighting in June," Wirthlin said, "plus we got some pick-up from the China trip and the meeting with the pope."

Part of the Rose Garden strategy had entailed Reagan visiting the Vatican and Beijing.

"If Mondale can break through the 'qualified to be president' barrier," Wirthlin continued, "we'll have a real horse race around fall."

He went on to explain that voters weren't convinced that the country's economic woes were over and worried that the economic recovery wouldn't last.

"Am I right that we're back to Napoleon's axiom, never interfere with the enemy when they're destroying themselves?" Atwater spoke up. "I think that's a mistake. Jackson is the most dominant Democrat in the country right now and we need to join Jackson and Mondale at the hip. That will give us the South and the blue-collar voters."

Atwater and Khachigian made their case for going on the attack, but they were in the minority. The consensus by the end of the conference call was that the target of opportunity was Mondale's leadership qualities. Our campaign should withhold further on-the-record comment about Mondale's vice-presidential selection process. It appeared that Geraldine Ferraro had been passed over for vice president. The longer Mondale's search dragged on, the more of a liability it would become. The press would do the work for us.

*   *   *

Five days later Walter Mondale announced Geraldine Ferraro as his vice-presidential running mate in front of an enthusiastic crowd at the state capitol in St. Paul, Minnesota.

Mondale might as well have set off a bomb at Reagan-Bush headquarters. For months the atmosphere on the fourth floor, where the campaign's executive suites were clustered, had been placid. With no primary opponents, the Reagan team spent its time leisurely developing its organization in all 50 states and honing the reelection strategy.

The morning after Mondale's announcement was different. Phones rang up and down the corridor. Young aides hustled between offices. The clattering of IBM Selectric typewriters and the screech of dial-up modems was incessant and the blue haze of cigarette smoke was more intense than usual.

Mondale blindsided us with his choice of Ferraro. Never before had a major party nominated a woman for vice president. Despite rumors that the congresswoman from Queens was being pushed by House Speaker Tip O'Neill, the campaign leadership considered Ferraro so unlikely a choice that they focused their attention on other possible running mates.

The press office was bombarded by reporters wanting the campaign's response. Jim Lake had his hands full dealing with journalists. Deputy Press Secretary John Buckley, who fielded most of the calls, kept darting out from behind the Christie Brinkley swimsuit poster that screened the glass partition of his office to go down the hall to Ed Rollins' suite. John was in his mid–20s and had gotten his start in writing as a rock critic for *Rolling Stone* and the *Village Voice*.

Buckley, normally light-hearted and easy-going, looked harried. He had to pass my office to see Ed's longtime assistant and girlfriend, Michele Davis, who was next door to me. You could measure the campaign's consternation by the number of lines lighting up on the phones outside Rollins' office and the number of aides asking Michele when they could get a few minutes of his time.

We had no idea how to respond to a woman on the Democratic ticket. No polling had been done on the contingency that Mondale might pick a female running mate. Despite Nofziger's intuition in Normandy, the campaign simply had not focused on Ferraro. We knew nothing about her: her history, her voting record in Congress, or her positions on major policy issues. We hadn't tested themes or talking points, and we didn't know what kind of statements would be politically productive or counter-productive.

This was the second time we had been caught flat-footed. The first lapse was when Senator Gary Hart unexpectedly surged in the Democratic primaries and looked like he might wrest the nomination away from Mondale. Wirthlin's first estimate gave Hart a 50-50 chance of winning the nomination. No opposition research had been done on Hart because he seemed like a long shot. Nancy Reagan seethed when she learned that the reelection team didn't have a strategy for handling Hart in case he broke through and beat Mondale for the nomination.

I lit another Marlboro while listening to the squawk of my dial-up modem connecting with our "Voices for Victory" computer bulletin board. The state-of-the-art system connected Reagan-Bush headquarters with state campaign offices and key officials. In addition to disseminating talking points, it was used to share information. Ferraro was scheduled to hold her first news conference after Mondale's announcement and I wanted to see what guidance, if any, we were putting out. Wirthlin was hurriedly taking a poll on the reaction to Ferraro. Until he had results, the guidance was to refrain from saying anything about Ferraro.

In his corner office, next to Michele's, Rollins had CNN tuned in. Buckley turned away from Michele's desk. As he stepped into the corridor I stopped him.

"John, do me a favor," I said. "Can you get me the wire copy on Ferraro's news conference when it's available?"

"Sure," he said. "I'll drop off one for you along with Ed's."

He looked like he would have preferred that I make my own copy. John

Geraldine Ferraro at a union rally, Detroit, Michigan, October 1984 (photograph by Manny Crisostomo, copyright Detroit Free Press/ZUMA Press).

wasn't really sure what my role was on the campaign.

It was only a hunch but I thought Geraldine Ferraro was worth watching closely. One thing I'd learned about conventional wisdom is that it only applies in conventional circumstances. Ferraro's candidacy for vice president was unprecedented. That meant no matter what past experience showed regarding voters casting their ballots for the bottom of the ticket, voters had never had a choice like this before. We were in uncharted territory where statistical data from past elections was irrelevant.

Among the flood of calls that inundated campaign headquarters was one from Mike McManus, Deaver's deputy. McManus said that Roy Cohn had jumped on a plane to Washington as soon as he learned of Ferraro's

Geraldine Ferraro greets crowd of supporters at the ropeline, Flint, Michigan, September 1984 (copyright Detroit Free Press/ZUMA Press).

nomination. Cohn was a longtime intimate of Ronald and Nancy Reagan, dating back to when Reagan was president of the Screen Actors Guild. He had been Senator Joseph McCarthy's chief counsel during the 1950s' "Red Scare," when fears of Communist penetration of the State Department featured in McCarthy's hearings in the Senate Permanent Subcommittee on Investigations. A few years earlier, in 1947, Reagan had testified before the House Un-American Activities Committee about the importance of keeping Marxist influence out of Hollywood.

Somewhere along the way the Reagans and Cohn forged an enduring relationship. When Reagan decided to run for president in 1980, Mike Deaver gave Roger Stone, Reagan's regional political director for the Northeast, Cohn's name and number. Deaver told Stone to get in touch with Cohn for help on the campaign.

McManus told Rollins that Cohn had come to the White House with inside information about Geraldine Ferraro. A meeting was set up for 11:00 a.m. on July 13 between Rollins and Cohn. I was told to attend. When I asked Michele if she had any idea about the nature of Cohn's information, she shook her head and smiled. I'd worked with Michele on the 1980 campaign and knew that smile well. It meant she wasn't going to tell me anything, but she knew I would like what I found out.

The following morning I skipped Lyn's Attack Meeting. I was reading everything I could lay my hands on about Ferraro before the meeting with Roy Cohn. I wanted to get some context for whatever information he had. After leaving the Senate, Cohn practiced law. He had some interesting clients. One of them was Carmine Galante, at one time the "capo di tutti capi" or godfather of America's five Mafia crime families. Another was Anthony "Fat Tony" Salerno, godfather of the Genovese family.

I had a fresh shot of coffee before the meeting began, straightened my tie, and went to Rollins' office to wait for his arrival.

Cohn had a suntan that made him look like he had either just come from a beach vacation or a tanning bed. His gray hair was close-cropped, and his piercing blue eyes seemed to conceal a thousand years of experiences. He was amiable but got straight down to business.

He said that Geraldine Ferraro and her husband, John Zaccaro, had ties to the Mafia. He told us that Zaccaro ran a family real estate business and rented one property to a major pornography distributor linked to organized crime.

Cohn said the Gambino branch of the Mafia had links to Ferraro and Zaccaro. He said if Ferraro's campaign contributions and her husband's business associations were scrutinized, we would find the connections. Cohn offered to hold a series of news conferences and personally make the allegation

Roy Cohn, Ronald Reagan and Nancy Reagan at a White House reception for the Eureka College Scholarship Program, June 28, 1982. Eureka College was Ronald Reagan's alma mater (courtesy Ronald Reagan Presidential Library).

that Ferraro was "mobbed up." That would lead the press to do its own investigating, he believed.

I was astounded.

If what Cohn said was true, it would be devastating to the Mondale-Ferraro ticket. But if it wasn't true or couldn't be backed up by evidence, it might backfire on us.

Rollins explained that the campaign was doing some polling on the most effective way to handle Ferraro's candidacy. It would take some time before Wirthlin had the results. He asked Cohn to hold off on raising any charges until we could do some analysis. The meeting ended cordially. Cohn and I exchanged numbers and agreed to stay in close touch.

While we were meeting with Roy Cohn, Walter Mondale and Geraldine Ferraro were kick-starting their campaign in Elmore, Minnesota. It was a small town of several hundred people, a perfect setting for the press to photograph the duo in scenes that looked like they were straight from Norman Rockwell paintings.

As she and Mondale came out of a church, Ferraro was asked by a reporter how she reconciled her Catholic faith with her pro-choice position on abortion. Her reflex was to turn the attack around on her opponent.

"President Reagan walks around calling himself a good Christian," she retorted. "I don't for one minute believe it."

She went on to justify her remark by saying the effect of his policies on the poor and minorities wasn't consistent with the religious values he proclaimed.

I was stunned by Ferraro's comment. It was an amateurish mistake. Ferraro wasn't even officially on the ticket yet, and she'd already given journalists a headline that would define her debut on the national stage, a mean-spirited attack on Reagan's religious convictions certain to invite retribution.

The game was on, and it was going to be hardball.

Stu Spencer called me into his office and shut the door. With him was a studious-looking black man in his late 30s. He was trim and immaculately dressed.

"Do you guys know each other?" Stu asked. We shook our heads.

"This is Art Teele. Art, meet John Roberts."

Teele's grip was firm and his palm dry. He gave me a wry smile.

"Nancy just called and she's mad as hell," Stu continued. "She wants to know what we're going to do about Ferraro. Do you have any time on your hands?"

I could imagine what the call must have been like. I remembered Nancy's reaction to a reporter, Judy Bacharach, who wrote a story mocking her for handing out candies on the campaign plane during the 1980 election. Nancy organized a full-fledged campaign against Bacharach ranging from orchestrated complaints to her editor and publisher to bundles of letters critical of her reporting. In comparison to Ferraro's comments, Bacharach had only committed a minor slight.

"Yeah, I can take it on," I said, "but there's a lot of catching up to do."

"Good. I'll clear it with Ed," Stu said. "This is your top priority. Keep it quiet. Don't go telling everybody that Nancy wants something done. You two are going to figure out what we do about Ferraro."

He paused as if waiting to see that we understood the need for discretion. I was no stranger to this kind of message. I'd heard it since early adolescence.

After several days of IQ tests when I was 12, I was cautioned never to discuss my scores with anyone because it would make them uncomfortable with me. When I started college at 14, I kept my age a secret. At 18, I'd been invited to a meeting in Room 2E-10 of the federal building in Lawndale, California. The appointment letter said not to tell anyone, not even family members, about the meeting. To reinforce the point, the meeting began with the Central Intelligence Agency's West Coast representative handing me a palm card that said not to disclose the meeting to anyone or I could compromise my usefulness to the organization. There were confidential matters from the 1980 campaign I'd never disclosed. I knew how to handle secrets, but I was always grateful to be reminded I'd just been entrusted with another one.

To deflect Nancy temporarily, Stu told her the campaign was waiting for the results of Dick Wirthlin's polling on the public reaction to Ferraro's nomination before formulating our strategy.

I looked at my new workmate. I knew less about Art Teele than I did Gerry Ferraro. In the process of writing the reelection strategy, I'd developed a working relationship with Stu Spencer. I liked his wit and respected his intelligence. Whoever Art Teele was, Spencer clearly trusted him.

"Start by keeping tabs on all the tips that are coming into the campaign," Stu said, "and get all the basic stuff started."

I gave Teele and Spencer a quick summation of the meeting with Roy Cohn.

"McManus sent him to us," I said, "so the White House has the same information."

Spencer had a serious look on his face that I hadn't seen before.

"How long will it take Wirthlin to complete his poll?" Art asked.

"Two, three days," Stu said. "You have any questions you want included in it?"

Teele and I looked at each other.

"Let us think it over," he said. "We might."

"If you come up with anything, let me know today so I can get it to Wirthlin in time."

President Reagan thanking Arthur E. Teele, Jr., in the Oval Office for his achievements as administrator of the Urban Mass Transit Administration at the Department of Transportation, August 11, 1983 (courtesy Ronald Reagan Presidential Library).

The Reagans trusted Wirthlin, a former Utah college professor, more than any other pollster in the Republican Party. His bond with them gave him extraordinary power inside the White House and Reagan campaign. Atwater and Rollins preferred a different pollster, Bob Teeter, who was also on the campaign payroll.

Duplicate or overlapping structures and fiefdoms abounded in the 1984 Reagan-Bush organization. Ken Khachigian was in charge of the campaign's research into Walter Mondale but Lee Atwater had an entirely separate research effort underway behind closed doors. In a series of small cubicles surrounding a bullpen area, some of the GOP's most ardent opposition researchers, like Gary Maloney, toiled in what was called "the Swill Hole."

The Republican National Committee had its own research team under the direction of Communications Director Bill Greener and Mike Bayer, an army reservist and former Senate aide. They were compiling a computerized "Quotes and Votes" system for use by the campaign, allowing us to quickly find things Mondale had said or done when he was in Congress with a reasonably simple search system. They would be scrambling to find information on Ferraro, too, entering her votes, Congressional Record remarks, and scanning her past speeches and court cases as a prosecutor.

The first challenge Teele and I faced was bringing these disparate groups under control to assure that we didn't waste time or resources duplicating work. The other was to keep the researchers in line to prevent freelancing—digging up information on Ferraro to feed to their favorite reporters or political friends. Instilling discipline wouldn't be easy.

But that's the nature of campaigns. At the presidential level, there really aren't teams in politics. It's more like a confederacy of pirates, temporarily banded together to beat the other side as a prelude to dividing the spoils.

Spencer had a lot of phone calls to return so we got out of his way.

"Come on and I'll show you my office," I said to Teele. "We can grab some coffee and figure out where to start."

Art looked around the walls. Unlike most of the offices and cubicles, there were no campaign posters or photos of me with dignitaries. They were bare.

We settled into chairs, notepads in hand.

"I'm guessing this isn't your first campaign," Art said.

"I was in the press office in the '80 campaign," I replied, "working for Nofziger. How about you?"

"Voter groups. I headed up Blacks for Reagan. Funny we didn't run into each other."

Nancy Reagan and I at White House Staff Christmas party, December 15, 1983. The sign explains that she can't talk because of laryngitis (courtesy Ronald Reagan Presidential Library).

"I was either tethered to a phone or a typewriter most of the time. I barely left my desk to go to the bathroom."

Art smiled.

"Nineteen-eighty was a little more intense than this campaign," he said, "at least until now. Where were you before this?"

I gave him the brief version.

"Sounds very interesting," he said. "Do you plan to go back to the White House after the election?"

I shrugged.

"How about you? What have you been up to since 1980?"

"I was the administrator of UMTA," he said.

I knew what that meant. The Urban Mass Transit Administration was part of the U.S. Department of Transportation. The administrator was responsible for a multi-million-dollar budget and federal grants for light rail, subways, and buses in cities across the country. No doubt Teele had made a lot of connections and had contacts in state and municipal governments nationwide.

"What's your background?" I was curious about how he'd gotten into the Transportation Department.

"I studied law. And you?"

"I got a degree from Oxford in philosophy, politics, and economics," I said, "sort of the English equivalent to political science. Then I went to work for Reagan's political action committee."

"Is that where you met Nofziger?"

We were sizing each other up, trying to figure out lines of patronage, loyalties, networks. We were going to be working together on a sensitive project and I wanted to know Art's political lineage as much as he wanted to know mine.

"So how do you see getting this thing started?" I said.

"The first thing is to get the troops under control."

We issued guidance to all the campaign staff at headquarters and in the state offices and to our surrogates. It explained the challenges of handling Ferraro's candidacy and ended with the following command: "In short, we want all surrogates in at least the next 48 hours not to attack Ferraro, or for that matter, say ANYTHING negative about her. Most importantly, DO NOT raise or discuss her gender—the issue for the campaign will be her experience and qualifications, and those alone."

*   *   *

From Minnesota, Mondale and Ferraro went to Lake Tahoe, California, to prepare for the Democratic National Convention. The Olympic torch was passing through on its way from Greece to Los Angeles. Mondale and Ferraro got a great photo op as the torch bearer ran by on Highway 50. Ferraro got an opportunity to qualify her remarks about Reagan and religion when reporters pressed her for elaboration. Instead, she doubled down, calling Reagan's policies "un–Christian."

She couldn't have picked a worse place to continue her attacks on Reagan's character. Lake Tahoe, known as the "Jewel of the Sierra," was deeply important to both Ronald and Nancy Reagan and to Paul and Carol Laxalt. The couples became friends when Reagan was governor of California and Laxalt was governor of Nevada.

Ron and Nancy vacationed often at the Laxalts' Marlette Lake property overlooking the Tahoe Basin. Concerned about over-development of the lake, the two men formed a bi-state compact to protect it. Environmentalism was just in its infancy in 1968 when the two Republican governors pushed the bills through their state legislatures. The legislation allowed the two states to jointly control development at the lake.

The towering Ponderosa pines and crystalline waters of Lake Tahoe that Ferraro probably took for granted were a direct legacy of Ronald Reagan and Paul Laxalt, now a U.S. senator and Reagan's campaign chairman. Nor could she have imagined how far off the mark her comments were about Reagan's Christianity. He wasn't just religiously observant in the way many politicians are; he was devout.

In 1982, when Nancy's stepfather was dying of congestive heart failure, she despaired over his atheism. Davis, a highly-respected neurosurgeon, couldn't reconcile religion with his knowledge of science. Ronald Reagan shared Nancy's concern about her father's afterlife, so he penned his father-in-law a four-page handwritten letter urging him to accept God.

The letter recounted how Reagan had developed an ulcer in his first year as governor. It troubled him so much he'd become dependent on Maalox, until one day when he suddenly felt he no longer needed it.

That morning his secretary, Helene Von Damm, brought him his correspondence. The first letter was from a woman in Southern California who said she was part of a group that prayed for him every week. The second letter was from a man with a similar prayer group. Next, a young aide brought in a memo. As he left he told Reagan that he and a few others gathered each morning to say prayers for him.

Reagan attributed the disappearance of his ulcer to the power of prayer, and he urged Loyal Davis to have faith. Noting the impact Jesus had on the world, Reagan wrote that "either he was who he said he was, or he was the greatest faker and charlatan who ever lived."

"All that is required," Reagan wrote in closing, "is that you believe and tell God you put yourself in his hands. Love, Ronnie."

I shook my head. Ferraro was clearly clueless to the impact of her words. She had no idea what she had started.

5

Promise and Peril

Reagan-Bush Headquarters
Washington, D.C.
July 15, 1984

When the morning Attack Meeting wrapped up, Lyn beckoned me into his office to talk about Ferraro. He knew the sensitivity of what Teele and I were embarking on and didn't want to put me on the spot discussing it in front of the Attack Meeting group.

"Johnny-boy," he began, "I always said if a woman ever ran for president I was going to find a way to make her cry. Vice president's just as good. Do you have any ideas?"

I started to talk about the tip from Cohn but Lyn already knew all about it.

"What you have to do," he said, "is go at this like a reporter would. You don't need just one source, you need two. Three, if you can get them."

Before he'd gone to work for Reagan in 1966, Lyn was a reporter for Copley News Service. He knew what he was talking about.

I knew I could talk freely with Lyn about Ferraro. I told him about Nancy's personal interest in the matter. We brainstormed ideas, and Lyn offered free use of his surrogate network.

Ferraro was a triple-threat to the reelection strategy. She was Catholic, which might cut into Reagan's strength with Catholic voters. She was Italian-American, which constituted one of the country's largest voter groups. And she was female, which cut to one of Reagan's greatest vulnerabilities: the Gender Gap.

Throughout his first term in office, there was a dramatic difference in Reagan's approval ratings between men and women that became known as "the Gender Gap." Men gave Reagan's presidency much higher marks than women did. The gap was about 20 percent in most polls. Starting in 1982, Mike Deaver began chairing meetings at the White House with the Administration's female appointees to try to create strategies to close the gap between men's and women's approval ratings for Reagan. One of my bosses, Anne

Graham, was a regular attendee at these sessions. None of the strategies had worked. The Gender Gap was widely believed to be Reagan's greatest political vulnerability.

That made Ferraro Mondale's precision weapon, and she was aimed right at our Achilles' heel. With Ferraro on the ticket, it was suddenly conceivable that we might lose the race. Lyn was convinced that Ferraro could become a detriment to Mondale. But we didn't solve the question of how before the meeting broke up.

"Be careful of Nancy, Johnny-boy," Lyn said as I got up to leave. "Let Spencer handle her and try to stay in the background."

It wasn't the first time I'd heard that advice. When I started working at CFTR, I was

Geraldine Ferraro at the podium, July 31, 1984 (David Andersen/The Plain Dealer. Copyright 1984 The Plain Dealer. All rights reserved. REPRINTED/USED with permission).

warned about the "icy stare" that meant she disapproved of you in some way. Recipients of Nancy's icy stare considered their days numbered. I'd met her several times and served on the First Lady's Council on Drug Abuse Education and got on well with her staff. But I'd never had a high-profile assignment like this with her.

The First Lady was protective of her husband not only because he was the man she loved, but also because Ronald Reagan's trusting nature and tendency to give those around him the benefit of the doubt led some aides to pursue their own agendas. Being in politics is like swimming with red-bellied piranhas: it isn't dangerous until you shed a drop of blood in the water. Nancy wanted to ensure that the people who surrounded the president were not only competent but loyal to him.

I went to Stu's office and found Art Teele going through the news clips. Teele brought up the phone calls coming into the campaign. One tipster claimed that Ferraro had had an adulterous affair with a judge, but the man had no proof whatsoever. Another alleged she used her influence in Congress to line up public housing funds for her husband's real estate business but offered no specifics. I was dismissive of these kinds of tips. I wasn't interested in Ferraro's private life and not about to waste time trying to prove vague allegations.

"What do you think about letting Cohn break the Mafia stories?" I said.

"If he knows about this because of his work for mobsters," Teele said, "he's got a problem with attorney-client privilege, doesn't he?"

I was thinking about other problems. By meeting with McManus, Cohn had opened a pipeline of information certain to reach Mike Deaver and the First Lady.

"When Nancy gets word of this she's going to want us to work with Cohn," I said.

Teele's brows furrowed.

"Stu should be able to deal with Nancy," he said, a soft Southern drawl noticeable in the way he said her name. "We need to figure out how to deal with Cohn. What's he want out of this?"

"Maybe he's trying to curry favor with the Reagans? Or trying to settle a score?"

"We'd better figure out his angle before we use him," Art said. "We need to know his motivation if we're going to be able to control him."

I was starting to like Teele. He was intelligent, but there are lots of bright people on presidential campaigns. Art had people sense.

I grabbed a sheaf of papers and started reading to kill time until our next meeting. We hadn't really talked about how to approach our joint responsibilities. We had no idea yet what we were going to do. Three days had gone by since Mondale's announcement. Dick Wirthlin's poll was complete and we were about to learn the results.

*   *   *

I took a seat in the conference room. Teele sat beside me. We were both hoping that Wirthlin's research would show us a way to get the job done.

Chuck Rund, the campaign's director of survey research, presented the findings.

"There's a lot of excitement about Ferraro's candidacy," Rund began, "mainly among women, but not just among women. Independent women, Democratic women, even Republican women are enthusiastic about a woman on the ticket."

Teele and I exchanged glances.

"The Democratic base is energized by this," Rund continued. "It's injected energy into Mondale's campaign."

Rund outlined Ferraro's demographic and geographic strengths. As a Catholic and Italian-American, Ferraro would appeal to two voter groups that traditionally backed Republicans. She would appeal in the Northeast but also among suburban and college-educated women across the country.

"We expect between half a million and a million more women to turn out in 1984 than did in 1980," Rund said. "That was our estimate before we knew Ferraro was on the ticket."

I listened closely and, in my trademark style, took thorough notes. Teele listened intently, too, but he only took notes on points which seemed to catch his interest.

"Whatever you do, whatever you say about her," Rund cautioned, "don't appear to question her qualifications. That's the one red flag. Women perceive that as an attack on her gender, in effect saying a woman can't be vice president or president."

That ran contrary to the guidance we'd put out around the campaign about making her experience and qualifications the issue.

"What can we say about her?" Teele asked.

"Until the euphoria dies down, about all you can do is to say you welcome a chance to compare her record with ours."

"What about whether she's got the experience?" Atwater asked. "Can we compare her resume with the vice president's?"

It was a natural question. Bush was a World War II fighter pilot, successful businessman, congressman, ambassador to China, and director of the CIA. Ferraro was a prosecutor and a three-term representative from Queens.

"No." Rund was emphatic. "That will come across as questioning her qualifications."

Lee persisted. His nervous tic—bouncing one leg by the ball of his foot— was in high gear. Restraint wasn't Lee's strong point.

"What if we have surrogates attack her?"

Ferraro had low national recognition, which meant her public image was a blank slate. If Mondale had put a man on the ticket, this would be the ideal time to attack and attack hard, driving up his negative ratings. Atwater had distilled negative attacks into a formula. When a candidate's negative-to-positive ratio exceeded 2:1, Lee believed the candidate became unelectable. He was notorious for a South Carolina state senate race in which he disparaged the Democratic incumbent, Tom Turnipseed, for being "hooked up to jumper cables" when being treated for depression as a teenager. Turnipseed's mental health history weighed heavily on his campaign and Atwater's candidate, Floyd Spence, sailed to victory.

Rund shook his head.

"Not if they're Republicans. It won't matter that they're not in the White House or the Reagan campaign. Women will see it as us attacking her qualifications. In fact, right now it's just better not to try to attack her at all."

Teele shot me a glance. I thought I saw in his eyes the same realization that had hit me. This was going to be tough. Very tough. If we couldn't find a way to attack Ferraro, we would end up getting our asses kicked by Nancy Reagan.

After Rund's briefing, we sat down to compare notes. Although there were lots of leads, mainly from self-serving tipsters who wanted to earn Brownie points with the White House, in fact we knew next to nothing about Ferraro. We did know we'd pay a price for any useful tips. Information is power in politics and a form of currency. Our tipsters would want to be paid back in anything from political appointments to White House tours or tickets to the presidential box at the Kennedy Center. But every tip would have to be checked out, and at this point we knew nothing that was verified. Teele and I agreed that chasing each individual tip would be fruitless and undisciplined.

We could never hope to understand Ferraro until we knew everything about her. We had a lot of ground to cover. We had to start with the basics, beginning with her voting record in Congress. Next we had to get to know her political allies. We needed to scrutinize thousands of pages of Federal Election Commission reports to learn about her contributors. We needed to know the details of her biography, starting with her birth.

We needed to know about John Zaccaro's business, which Geraldine claimed was entirely separate from her career. We needed to know how he made money, what investments he held and managed, and who his associates were.

We needed to know what it took to support the family's lifestyle, whether the kids attended public or private schools, and what kind of cars the family drove. We needed the probate papers from Zaccaro's parents to see whether he had inherited money. We needed to know about the family residence and any vacation properties. That would allow us to figure out the tuition and car payments and mortgages, helpful information in determining whether the Ferraro/Zaccaro family lived within or above their means. If the latter were the case, we'd start looking for sources of undeclared income or outside support in the form of illegal contributions or political graft.

We had to carefully separate verifiable facts from rumors, suspicions, and deductions. We needed to pull public records. It would take legwork, people. And right now, we were the people.

Teele and I recognized that we had two problems. The first was that we had to learn a lot in a short time. The second was that even when we had all this information, it wouldn't mean we had sorted out Wirthlin's strategic dilemma. So long as it remained true that any attack on Ferraro could backfire, there could be no attacks in campaign advertising, speeches or news conferences by surrogates or comments to reporters. Even push-polls—a technique whereby pollsters insert damaging information into the questions they ask voters in order to spread the information around—would be too risky. If anyone learned that the campaign had commissioned the polls, it would backfire.

The longer it took us to get into action, the more likely it was that others in the campaign or White House would try to fill the void. We had to restrain the members of our own team from going after Ferraro, but we couldn't offer them an alternative strategy until we developed more information and tested its effectiveness. We respected Wirthlin's sense of caution, but I had no idea what Bob Teeter might be telling Atwater or White House Chief of Staff James A. Baker III.

We had a wild mustang by the reins, and we were hoping to get on its back and start riding without being thrown off first.

6

Just Because You're Paranoid...

Reagan-Bush Headquarters
Washington, D.C.
July 16–31, 1984

Over the next few days we got more tips. An anonymous pen pal who called himself "Quixote" claimed that Zaccaro was landlord to a gay bar. I didn't consider it damaging information, but to Moral Majority types and social conservatives it wouldn't play well. A few years before, in London, I'd seen the French movie *La Cage aux Folles*. (Later it was remade as *The Birdcage* with Robin Williams in a starring role.) The film centered on a conservative politician whose daughter is engaged to the son of a gay couple who own a nightclub. The movie was hilarious. I wondered if Quixote had seen it too and was playing some kind of joke on us.

I was on my way to Nofziger's morning meeting when Ed Rollins called me into his office. He told me about a phone call he'd gotten from a New York City official. The man said that Ferraro's husband, John Zaccaro, was a slumlord with numerous building code violations and citations.

"I'll check it out," I said.

He looked pensive, like there was something more he wanted to say, so I sat and waited.

Ed told me he didn't want to know the details of how we handled Ferraro. He said that after the election was over, he wanted to be able to get Senate confirmation without having to answer questions about it.

Michele had told me Ed wanted a Cabinet position or Postmaster General if Reagan was reelected. Her preference was for him to make a play to become ambassador to Australia so they could spend the next four years down under. The jobs entailed public confirmation hearings before the relevant Senate committees, followed by a full floor vote.

Teele and I had to get the job done, but without leaving a trail leading back to the campaign. It was clear that if anything blew up in our faces, we would be on our own.

We both knew that after the 1980 election Congress had launched two investigations into the Reagan-Bush campaign. One centered on whether we had thwarted President Carter's plans for an "October Surprise" by entering secret negotiations with the Ayatollah Khomeini to delay the release of the U.S. embassy hostages in Iran until after the election. The other concerned how the Reagan campaign had gotten hold of Carter's presidential debate briefing materials. A number of people who had worked with me, including one who volunteered on one of my programs, were drawn into the investigations. I'd been asked to safeguard our office files for several days after the 1980 election, until senior staff could return from California and take custody. Other campaign offices hadn't been so careful. Many had discarded files in the trash. I'd watched from the upper-level window as Dumpster divers looking for political memorabilia carted away satchels of documents. Some of them formed the basis for the congressional probes. The overall experience had made me duly cautious.

"We won't break any laws," I told Ed, "and we won't leave any fingerprints. I'll let you know when we've got something, but I'll leave out the details about how."

*   *   *

The week of the Democratic National Convention was a honeymoon period for Ferraro. Doug Watts had penned a memo on June 6, while I was in Normandy, recommending that the campaign "bracket" the convention with negative ads aimed at Mondale. The idea was to launch the attacks before the convention started, go off the air during the three days it was in progress, and then come back up with more negative ads for several days afterward. It was a good technique for influencing voter attitudes toward what would otherwise be three days in which the Democrats would dominate the news.

Watts' memo also outlined two alternative approaches, both of which involved some positive advertising about Reagan's economic recovery. James Baker recommended starting with the positive ads and going negative on Mondale immediately after the convention. It would have the effect, to some extent, of inoculating public opinion against the attacks on "Reaganomics" that we expected from the Democratic convention speakers.

Stu Spencer went to Chicago for a few days during the convention. When he returned, he gave Art and me a debrief of his weekend.

"A friendly mobster invited me to a ballgame this weekend," he said, closing the door. "Someone sent me a ticket, and when I found the row and sat down, there he was next to me. He said John Zaccaro is vulnerable."

I wondered if it was just a coincidence that we seemed to be getting confirmation of Cohn's information less than a week after he told us or if Cohn might have put Spencer's contact up to it. He could have been chumming the waters to make us eager to take Cohn up on his offer to go to the press about Ferraro.

"Is he under surveillance?" Art asked. "Do you think that's why he wanted the separate entrances? So it didn't look like an actual meeting, just a coincidence that your seat was next to his?"

"I don't know," Stu grinned, "I just got word he wanted to meet through an intermediary."

"Who is he?" Art asked. "Why's he telling you this?"

"He doesn't want his name used. Let's just say he's a Republican-leaning mobster."

We discussed the pros and cons of trying to verify the allegations about Mafia ties to Ferraro and Zaccaro. The media were already digging into it, and if we developed additional leads, we could feed their stories anonymously or through cut-outs—people without any direct connection to the GOP willing to pass information to the press. On the downside, if the Reagan-Bush team was revealed to be behind damaging leaks about Ferraro, there could be a nasty backlash from female voters.

In 1983, Reagan had established a blue-ribbon panel of experts called the President's Commission on Organized Crime. The Commission's charter was to investigate and publicize the extent of organized crime activity in the United States. But because Congress didn't initially grant it subpoena powers, the commission had gotten off to a slow start in its first year. Without the use of subpoenas, the commission couldn't compel witnesses to appear before its investigators or require documents to be turned over to it. Congress had only recently corrected its error by giving the commission power to use subpoenas.

I was dubious about how much success we would have in uncovering evidence linking the couple to organized crime, given that we had only slightly more than three months before Election Day and no formal investigative powers at all.

"I'm going to tell Nancy you're working on it," Stu said. "That will keep Cohn in line. But be careful."

Spencer didn't have to finish his thought. We all knew this could become dangerous.

In the 1980 campaign, I worked closely with Nofziger's deputy press secretary, Ken Towery. Ken was a lean, soft-spoken Texan. He enlisted in the army when he turned 18 and was stationed in the Philippines at the start of World War II. After the Battle of Corregidor, he was taken prisoner by the Japanese. For three and a half years, Towery and his fellow POWs were beaten and starved. When he was freed, he weighed only 90 pounds. After the war, Towery became a newspaper reporter in Cuero, Texas. While he was investigating corruption in a veterans' program, his car caught fire in his driveway. The police determined that a fault in a car bomb caused the bomb to go off prematurely. It was intended to kill Ken when he started the car to drive off to work.

*   *   *

Teele and I asked Bill Greener from the Republican National Committee to meet with us at campaign headquarters. This was going to require heavy legwork, and we needed to outsource it. He brought along several of his staff, including Michael Bayer and Candace Strother. We introduced ourselves and got right to the point.

"We're coordinating the Ferraro research," Teele said, "and we need your help and cooperation."

Greener was all ears. I'd dealt with him on the Saturday morning weekly conference calls coordinating the campaign's efforts. His analysis was good, his political instincts were sharp, and he was strong on follow-through.

Teele laid out what we wanted from him.

"First, we have to go through Justice Department and Senate reports on organized crime families, especially the Gambinos. We need to pull out all the names we can, along with a description of the role and activities of any individuals identified in the report as foot soldiers, underbosses, et cetera."

Bill's eyes widened.

"Why can't you just go to the Justice Department and ask them to do it?" one of Greener's staff said.

"Isn't there a presidential commission on organized crime that could help?"

"That's the last thing we want," Art said. "The Administration has to be clear of all of this. We can't ask anyone in the entire government to do anything officially or unofficially. Work with the public reports in the Library of Congress."

"This isn't because of the Hatch Act," I said. The act prohibited federal employees from participating in a political campaign, with a few exceptions for presidentially-appointed officials.

"It's because of Watergate," I went on. "There's no way we can involve the Justice Department or any other federal agency in investigating the Democratic vice-presidential nominee on behalf of the campaign. That's how people end up in jail."

Greener nodded.

"How soon do you need this?" Mike Bayer asked.

"It's the first priority," Teele said, "even if you have to pull some people off the Quotes and Votes project."

Bayer looked like he was ready to go back and get started. I had the feeling the Quotes and Votes project was not as exciting as delving into organized crime.

"There's more," Teele said. "We need to cross-check all the organized crime names you get against the Federal Election Commission reports of her campaign contributions. Maybe we'll get a match. Start with her first congressional campaign and go from there."

"All right," Greener said. "Anything else you need?"

"Yes," I spoke up. "We don't want to talk this around town. This whole operation is confidential. So if you find anything don't shop it to reporters yourselves. We'll handle that end of it."

As the RNC's director of communications, Greener spent most of his day talking to journalists. Bill was a professional and I doubted he would freelance any hits on Ferraro, but I had to make sure he got the message.

"Would it be useful to you if we identified properties listed as organized crime clubs or residences in the reports," Mike Bayer asked, "and then overlaid it on a map of Zaccaro-owned or managed properties?"

I didn't know Mike well yet, but this was the soldier in him and I liked it. He wanted to map the target. We wrapped up the meeting confident we had something underway. What we would do with the results was still an unknown.

*　　*　　*

President Reagan held a news conference a few days later, on July 24. Helen Thomas, a veteran reporter from UPI who had covered three previous presidencies, asked him what he thought about Ferraro's remark that he wasn't a good Christian.

"Well, Helen," he said with a smile, "the minute I heard she'd made that statement, I turned the other cheek."

When the reporters stopped laughing, Reagan went on to defend his economic policies. It was their impact on the poor that Ferraro said justified her claims about Reagan's lack of faith.

Helen asked a follow-up question.

"Ed Rollins said today that the Ferraro nomination to the number two spot could be one of the biggest busts in history. And do you think so?"

"Helen," Reagan said, "I wouldn't touch that question with a 10-foot pole. I understand he's retracted it already."

Ed's need to retract his quote about Ferraro was typical. Rollins had a penchant for making statements to the press that made irresistible copy. It often got him into trouble. Early in Reagan's first term, he had been forced to apologize to a congressman after saying the White House had "bashed his brains out" and "lined him up in front of his open grave" in order to get his vote on a crucial piece of legislation. We cringed whenever Ed was invited to the Sperling Breakfast, an informal weekly get-together between the press and a newsmaker to discuss events, especially when it was a slow news day.

That raised the odds that a Rollins quip would become a headline. But the tough talk and hardball bravado was part of Rollins' persona. The press loved him for it and so did rank-and-file Republicans.

Ed wasn't alone in talking to the press about Ferraro. Almost everyone on the campaign's fourth floor had special relationships with individual reporters. Other senior aides were complaining to reporters on background that Wirthlin had kept them muzzled about Ferraro's qualifications.

Andrea Mitchell, a correspondent for NBC, said that senior Republicans were complaining the media had a double-standard in covering Ferraro and that if a man had questioned his Christianity the press would have been more critical. Mitchell asked Reagan if he agreed that there was a double-standard.

"I have never been one to campaign against opponents," Reagan said. "I prefer to campaign on our record ... that's the way I'm going to conduct myself in this campaign."

Mitchell had a follow-up.

"What kind of strategy are you going to use against the first woman vice presidential candidate?" she asked.

"Well, I think this is a decision for those who are working on the strategy of the campaign to deal with, and I'm going to let them do that."

I felt like Reagan was speaking directly to me and Teele. I wondered how much he and Nancy had already discussed Stu's reassurances that the campaign was working on how to get Ferraro.

It was becoming apparent that disciplining our own team was vital. The GOP convention was due to open in a matter of weeks. Literally scores of thousands of Republicans eager for blood would rub elbows with thousands of journalists eager for stories. Speaker after speaker would line up in front of microphones at news conferences and on the podium to extol Reagan's praises and denounce Mondale and Ferraro. They would bump into reporters at the convention center, in their hotels, at restaurants and bars, and in the men's and ladies' rooms. From the lowliest delegate to the Senate majority leader, the convention-goers all had the super-sized egos of politicians. They would be difficult to control sober, virtually impossible to control when a bit drunk.

There was, however, one possibility that we might discover a way to put Ferraro on the defensive without seeming to question her qualifications. Ferraro was likely to follow Mondale's lead and release her tax returns. Maybe we'd find something useful there.

On July 25, Ferraro did indeed announce that she would disclose several years of her tax returns and those of her husband sometime within the next 30 days. Stu Spencer set up a meeting for Art and me with Don Alexander, a partner in the Washington office of Morgan, Lewis & Bockius. Alexander was an expert tax attorney.

After a hot cab ride from Capitol Hill, Alexander's office was a cool relief. Not all D.C. taxis had air-conditioning, and beneath my suit jacket my shirt was soaked.

Alexander welcomed us cordially and asked how he could help. He was in his 60s, a former IRS commissioner and World War II combat veteran who had won the Silver Star and the Bronze Star. After the war he'd gotten his law degree at Harvard.

Stu had already made introductions for us over the phone so we got right to business. Alexander had already agreed to help, so the meeting was really a formality and a chance to size one another up.

"We'd like you to head a group of lawyers and tax experts in analyzing Representative Ferraro's returns as soon as they become available," Art said. "We need to know how to advise the campaign and the White House to react to what's in them. Neither of us are experts."

Alexander's reputation was impeccable. When he was appointed IRS commissioner, Alexander discovered that the Nixon White House had set up a secret unit in the IRS called the "Special Service Staff" to audit groups and individuals on the left and the right. Within three months of taking office, Alexander disbanded the unit and refused to allow the IRS to be used to harass and persecute those on Nixon's "enemies list." He began lobbying Congress to pass taxpayer-confidentiality protections. When President Nixon was selected for a random audit by the IRS, he was furious, but Alexander persevered with the audit. Nixon ended up owing $400,000 in back taxes and penalties.

"If there's nothing unusual in their tax returns," Art said, "that's all we need to know. And of course if anything stands out, we'd like to know that too."

"We may not be able to tell much about his business without the company tax returns," Alexander cautioned. "My hunch is they'll be more interesting than the 1040s."

We offered to suggest names to help with the analysis, but Alexander said he'd have no problem pulling his own group together.

"If we do find something about their tax returns that needs to be explained to reporters," I said, "do you have any problem if we give them your name as someone willing to speak on background?"

"I'll go on the record if you want," Alexander said. "I'd say the same thing on the record that I'd say on background. Is there anything else?"

"Yes," I added. "We need to analyze the returns at least as quickly as the press does. Preferably faster."

"We can start as quickly as you can get them to us," he said.

I jotted a note: "RB84 action item, pick up and distribute tax returns." I preferred not to leave this detail to a courier service.

On the way back we lucked out. The first cab we hailed was air-conditioned.

"Can you imagine standing up to a president like Nixon?" Teele said.

"Takes some balls, that's for sure."

I told Art what I thought our next priority should be.

"We need an understanding of Zacarro's business, P. Zacarro and Company. What's their line of work, how many properties do they own, what rentals do they manage, who are the tenants, the owners? The works."

"Um-hmm," Teele said. "Maybe we can get a law firm in New York to pull together the articles of incorporation and property records. Someone who does real estate deals."

"Yeah. We could put them on checking for building code violations, mortgages."

"You don't think Greener's people could check into any of that?"

I shook my head.

"I think it's better if we divide responsibilities and accountability. Don't overload anybody."

"That makes sense," Teele said, but he looked at me as if he wanted to hear my real thoughts.

I wasn't ready to articulate my reasons, or maybe they were still percolating in my subconscious, but I felt sure about the compartmented structure I was suggesting. There was no reason Don Alexander, for instance, needed to know what Greener's group were doing about organized crime connections. If we found anything interesting in the real estate business, there was no reason Greener's group or Alexander's needed to know about that.

When we returned to headquarters Stu wanted to know how the meeting went. We gave him the upshot.

"He won't let us down," Stu said. "Alexander's reliable."

We told him about our idea to engage a law firm to pull the paperwork on Zaccaro's real estate holdings. He agreed, on the stipulation that we go through the Reagan-Bush committee's attorneys to find a politically-reliable firm.

Over the next 10 days we stayed busy building a basic understanding of Ferraro. We read the biography that had been hastily compiled to satisfy public interest in her. Her parents had run a nickel-and-dime store in Newburgh, New York. Her father died of a sudden heart attack when she was eight years old. Her mother sacrificed and only ate meat once a week to give her daughter a good education. Geraldine studied law and wanted to become a prosecutor, but when she interviewed with New York County Prosecutor Frank Hogan, he rejected her application as soon as he found out she was engaged. According to Ferraro, Hogan didn't think that a woman could have a demanding career and be a wife and mother. The sexist discrimination awakened her to feminism. She practiced law on her own, took time out to raise her children, and with determination finally became a public prosecutor in 1974, the same year Frank Hogan died. It became her springboard to Congress.

Geraldine Ferraro's narrative was the epitome of a late 20th-century

Ronald Reagan and Roy Cohn in the Oval Office, Rupert Murdoch in background, January 18, 1983 (courtesy Ronald Reagan Presidential Library).

woman's American dream, a hard-working, multi-generational immigrant success story. Or so it seemed.

*   *   *

Roy Cohn called and gave me the phone number for Bruce Rothwell, an editor from the *New York Post*. I knew that Cohn had done legal work for the paper's owner, Rupert Murdoch, and accompanied the Australian media mogul to a meeting with President Reagan in the Oval Office.

Cohn said that Rothwell would work with us in getting out stories on Ferraro. The problem was we had nothing to offer. I was uncomfortable with Cohn making media contacts on our behalf, but I put Rothwell's name and number in my Rolodex, just in case. We were laying the groundwork, but we still had no idea how to take action against Ferraro that wouldn't backfire.

7

Yours, Mine and Ours

Reagan-Bush Headquarters
Washington, D.C.
August 1–20, 1984

Compartmented is the term my CIA friend Howard Bane used.

The month of August, Howard and his wife rented a beach house in Ocean City, Maryland. They invited my wife and me to bring our 17-month old son, Benjamin, to stay for a weekend. I'd known Howard since 1980 and we'd collaborated on several projects, including political research I'd done in Spain while I was a graduate student at Oxford University.

I was happy to get out of the Washington torpor and spend some time with Howard at the beach. During our stay I told him about the Ferraro operation. We discussed the problems of how to get the information we needed and set up an operation that couldn't be easily exposed through leaks or an inside informant. Over the weekend, we refined the details of how to investigate Ferraro.

Creating a compartmented organizational structure to handle the various aspects of the probe was key. My instinct had been right. Teele and I would know what each component of our team was doing, but the individual components would be on a need-to-know basis. In some instances, they wouldn't even know the other components existed. Aside from Stu Spencer, we were the only ones who would have the full picture of the Reagan-Bush campaign's investigation into Geraldine Ferraro.

When I got back from Ocean City, I proposed to Spencer that we hire Howard as a consultant for the project.

"How well do you know him?" he asked.

"I worked with him in a couple of different capacities," I said. "I trust him completely."

"I don't know," Stu shook his head. "When you use CIA guys they have you in their pocket forever."

Stu's political consulting business had foreign clients, and I thought maybe he didn't want to feel beholden to the CIA.

I let it drop. I knew if I asked for Howard's help again, he'd give it.

*   *   *

After the weekend at the beach I started building our teams by interviewing people we'd identified who had the right credentials and wanted to help reelect Reagan. Like corporate headhunters, we knew the kind of qualifications we wanted and where to begin looking—among the scores of professionals who had volunteered to work on the campaign. Many of these people had contacted the campaign and filled out forms outlining their experience and were literally waiting to be asked to help. In other cases, senior aides like Nofziger, Spencer and Rollins knew of individuals they thought we should approach about aiding our investigations.

Myles Ambrose was a tall Irish-American in his late 50s who had been an assistant U.S. attorney in New York and gone on to fight organized crime at the Treasury Department. We met in my office at campaign headquarters. I explained the confidential nature of the assignment and then outlined the work we had to do.

"We're going through all the public congressional and Justice Department reports on organized crime and matching names against Ferraro's Federal Election Commission campaign contributor filings," I said, "but that's only the beginning. We're also reviewing Zaccaro's real estate business. If we find ties to organized crime figures, we'll need to know as much about those people as possible. Some of this may involve legwork."

Myles volunteered to organize a group of ex-detectives with experience investigating the Mafia. One was Arthur Grubert who'd been on the New York Police Department's organized crime squad. Another was Bill Sirignano.

Ambrose called them his "Guinea Chasers." It was a construction industry term for the workers who followed heavy road-grading equipment on foot, looking for exposed markers that indicated whether dirt had to be added or removed from the roadbed. I liked the analogy. Myles' Guinea Chasers would be the ones to get out on the streets examining the leads we uncovered.

One tip was about a character named Nick Sands, a.k.a. Dominic Santiago, who had been shot eight or nine times with a 9mm pistol while sitting in his Lincoln Town Car and survived. An anonymous, handwritten letter addressed to Al DelliBovi had tipped us off to Sands' connection to Ferraro. Bill Greener's group at the RNC sent over a copy of it. Sands had chaired a fundraising dinner for Ferraro's 1978 campaign for Congress. DelliBovi had run against Ferraro. I asked Ambrose to get the Guinea Chasers started on finding out everything they could about Sands.

Bill Callahan also volunteered his service. He was the founder of Unitel, a private intelligence and security firm based in Manhattan. Callahan was a former federal prosecutor who played a key role in dismantling a heroin-smuggling network. After hearing some of the same rumors about Ferraro that had reached the White House, he called the campaign to offer his help.

Callahan's call was routed to me. Because of the need to keep the campaign staff from attacking Ferraro in the days immediately after Mondale's announcement, the campaign senior staff had been told that Art and I were developing the campaign's strategy for handling her candidacy. No one was to do anything about her without checking with us. That meant almost any call that came in about Ferraro was referred to me or to Art. While we kept the details about what we were doing secret, the top players in the campaign knew we were up to something. They just didn't know exactly what we were doing or how we were accomplishing it.

Callahan's contacts were wide-ranging. We discussed how we might work together, and I suggested that when we had developed as much information as we could about an individual or organization we'd taken an interest in, I would call to ask what he could find out about the person or entity. He agreed and said he'd call us when he came across something or someone he thought could be helpful to us. I took him up on his offer and asked him to check into the tip about Nick Sands.

It didn't take long to get these investigative assets in place. But we couldn't put them to full use while the tedious work of cross-checking Ferraro's contributor names against known organized crime figures was underway.

I was impatient for leads. Almost a month had gone by since Mondale's announcement of his running mate, and we still had no way to safely go after Ferraro. Any day now I expected a phone call from the White House telling us to take up Roy Cohn on his plan. I got a four-inch-thick binder of the Federal Election Commission (FEC) reports on Ferraro's campaign contributors and started going through the names myself.

We did get some relief. We weren't the only ones scrambling to learn about her. The press was also doing its job. In the second half of July the Associated Press and United Press International reported that Ferraro's 1978 congressional campaign had taken $110,000 in illegal loans from her family, including the children. They claimed they'd misunderstood the rules and only paid a minor fine of $750. The *Wall Street Journal* ran an article analyzing Ferraro's failure to disclose her husband's assets on FEC reports. *Newsday* ran a report that said there were 106 pending violations cited against Zaccaro's real estate firm by New York housing authorities. The *New York Times* reported that Ferraro failed to list her husband's assets and their joint holdings in required House of Representatives financial disclosure forms.

The most damaging press coverage was a story in the *New York Tribune* about one of Zaccaro's tenants, Star Distributors. The company was one of the largest distributors of pornography in the country. The newspaper reported that Star Distributors was controlled by the DeCavalcante crime syndicate. At the end of July, the *Washington Post* reported that John Zaccaro owned a half-interest in the building used by the pornography distributors.

In early August, a conservative non-profit organization called the Washington Legal Foundation filed a complaint with the House Ethics Committee claiming that Ferraro had failed to properly disclose her financial holdings.

The Reagan-Bush campaign had nothing to do with this early investigative reporting into Ferraro, but I wondered if Roy Cohn had given some reporters a nudge. In any case, we welcomed the media scrutiny. Nancy was pleased with the negative coverage, and it bought us time while we planned our own approach. The stories took some of the pressure off, at least temporarily.

*   *   *

On August 13, Gerry Ferraro solved our quandary.

She told a reporter that although she would release her tax returns, her husband wouldn't disclose his because of sensitivities regarding his business. The couple had filed separate tax returns beginning in 1979, when she first took her seat in Congress. Ferraro explained her husband's position: "[His] reaction was, 'Gerry, I'm not going to tell you how to run the country, you're not going to tell me how to run my business.' You people married to Italian men, you know what it's like."

It seemed ironic that Ferraro, who complained when negative news stories appeared earlier about the biased media treatment of Italian-Americans, was now resorting to a stereotype to rationalize her husband's objections to disclosing his tax returns.

The issue exploded. Wirthlin did some testing and confirmed that Republicans could safely pile on and demand that Ferraro disclose her tax returns.

Now a new round of tipsters began calling the White House and the campaign. They included major real estate developers, who briefed us on all the ways income could be sheltered from the IRS in the real estate business. They speculated that Zaccaro had a multi-million-dollar gross income but paid only a negligible amount of tax. The more Zaccaro dug in his heels and refused to release his tax returns, the more convinced our side became that the returns would be a major embarrassment for Ferraro.

We scrutinized Ferraro's congressional financial disclosure statements, required under the Ethics in Government Act. They didn't suggest anything remotely like what the campaign brass and White House were expecting from Ferraro's tax returns. Her income and assets were relatively modest. His income and assets were excluded from the statements because Ferraro maintained that their business affairs were kept separate.

"Why do you suppose she's fighting so hard on the tax returns?" Teele asked one afternoon while we pondered their significance. I shook my head.

"I've got a question for you," I said. "Do you believe the number 13 is unlucky?"

"What?"

"On the 13th of July she screwed up by questioning Reagan's Christianity. Now it's the 13th again, and she steps in it with the tax returns."

"It might be unlucky for her," he said, "not for us."

"I can't wait to see what happens on September 13th."

Art laughed.

"The question I always ask myself is how someone made their first million," he continued. "If they're going to cut corners or do anything crooked, that's where you'll find it."

I pointed out that Ferraro's declared assets didn't reach a million dollars.

"There's something about those tax returns," Art said. "We have to understand those returns before anyone else does."

"There's something I've been thinking about. We need a second group of tax attorneys and accountants to go over the returns."

"You don't trust Alexander?" Art looked at me oddly.

"No, I do. I mean, yes, I trust him. But I still think we need a second group."

"Why? The more people become involved, the higher the likelihood it will leak."

"Look, everyone expects us to find something big," I said. "There's going to be a lot of pressure to do something when those returns come out. We have to be absolutely right that the first shot we take isn't a dud."

"What are you getting at?"

"We need an A Team and a B Team," I said. "They shouldn't know about each other. Each one should think they're the only group analyzing the tax returns. Then when we get the analyses, we compare both results, and we only use what overlaps. At least in the first 24 hours. That way we don't get off on a tangent."

"That's a good idea," Teele said. "Did you come up with that yourself?"

"The CIA uses it."

"Do you have anyone in mind?"

"Ron Robertson. I think he can pull together a second group for us."

Robertson was general counsel for the reelection campaign.

"At the rate this disclosure is going, we should have one team based in Dallas during the convention," I said.

The controversy over Zaccaro's returns was delaying Gerry's disclosure of her own tax returns. We were now less than a week from the start of the Republican National Convention on August 20. It would conclude on the 23rd.

We took the idea to Stu. He agreed with our reasoning. His credibility was on the line too. He'd persuaded the First Lady to be patient while we came up with an effective way to go after Ferraro, and everyone from the president down was waiting for results. There would be a hurry to get our spin on Ferraro's tax returns into the first 24-hour news cycle. If we went with something flimsy and half-baked, we risked losing the confidence of the White House, not to mention those on the campaign like Lee Atwater who were itching to take over the Ferraro operation.

*   *   *

Demanding the release of John Zacarro's tax returns didn't run afoul of Wirthlin's warnings about attacking Geraldine Ferraro, so we turned the surrogates loose. The press did the rest.

The evening of August 15, Lisa Colgate scrawled a note on an AP wire story with a Portland, Oregon, dateline: "John—This isn't really 'new' but I thought you'd like to see it—Lisa." The wire story summarized John Zaccaro's interview on NBC's *Today Show* in which he said he was "reconsidering" the release of his tax returns.

After a few more days of pressure, Ferraro announced that her husband would also disclose his tax returns.

*   *   *

Twenty minutes after noon on August 17, Art and I met with Chuck Rund and his associate, Deborah Deane. Since the last briefing, they had collected and analyzed 10 months of data on women voters. Dick Wirthlin's firm, Decision Making Information, had also completed fresh polling and focus group research on Ferraro. This was the most definitive study undertaken on Ferraro's candidacy and its potential to change the election. We were eager to hear the results.

"She will have an impact never before seen in a presidential race," Chuck began. "She'll pull votes from us, mainly from women, mostly Democratic women but also Republicans."

"We expect the 1984 electorate to be 53 percent female," he said, "between 500,000 and a million more women will turn out than in 1980."

"This is due to Ferraro on their ticket?" Art asked.

"That was our expectation before Ferraro," Chuck said. "Given the polling results, turnout could be even higher."

He went on to elaborate her demographic strengths and weaknesses and pointed out that her image with the voters was still relatively undefined. By "defined," Rund meant that the voters would have a good grasp of the issues and policies she supported and a sense of her personality and character.

"We don't expect her candidacy to be well defined in the voters' minds until early September," he said, "and possibly not until late September. Last week her negative rating was 29 percent."

That was good news on two fronts. The controversy over the tax returns and the poor publicity Zaccaro was getting were having an effect. The fact that her image was still poorly defined gave us time to launch an offensive to drive her negative ratings higher before she was able to define her candidacy and the voters formed solid opinions about her.

Rund went into detail about attitudes toward Mondale compared to Ferraro. Mondale's ratings were poor. His positive/negative ratio was 1.2 to 1. Once a candidate's positive/negative ratio reaches 1:1 they're virtually unelectable.

In contrast, Ferraro's positives were twice as high as her negative ratings.

"She's his strength," Rund said, "and 52% of the voters say they've already made up their mind on her, but 48% haven't."

If Ferraro's appeal to women voters grew, she posed a major threat to Reagan's reelection. Her popularity might be enough to put Mondale into the Oval Office, especially if Reagan couldn't narrow the Gender Gap and female turnout on Election Day was high. Conversely, if her appeal weakened, Mondale's lackluster ratings wouldn't be able to buoy the Democratic ticket and Reagan's prospects of reelection would strengthen substantially.

Chuck's advice was intriguing.

"Don't define her," he said. "The longer she stays undefined, the tougher it is for Mondale to go on strategic offense."

He pointed out that the Mondale-Ferraro ticket had dropped from 44 percent on August 11 to 40 percent on August 13, attributable chiefly to the impact of the financial disclosure issues. The Reagan-Bush ticket had risen from 46 percent to 52 percent on the same dates. On August 11, at 46 percent to their 44 percent, the race was a dead heat, within the poll's margin of error. Two days later we had pulled ahead.

The data was clear. The fate of the president's second term depended on how our campaign handled Geraldine Ferraro's historic candidacy.

*   *   *

On the eve of the Republican Convention, speculation about Zacarro's tax returns was at a fevered pitch. Republican developers and real estate barons alerted the campaign and White House to be on the watch for very high deductions for depreciation. The campaign's senior management anticipated that the tax returns would show a high level of gross income but a low percentage of taxes paid. The most optimistic hope was that Zacarro had filed tax returns with excessive deductions and would be forced to file amended returns. If so, it would be a serious political embarrassment.

I knew something was wrong with those scenarios when Gerry Ferraro's arrival at the accounting firm of Arthur Young & Co. for a nine-hour briefing on her husband's finances was covered by the media. The press had obviously been alerted in advance about the photo opportunity. Television crews covered both her arrival and her departure.

I tracked down Art.

"She doesn't need this briefing," I said. "Their campaign has staged this as a press event. They could just as easily have scheduled a private briefing at the family residence."

"It's a smart move," Art said. "She looks like the innocent spouse who doesn't know what her husband is up to. It insulates her from any bad news when the returns are released."

"Yeah, it's smart, all right. It makes it look like she was so uninvolved in Zaccaro's business that it took the experts nine hours to explain it all to her."

The couple's tax returns were scheduled to be released on August 20. The day before their release, it hit me. The Mondale-Ferraro team wasn't concerned about disclosure of the tax returns.

"I think I know what's got them worried," I told Art. "It's not the tax returns. It's the Ethics in Government Act."

"You think there are problems with her financial disclosure forms?"

"She's left Zacarro's businesses out of her filings for years. She says she isn't required to report finances and assets, because they keep their financial affairs separate."

"So when the Mondale team brought in the high-powered accountants to review the tax returns before their release," Art said, "they would have examined her claim to an exemption from the Ethics in Government Act requirements. They must have discovered she's vulnerable."

"We've been looking in the wrong direction," I said. "That explains why the Mondale team's trying to create the perception that she was in the dark about his finances. Zaccaro's the fall guy on this one."

Art looked thoughtful.

"That could be," he said. "If so, we need to be ready to analyze those financial disclosure statements from Dallas. A lot of people are going to be disappointed if there's nothing in the tax returns."

The executive offices of our campaign were emptying out as one after another of the top staff left for Dallas, where the Republican National Convention was just about to take place. Art left for the convention before I did. I was waiting for the release of Zaccaro's and Ferraro's tax returns on the 20th.

That morning I composed a memo titled "Ferraro's Press Strategy" and faxed it to Dallas for hand delivery to Ed Rollins on arrival. Lee Atwater and other senior members of the campaign were already there, along with top officials from the White House. Stu was with the president and First Lady.

My memo outlined the Mondale campaign's elaborate media stagecraft and my suspicions that there were no bombshells in the tax returns. I didn't want Rollins to inadvertently raise expectations about political fallout from the returns in discussions with the press or our own team in Dallas. Instead, I counseled lowering expectations about the tax returns and shifting the focus to her financial disclosure statements. The Washington Legal Foundation complaint had set the clock running on a review of the complaint by the House Ethics Committee. Under the rules, the review of whether or not an investigation was warranted had to take place by September 12.

Later in the day, the couple's joint tax return from 1978 was released along with their individual returns for the past five years. I made sure Don Alexander got copies, then I took two more batches and went straight to National Airport and caught a flight to Dallas. I kept the tax returns with me as I took my seat in a smoking row toward the rear of the airplane.

After takeoff, I lit up a Marlboro and thumbed through some of the pages. I didn't bother to read closely. We had two teams of experts to do that for us. I ordered a gin and tonic and read John Updike's *Bech Is Back* for the rest of the flight.

As the plane descended, I could see the small cluster of high-rise buildings that comprised Dallas' downtown. The rest of the town sprawled around it for miles, rings of freeways, suburbs and ex-urbs. This was about as much of Dallas as I was likely to see on the trip. I'd be lucky if I got out of the hotel.

I didn't bother checking in when I got to the Loews-Anatole Hotel. I went straight to the back room where Bob Charrow and his team waited and gave them a set of the tax returns.

"When you finish going through these, talk to me or Art first," I said to Bob. "Don't let anyone else from the campaign or the White House know your findings until we do."

"How am I going to do that if Mike Deaver wants them?" he asked. "Or Jim Baker?"

"Just tell them you're not finished yet. Tell anyone who asks you you're not finished, until you brief us. Got it?"

Bob nodded.

I wasn't naïve. I knew that within a few hours of reading Ferraro's tax returns, our team members would spread word about their contents to every political insider and reporter they knew. In politics, everyone loves to be in the know, and those who aren't want to be thought to be in the know. One way people show they're insiders is to gossip and leak information. We recognized this would be an ongoing challenge in the Ferraro operation.

I didn't care what they said later. I cared what they said first. It was crucial for Teele and me to understand the tax returns' implications and then explain them to Spencer so we could present a unified judgment to the White House about the message we should use. The last thing we needed was for tidbits of the analysis to leak out piecemeal and for somebody to jump the gun with the press and put out inaccurate spin. Once we had developed our spin, all and sundry were welcome to it.

Because they'd had a head start of a couple of hours over the Dallas team, the Alexander group's analysis came in first. By early evening, Teele and I had gotten preliminary assessments from both teams.

There was nothing unusual.

Ferraro and Zaccaro had a net worth of about $3.8 million. Based on their income, they paid tax in the right bracket. In fact, according to our experts, it appeared they weren't aggressive enough in taking deductions and depreciating assets. The tax they paid put them safely above the range likely to trigger an audit.

We were scheduled to brief a dozen top White House and campaign officials in Ed Rollins' suite later that evening. It appeared from the tax returns that we might have to disappoint them. Then it hit us.

Seen in a vacuum, the tax returns were unremarkable. So were Ferraro's congressional financial disclosure statements. But when the two sets of financial documents were assessed together, a different picture emerged. I raced to get copies of the congressional filings to our tax review teams and asked them to cross-check them against the returns.

The result was political pay dirt. The tax returns showed that Ferraro was involved in her husband's business to an extent that made disclosure in the congressional filings mandatory but no disclosure had been made. She received income from the business and was listed as an officer of the company. She had omitted her husband's sizeable assets by improperly claiming an exemption. It was a clear violation of the Ethics in Government Act.

When we arrived at Rollins' suite, Teele and I were surprised and a little alarmed at the size of the group waiting for our briefing. White House Counsel Fred Fielding's deputy, Sherrie Cooksey, was present. Margaret Tutwiler, a protégé of Chief of Staff Jim Baker, was there from the White House Political Affairs Office. So was Deaver's deputy, Mike McManus. Pollster Dick Wirthlin was there, as was the reelection campaign committee's attorney, Ron Robertson. Deputy campaign manager Lee Atwater was pacing the room in his usual frenetic manner, while Ed Rollins sat patiently. Only Rollins had been told in advance that we had good news.

Teele opened our briefing, taking his time to go through what the tax returns showed in great detail. The result was anticlimactic. Everyone had been expecting political dynamite. The disappointment in the room was palpable. It was like someone had let all the air out of the party balloons.

Art turned the floor over to me. I launched into the conflicts between the House financial disclosure forms and the tax returns.

"If we're right," I concluded, "we can trigger a House Ethics Committee investigation. And if we've read this information right, she's in trouble. She'll either be reprimanded or censured, but this isn't even close to a gray area. She's way over the line."

We stopped short of outlining how we proposed to get the investigation started. There was no guarantee that the Ethics Committee would act on the Washington Legal Foundation complaint. If we wanted an investigation to start and finish before the election it was going to take political pressure.

The group in Rollins' suite were seasoned pros. They understood without any need for explanation that we had reached the limits of what was prudent to discuss. The group was too large for any in-depth discussion of the pros and cons of approaching various members on the Ethics Committee. If word of their involvement was revealed, it could lead charges that the White House was politicizing the process.

Teele and I had little time to savor the moment. We went over the tax returns and congressional financial disclosure forms with our teams again to make sure we understood the nuances. The findings were reduced to succinct bullet points to make it easy for lawmakers and reporters to get the key points. We checked and double-checked the work.

Nancy was elated when Stu Spencer told her that we finally had a plan.

8

Frenemies

Some of the most original costumes in America are on display at political conventions. Delegates covered head to heel in campaign buttons and red, white and blue garments resembled the Cockney Pearly Kings and Queens I'd seen in London on my first visit in the 1960s. There were so many buttons stuck to some delegates that their clothes would probably fall to pieces if the pins were pulled out.

Teele and I didn't have much time to admire the political pageantry. We had a full-time job trying to contain the damage caused by Lee Atwater. Lee encouraged Republican officials attending the proceedings, including Senate Majority Leader Robert Dole, to attack Ferraro by comparing her credentials to George Bush's resume. It was a direct contravention of Wirthlin's guidance and openly flaunted Rollins' directive that no attacks be launched on Ferarro without first being cleared by us. Every time I heard about one of these capers, I tracked down Rollins or Spencer to tell them they needed to yank Atwater's chain and get him back in line. Atwater would protest that he hadn't been able to control the remarks of the offending official, but I thought he had a strong motive for encouraging the tactics.

Lee wanted the credit for driving up Ferraro's negative ratings in order to bolster his standing with Vice President Bush. Atwater was already angling to run Bush's political action committee and presidential exploratory effort starting the following year. Lee's ultimate goal was to become Bush's campaign director in 1988, and he was orchestrating attacks on Ferraro at the convention to demonstrate his value to Bush.

* * *

On the morning of August 22, Ferraro held a news conference in a hotel ballroom at Kennedy International Airport to answer questions about the tax returns. The news conference was televised live, and I watched it from my Dallas hotel room.

Statements by Ferraro and her accounting team were followed by questions from the press. The line of inquiry quickly shifted to the unsavory revelations about Zaccaro's tenants. Although she was on the defensive for almost two hours, she coolly parried reporters' queries.

I was surprised to see a young man among the reporters, Gregory Fossedal, who had briefly worked for me at the U.S. Department of Education. He identified himself as a correspondent for the *Wall Street Journal*. When he felt that Ferraro was dodging his question, he shouted at her to answer it. You could see the atmosphere of the news conference change. Fossedal's rudeness swung the pendulum in Ferraro's favor.

At 1:15 that afternoon I had a lengthy phone conversation with Mike Saperstein from Bear Stearns in New York. He had studied the couple's tax returns and watched her news conference.

Saperstein knew the real estate market. He estimated the value of their real estate holdings between $10 to $20 million. Assuming average leverage on the properties and their estimated market value, he figured the couple's net worth to be just under $4 million. The cash flow from the buildings was in the $1.5 to $2 million range annually. He advised pulling records on Zaccaro's partnerships in Albany to find out who his business partners were. Then he said there was an expert at NYU who thought the value of their holdings could be far higher than the records indicated. It was an intriguing lead. Understanding the couple's assets was a vital step if we were to be able to identify gaps in her House financial disclosure forms.

My convention credentials gave me access to everything, but I spent very little time on the convention floor. I had been in the room for Reagan's speeches and with him in small group meetings in the Roosevelt and Cabinet rooms many times since I first went to work for his political action committee, Citizens for the Republic, back in 1979.

I preferred to watch the campaign speeches on television. The image on the screen showed what was real to most voters, not what was happening in the room where the speeches took place. In politics, perception is reality.

When I wasn't following the convention action, I found it productive to network in the receptions, where the drinks and conversation flowed. Roy Cohn threw a party at the convention and invited me.

A few days before the start of the convention, *New York Magazine* released its August 27 issue containing an account of how John Zacarro's real estate management company, P. Zaccaro Co., Inc., managed a property for the underboss of the Gambino crime family, Aniello Dellacroce. Because he

President Reagan and Vice President George H.W. Bush at the Republican National Convention, Dallas, Texas, August 23, 1984 (courtesy Ronald Reagan Presidential Library).

liked to evade surveillance by disguising himself as a priest, Dellacroce got the nickname "Father O'Neill." The magazine described Zaccaro as Anniello Dellacroce's "landlord."

The building, at 232 Mulberry Street, was owned by a Zaccaro partnership called Frajo and under the firm's management from 1963 until 1971. Gerry Ferraro was an attorney in private practice when the building was sold to a group of buyers in 1971. She represented the purchasers, one of whom was named Larry J. Latona. A decade later, those buyers sold it to another Gambino crime boss, Joseph LaForte, Sr. According to the magazine, Dellacroce continued to live on the premises throughout the changes in ownership.

The article bore Cohn's fingerprints. I suspected he'd tipped off the magazine so that the article would appear during the Dallas convention, a sample of the kind of coverage he could generate for us.

Roy Cohn knew how to host a party. He didn't lobby me about his news conference proposal. Instead, we talked about another Zaccaro property.

Cohn said we should take a look at 23 Cleveland Place. He said there had been a gambling raid on the property on April 11, 1981. A reporter named Guy Hawtin from the *New York Post* had started to check it out and told Cohn that a "Mafioso" had been busted in the raid. He thought the illegal gambling operation might be connected to Dellacroce or LaForte. Cohn was under the impression one of them had purchased the property from a Chinese owner.

He reminded me that Bruce Rothwell was eager to work with the campaign, and I confirmed that Rothwell had been in touch. I also took note of Guy Hawtin's name. It might come in handy.

But I was far from finished with the financial analysis on Ferraro and not quite ready to follow up Mafia leads.

Myself and Roy Cohn at his cocktail reception, Republican National Convention, Dallas, Texas, August 1984 (author's collection).

* * *

The next morning the phone jangled me awake.

"Hello?"

It was Ed Rollins. He wanted me to join him for breakfast in his suite. I glanced at the radio alarm clock. It seemed like I'd only gotten to sleep a few hours earlier.

"Sure," I said. "What's up?"

"We're having breakfast with Bob Novak."

I knew what that meant. Rollins wanted me to give Novak the scoop on Ferraro. Novak's nickname was "the Prince of Darkness." The Evans and Novak syndicated column was known for its formula of featuring a hapless protagonist trying to do the right thing being undercut by a wily opponent, generally featuring a behind-the-back betrayal often by someone supposed to be on the same side. In addition to his political column and newsletter, Novak was a regular panelist on John McLaughlin's new talk show, *The McLaughlin Group*. It was rapidly becoming Washington's top-rated political television show. The conservative columnist would ask the questions, Rollins would get to eat his breakfast in peace, and I'd be kept talking the whole time explaining the nuances of our financial analysis.

When I hung up with Ed I called Teele's room.

"Do you know what time it is?"

Teele listened while I explained my proposal to outline the basic conflicts between the tax returns and congressional financial disclosure forms. I said I would withhold any talk of our intent to get an Ethics Committee probe started.

"Whatever you do, stay away from that!"

"How far do you think I can safely go without Novak figuring out that's where we're headed?"

"Let him think it's his idea. If he suggests it or brings it up, just say you're counting on the press to get Congress to do its job. Just make sure Rollins doesn't get off message."

I hadn't worked with Rollins before the 1984 campaign. We met in early 1981, at Lyn Nofziger's office when Lyn was assistant to the president for political affairs and Rollins was his deputy. Lyn liked to hold Friday evening cocktail hours in his office, Room 175 of the Old Executive Office Building. Room 175 had been Richard Nixon's hideaway office, and on the wall Lyn had a framed letter from Nixon saying that during the Vietnam War he'd made the decision to mine the Haiphong harbor and bomb Hanoi in that office.

Lyn served Bombay gin and tonics. It was my favorite brand, so I attended whenever I could. More than a networking opportunity, Lyn's cocktail hour was a chance to let our hair down among friends where we could speak openly instead of in the guarded manner Washington requires. When I was introduced to Rollins, I was wearing a burgundy tie with eagles embroidered on it. He mistook them for pheasants and asked if I was a sportsman.

I still didn't have a feel for Rollins. He was smart, worked long hours, and aspired to serve in the Cabinet. He had an uncanny ability to dominate a meeting, not by shouting others down or stifling dissent but by the force of his personality. And he had a reputation for speaking too freely with reporters.

I hoped Rollins would be open to my advice on how to handle Novak. I was still straightening my tie as I hurried to Rollins' suite, hoping to have a few minutes to brief him before Novak arrived.

I was too late. There were half-eaten breakfasts in front of both men. It was clear they had been talking for some time.

I cautiously briefed Novak on the elements Teele and I had agreed were safest. The columnist asked good questions and took detailed notes. As he was leaving, Novak asked me to stay in touch regarding our discoveries about Ferraro. I was relieved that he hadn't asked whether we intended to demand an ethics probe.

"You did a good job," Rollins slapped me on the back. "It's going to be a great column."

"He doesn't know we want to start an investigation, does he?"

If we were to have any chance of launching an Ethics Committee probe, it had to appear non-partisan. The Democrats controlled the House of Representatives, which meant they controlled the House Ethics Committee too. A column saying Reagan-Bush officials wanted a probe would be counter-productive and taint it from the start.

Rollins must have sensed my qualms. Ed said they'd been talking about other aspects of the campaign before my arrival.

I hurried off to give Teele the low-down on the Novak encounter. There was a look of concern on his face when he opened the door to his room.

"There's no need to worry," I said. "It went fine."

"That's not what concerns me. Stu has set up a conference call between us and Fineman."

He meant Howard Fineman, the Washington bureau chief of *Newsweek*. Teele shut the door unnecessarily hard.

"Every damned body on this campaign who thinks he has a special friend in the press is going to start peddling our names and saying we're the guys with the dirt on Ferraro. Coffee?"

"Yeah, thanks." I sat down.

Art shook his head.

"We don't have this under control," he sighed, "and if we're not careful it's going to spin out of control."

Teele walked to the window of his suite, his back to me. There was an expansive view of the Dallas skyline.

"I've been thinking about this," he said. "You know what I've come up with?"

"No."

"Our own people are the enemy."

"What?"

"We're not in danger from the Democrats finding out about this. We're in danger from our own people talking all over the place. What if Ferraro really does have Mafia friends? Think about that."

I thought Teele was having a bad morning. But I didn't know him well enough, and in any case, I was too diplomatic to say he was becoming paranoid.

"Let's say we find out about mob ties. Let's say we get an investigation started. What does it look like to you when we put this out on the street?"

I hadn't thought that far ahead. I was still preoccupied with how much we didn't know about Ferraro and how much work lay ahead of us in the coming months.

"It looks like dirty tricks, that's what. Like Jeb Magruder and CREEP."

I knew all about Nixon's 1972 reelection and the Committee to Reelect the President's dirty tricks. It had destroyed his presidency. People had gone to prison.

"I don't know about you, Art, but I have no intention of breaking any laws."

"Can you say for certain no one else in the White House or campaign will?"

I was silent.

"And if they do, whose names are associated with this? Yours and mine, buddy."

We were interrupted by the phone. It was Spencer. He reminded Teele about the Fineman call and then asked for me.

"I've got someone I want you to brief in D.C. when you get back," Stu said. "Bob Schackne, from CBS."

I hung up and told Teele. He turned back to the skyline.

"We've got to get this under control. We've got to get out from briefing the press one by one. In fact, we've got to figure out how to do this so that our fingerprints aren't all over it. So that when it blows up—and it will blow up—we don't get burnt."

He turned around and looked hard at me, searching my eyes.

"Who do you trust on this campaign?"

In truth, there was no one I completely trusted other than Lyn Nofziger. Rollins had given me no reason to distrust his motives, but his habit of talking too freely could pose trouble.

"I trust Stu, and only Stu," Teele said, "but I'm not going to give Fineman anything he can use. Starting right now, I suggest we try to make ourselves boring if anyone else sets us up with reporters."

"How do you propose we do that?"

"Stick to facts and rumors that have already been reported in the press. Make it seem like we've got nothing to add."

"That doesn't solve the problem about getting information out."

Teele looked at me closely again.

"Let me work on that," he said. "Meanwhile, let's try to get through Dallas without attracting any more attention to ourselves."

He turned away again.

"Our own people are the enemy. The more successful we are, and the bigger this thing becomes and the more it hurts Ferraro, the easier it is to use it against us. We've got to trust each other and watch each other's backs."

Art's warning brought to mind a joke about working in the White House. How do you know your friends from your enemies? Your enemies stab you in the back. Your friends stab you in the front.

9

Implausible Deniability

Reagan-Bush '84 Headquarters
Washington, D.C.
August 24–31, 1984

"Make sure you take off your ID tag before you go," Spencer said, "and if there's anything on your briefcase, like luggage tags, that identify you as working for the campaign or White House, take those off too. They may have a hidden TV camera on you."

We all wore identification at campaign headquarters. It was required for access, and most people kept their ID on throughout the day. I wore mine on a metal ball chain that allowed me to tuck the card into my shirt pocket so it didn't dangle loosely around my neck. If someone really needed to see my ID I'd pull it out of my pocket and then put it right back in.

Stu set up a lunch meeting for me with CBS correspondent Bob Schakne at the rooftop restaurant of the Hotel Washington. It hadn't occurred to me that CBS might be preparing one of its trademark ambush interviews, the kind that made *60 Minutes* compelling viewing. Only this time it could be me in an uncomfortable close-up with sweat popping out of the pores on my forehead as Schakne grilled me.

Spencer's baby-blue eyes registered that I'd gotten his point.

I went back to my office and put my ID card and copies of our white papers about Ferraro and Zacarro's tax returns and discrepancies regarding the Ethics in Government Act in my briefcase. The campaign produced a daily news digest on legal-sized paper of television and news reporting by national and regional papers. I buried myself in the post-convention press coverage.

Everything had gone according to plan in Dallas. Reagan's acceptance speech was beautifully delivered. We had kept the message on Reagan's renewal of the American spirit and the economy and his commitment to peace through strength. "Morning in America" was the tagline for the coming wave of commercials produced by the campaign's Tuesday Team. The themes and press coverage of the convention pre-saged the ad campaign.

This was no time to mar things with a story on CBS about the Reagan campaign muddying Ferraro's reputation. The feature in *New York Magazine*'s August 27 issue had whetted the media's interest in the Mafia angle. Art arranged for a law firm to collect all the records related to any property owned or managed by John Zaccaro or Gerry Ferraro. I began researching the buyers who owned 232 Mulberry Street between 1971 and 1982 to see if any organized crime ties could be established. We had other mob-related leads, but none were fully developed to the point that we felt confident disclosing them to journalists.

Nancy Reagan was eager for the campaign to start hitting Ferraro for her mob ties, but I planned to hold back the organized crime leads we had already found when I met with Schakne.

It was a typical August day in Washington. The humidity was so high, the air was almost liquid. In the few minutes it took me to hail a taxi a film of sweat moistened my shirt. As we drove the 10 blocks down Pennsylvania Avenue the tepid flow from the cab's overworked air conditioner barely cooled me.

I tipped the cabbie an extra buck on the two-and-a-half-dollar fare and got out a block away from the Hotel Washington. It was 20 minutes before the meeting with Schakne, giving me time to reconnoiter the layout. I checked for vans parked near the hotel that might hold a camera crew. In the lobby I loitered a few minutes to see if there was a spotter, someone watching for my arrival to alert a production team. Nobody seemed to pay attention.

I rode alone on the elevator. The Hotel Washington's rooftop was a favorite spot for tourists and for dates because of the view of the White House, especially in the evening when it was illuminated. I scanned the diners and didn't see any familiar faces. I looked around to see if there was anyplace CBS might have concealed a secret camera. It didn't look like a set-up. I went back downstairs and took a seat in the lobby.

Schakne didn't notice me when he arrived. He was wearing a light-colored suit and tie, typical D.C. attire for the summer. He went straight to the elevator. I waited a few minutes then rode up to the restaurant.

Schakne had already taken a table. I introduced myself, and we ordered lunch. After the obligatory small talk, he got to the point.

"Stu Spencer says you've found out some interesting things about Gerry Ferraro."

Channeling my inner accountant, I launched into a spiel about the deficiencies in Ferraro's financial disclosure statements. Schakne's eyes began to glaze.

He tried to turn the discussion to organized crime ties, but I feigned ignorance. Beyond what I'd read in *New York Magazine*, I said I didn't have any information. I wondered if Roy Cohn had already given Schakne an earful.

My goals in the meeting were two-fold. I wanted to drum up press interest in Ferraro's financial statements in order to build pressure for an Ethics Committee investigation. The *Washington Post* had reported in its August 22 edition that it was unlikely that the House Ethics Committee would open an investigation in the few remaining weeks of the legislative session. It was accurate reporting, but by making a probe seem like a long shot it dampened the rest of the media's interest in the financial discrepancy angle.

At the same time, I didn't want to come across as an interesting source to cultivate. Teele and I hadn't yet decided how to safely disseminate the information we were developing without risking exposure. The mere fact that Spencer felt compelled to warn me about the potential for a secret camera persuaded me CBS wouldn't make the cut when we chose a media outlet for distributing the information we developed on Ferraro. Even if Susan Zirinsky was the producer, she was too junior in the corporate hierarchy to guarantee confidentiality.

Schakne's response was perfect. He was pleasant, thanked me for the meeting, and suggested we stay in touch.

Clearly, I'd bored him. He gave me his business card, I passed him the white papers, and we said good-bye.

"How'd it go with CBS?" Teele asked when I got back to headquarters.

"He didn't seem too interested," I shrugged. "I don't think I'll get any follow-up calls."

Art smiled.

"I've lined up a meeting for us with the *Philadelphia Inquirer* later in the week," he said. "I know an editor there I think we can work with."

*   *   *

Nofziger's morning Attack Meetings focused on getting campaign surrogates to demand an Ethics Committee investigation. Congressman Dick Cheney (R–Wyoming) was an avid supporter of our efforts. After the meetings, we would quickly draft one-minute speeches to send to Capitol Hill for Republican members of Congress to use in floor remarks. One day Nofziger caught me staring at a blank page in my IBM Selectric typewriter. A cigarette dangled from my lips.

"What's the matter?" he asked. "Why aren't you writing?"

"I'm stuck on the opening line."

"I'll tell you a trick I learned in deadline reporting," Lyn said. "Just start writing. Anything at all. It doesn't matter what the subject is. It can be nonsense. You'll beat writer's block every time."

It was a reminder that there were just over two months left in the campaign, and even less time before Congress recessed until after the election. If we wanted an Ethics Committee investigation it had to happen fast.

Meanwhile calls from reporters kept coming. Robert Novak called and asked me to get back to him on something "very important." Greg Fossedal left a message that he had to reach me because of an "emergency." A reporter at the *Wall Street Journal* I'd never had contact with left a message that the newspaper was about to print a story that would "interest" me. Since the convention, word had spread that I was the one to call about Ferraro. Art's meeting with the *Inquirer* couldn't happen soon enough.

Our research efforts were beginning to pay off. We had thousands of pages of public records about Ferraro and Zaccaro. We also collected federal and New York State reports on organized crime. By combing through the Federal Election Commission reports of contributions to her House campaigns and cross-indexing them to known organized crime figures, we found donations from Michael LaRosa, a.k.a. "Mike the Baker." He had a conviction for labor racketeering. In a 1981 court case, he was described in testimony as a conduit between organized crime and corrupt union officials.

We checked Zaccaro's real estate business and discovered that he'd been the managing agent for five LaRosa properties until November of 1977. In addition to LaRosa, there were several dozen other political contributors and Zaccaro business associates we were just beginning to check out, including some major organized crime figures. This was just the kind of information we wanted to make public, but we had to do it discreetly.

Zaccaro was becoming a problem for the Mondale campaign. In addition to his real estate business, Zaccaro's tax returns revealed that he had another source of income as a court-appointed conservator or guardian for a number of estates.

During the weekend of the Republican convention, the *New York Times* and the *Washington Post* scoured the couple's tax returns and financial disclosure statements and discovered that Zaccaro had made questionable loans to his business associates from the estate of an elderly widow named Alice Phelan. Zaccaro had been appointed as conservator of her funds.

Media coverage resulted in Zaccaro appearing before New York State supreme court Justice Edwin Kassof to defend his handling of Phelan's money. The *Philadelphia Inquirer* was one of the newspapers that covered the affair. I made a note to check court records to determine if Zaccaro had other conservatorships so we could gather his court filings and examine how he accounted for the funds.

* * *

Art Teele had on a dark suit and a studious demeanor for our meeting with Asa Green and Don Barlett at the J.W. Marriott. Green was one of the few African American editors on the *Inquirer* staff. He looked young enough to be in his 30s, perhaps a year or two older than me. I was just coming up on my 29th birthday. Barlett was a veteran investigative reporter on the Pulitzer Prize–winning newspaper. He'd covered Mafia and corruption stories. They'd arranged a room in the hotel where we could talk discreetly. The meeting was strictly off the record. Teele opened the conversation by explaining our roles as staff for two of the campaign's top officials, chief strategist Stu Spencer and campaign manager Ed Rollins.

"In that capacity, we've come across a lot of troubling information about Ferraro that we think the public has a right to know but that our campaign isn't going to touch." He looked at me. "John and I have decided on our own to get the information out, but we can't have it connected with us or the campaign or we'll get fired."

Barlett asked what kind of information we were talking about. I explained that tips came into the campaign from all kinds of sources, people in New York politics, attorneys, former state and federal officials, New York state detectives, even our anonymous tipster Quixote.

"We can't follow up these leads," Teele said, "but you can. We'd like to pass the information along to you, on the condition that you check it out independently. You have to verify it. If you decide it's newsworthy, you can't mention us at all."

"This can work both ways," I added. "We may have sources you don't. When you have a lead, run it by us if you want, and we'll check with our sources to see what they know."

"And you're doing this without the approval of the campaign?" Barlett seemed skeptical.

"Absolutely. We're lone cowboys on this one," I said. "We'd be in deep shit if anyone knew we were doing this."

Green looked slightly pained. He either had a headache, or he sensed that the paper was being used.

As an example of what we were offering, I outlined the LaRosa campaign contributions without going into excessive detail. Barlett looked intrigued. Art emphasized that we were genuinely concerned about the Mafia ties.

"What happens if she becomes vice president and the mob has some kind of hold over her? What happens if she's in the mob and she becomes vice president? What if Mondale has a heart attack? The public has a right to know about her before they vote."

We talked for more than an hour before we struck an uneasy alliance. They agreed to take our leads and independently verify them. If they published a news article, they wouldn't reference us or the campaign as sources. We agreed to deal with them exclusively. We traded cards and phone numbers. Barlett gave us three numbers on which we could reach him: the news desk, the city desk, and his direct line.

On the ride back to Capitol Hill we were ecstatic. The *Philadelphia In-quirer* was a respected newspaper with solid investigative resources. No one would suspect them of being a mouthpiece for the Reagan-Bush reelection committee. Better still, by dealing with the Philadelphia-based Barlett instead of a D.C. Beltway reporter, we minimized the inevitable gossip that would surround a journalist who was clearly getting leads about Ferraro that none of the other Washington press had. No one does as much digging as an envious reporter. A Washington reporter would likely think a Philadelphia paper was getting tips from sources in New York instead of us.

We'd developed the channel we needed to start pumping out the mob stories.

Back at headquarters, we downplayed our enthusiasm. We didn't want anyone on the campaign aside from Stu Spencer to know about our agreement with the newspaper.

"We're finally out of the retail business," Teele said. "From now on, when it comes to the Mafia, do your best to avoid briefing any other reporters about Ferraro."

On August 28, the *Philadelphia Inquirer* reported that Ferraro had received three campaign contributions from Mike LaRosa. The article included colorful details about LaRosa's trial, including that he had been identified by

Geraldine Ferraro speaks to reporters on the campaign trail, Flint, Michigan, September 13, 1984 (photograph by Turnley, copyright Detroit Free Press/ZUMA Press).

a Teamster official who was secretly being wiretapped by the FBI as the bag man for payments to New York's top five organized crime families.

When she was questioned about the article by the reporters who covered her on the campaign trail, Ferraro overreacted. She called the *Inquirer* article "inaccurate and offensive," thereby triggering a fresh round of stories which not only featured her reaction but rehashed the original article. This time, the Mafia tie appeared not just in the pages of the *Inquirer* but in newspaper pages and on television sets across the country.

It was a pattern we hoped would repeat itself many times before Election Day.

10

Watergate Redux

Reagan-Bush '84 Headquarters
Washington, D.C.
August 30–September 3, 1984

My morning routine still included Nofziger's daily Attack Meeting, but once it was over my full attention went into the Ferraro investigations.

A few days after the *Philadelphia Inquirer* story broke, one of the receptionists handed me a phone message.

"Dr. Jack Ferber called you," Erin Walsh said. "He wants you to call him back."

"What's he want?"

"He wouldn't say. He said he has to talk directly with you."

I had no idea who Jack Ferber was. He left a New York City phone number. I returned his call that afternoon.

Ferber said that a patient had told him Zaccaro owned a night club and had a criminal record. He said there was a prostitution arrest from the 1950s. When I pressed him for details, he wasn't sure who had been arrested. It might have been anyone with the same last name, or it might have just been rumor. I asked if he had any more information, and he said the arrest may have taken place in Union City, New Jersey.

Ferber said he would call again if he learned anything more. Before we hung up he asked if he could get four invitations to the presidential inauguration.

Roger Stone popped into my office. Stone had blond hair, dressed impressively, and was in his mid–30s. He was a regional political director with responsibility for the Northeast, the same task he'd had when we first met on the 1980 Reagan-Bush campaign.

"Somebody dropped this on my desk," he said. "It looks like it's about Ferraro so I'm giving it to you."

I looked at the cover page. It appeared to be a transcript from a tape recording. There were no names on it, no indication of its origin. People were identified only as Speaker 1, Speaker 2, and so forth.

"Where did this come from?"

"I don't know," Roger said. "It just showed up on my desk."

I flipped to the second page and saw Ferraro's name in a discussion. Zaccaro's name was there too, misspelled as Zacarro. Another name, Art Finkleston, was on the first page of the transcript. I guessed it was another misspelling and probably referred to Art Finkelstein, a highly reputable California pollster who had helped elect Alfonse D'Amato to the U.S. Senate. Whoever typed the transcript obviously didn't know the names being spoken about on the tape recording.

I put the document down until I'd gotten through my day's list of Ferraro action items. Passing Ferber's tip to Myles Ambrose was on the list. It sounded like a long shot but we still needed to check it out.

Afternoon came before I got back to the transcript.

The document was 54 pages long. From the context, it appeared to be an interview with Al DelliBovi, the Republican candidate who ran against Ferraro in New York's 9th Congressional District race in 1978. DelliBovi subsequently went to work as regional administrator for the Urban Mass Transit Administration at the same time that Art Teele was administrator.

The transcript wasn't dated but from the context seemed to have been a recent interview, probably soon after Ferraro's candidacy for vice president was announced. The interviewers asked DelliBovi every question conceivable about Ferraro, from what kind of candidate she was to her demeanor in a debate and whether her kids got into trouble.

A female interviewer, identified in the transcript only as "A Lady," wanted to know if Ferraro was "a pushy broad."

Superficially, the document was innocuous. Debriefing DelliBovi would be useful. It would help the team preparing Vice President Bush for the debate with Ferraro to know about her style and how she responded to pressure.

It wasn't surprising that Roger Stone had gotten a copy. The first name "Roger" was sprinkled throughout the document, chiefly in DelliBovi's responses to how his campaign was managed. Stone and Finkelstein had apparently run the campaign jointly.

But the more I read, the more bothered I became. Many names were blanked out. There were missing words. The transcript had been redacted.

Who was carrying out the interviews? Where else had they been? What other information were they after? Who were they reporting their findings to? Who did the redactions? What was so sensitive it had been omitted? Not least of my concerns, who else had a copy and where was the audiotape from which it had purportedly been transcribed?

About a third of the way through the document, I hit the roof, internally. In fact, I did everything I could to keep my composure, even though the words I saw on the page spelled extreme danger:

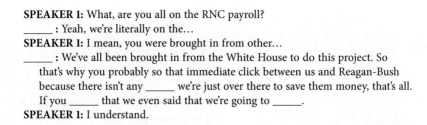

SPEAKER 1: What, are you all on the RNC payroll?

_____ : Yeah, we're literally on the…

SPEAKER 1: I mean, you were brought in from other…

_____ : We've all been brought in from the White House to do this project. So that's why you probably so that immediate click between us and Reagan-Bush because there isn't any _____ we're just over there to save them money, that's all. If you _____ that we even said that we're going to _____.

SPEAKER 1: I understand.

I lit a Marlboro Light. The blank lines bothered me. Someone had scrubbed the document to remove references they believed could be troublesome. From the omissions, it seemed it might be someone on our own team or working parallel to us.

Despite the redactions, the document in my hands was incendiary. Even if it was a forgery and no interview had really taken place, if it fell into the hands of a reporter no one would believe our denials. But if the document was real, it could cause incredible damage to the campaign. To link the White House to the opposition research into Ferraro was bad enough. But to do it on tape, and then produce who knows how many transcripts and spread them around the campaign and who knows where else was idiocy. All of our efforts to distance the Ferraro probes from the campaign would be gone in a puff of smoke if the press got a copy.

I tossed the transcript onto my desk and glanced out at the hallway.

Aides—junior, senior, and those stuck in the middle—bustled past my office on their way to Stu Spencer's and Lyn Nofziger's and Ed Rollins' offices in one direction or Jim Lake's press operation and Lee Atwater's political division in the other. Cigarette smoke wafted from Michele Davis' office while she fielded a call, while the phones on Erin Walsh's desk kept up their steady ringing. My dial-up modem squawked with updates from the Voices for Victory program. It was a normal day on the campaign, except that somebody had fucked up badly.

I hoped I wasn't holding the transcript of an interview conducted by Bill Greener's staff. If they were representing themselves as coming from the White House it was an outright fabrication. The only opposition research group that was composed primarily of people who had previous White House experience was Ken Khachigian's staff, but they were supposed to be focused on Mondale, not Ferraro. And there was no reason why they would say they were on the payroll of the RNC, unless they were trying to deflect attention from the campaign.

I snubbed my half-smoked cigarette in the ashtray and went down the hall past Atwater's lair and the Swill Hole toward Roger Stone's office. I caught him between phone calls. I thrust the transcript at him.

"Do you have any clue who's behind this?"

He shook his head.

"I can call DelliBovi and ask," he offered.

"I think he might be a Schedule C," I said, referring to a class of political appointee subject to the federal Hatch Act which constrained campaign activity.

"Let's leave him out of it," I continued. "I don't want to attract any more attention to this than we have to. Do you have any idea what was in these blank spaces?"

I showed him the gaps in the transcript.

"No, except that they're hiding something."

"I need to find that tape and I need every copy of this transcript that exists."

"I'll let you know if I find out anything," Roger said. He looked sincere.

I went back to my office and kept reading. What I came across next made me queasy:

> SPEAKER 1: ...John Zacarro's [sic] name was involved with some buildings in and around that vincinty [sic] ... it's usually a political process, you know, they give it to somebody who milks them even further. And the sense was, at least in this case, he had gotten a HUD building ... that would be interesting to find out. Did he get the HUD assignments and where did he get them and how did he get them and all that kind of thing.
>
> SPEAKER 3: We will have the HUD files over here tomorrow.

HUD meant the Department of Housing and Urban Development, a Cabinet-level agency headed by former New York judge Samuel Pierce, Jr. Secretary Pierce was the only African American in the Reagan Cabinet. And files from his agency might now be in the hands of the mysterious people who said they were from the White House and possibly on the Republican National Committee payroll.

It didn't matter that the documents might be public records available to anyone or accessible through a Freedom of Information Act request. What mattered would be the appearance. It would look like the Reagan campaign was using the federal government to investigate the Democratic vice-presidential candidate's husband.

The worst thing of all was that I didn't give a damn about the HUD files. It was an open secret in Washington that developers with connections routinely got HUD contracts. Even if it was true that John Zaccaro had been awarded a HUD contract, it would hardly elicit a shrug of the shoulders from cynical Beltway journalists.

But if those same journalists got hold of the transcript, they would see it as evidence that the White House was using the Executive Branch to find damaging information about Ferraro to use in the reelection campaign. Even though this wasn't the case, it would create a scandal that would progress to a congressional investigation by the Democrat-controlled House of Representatives, and depending on how much was happening behind my back, might end up with people going to jail and the president implicated in high crimes and misdemeanors and, in a word, impeachment.

* * *

I learned the hard way after the 1980 campaign what can happen with loose scraps of paper. Nofziger was the campaign's press secretary. He initially hired me in 1980 to handle special communications programs. I became a press spokesman in the fall, when Nofziger spent most of his time with the Reagans on Leadership 80, the campaign plane. Lyn was in California with the Reagans on election night and stayed there for about a week. That was when I saw the political souvenir hunters Dumpster diving through the campaign's trash.

Some of the papers they found that day featured in Representative Don Albosta's (D–Michigan) congressional investigation into how the Reagan-Bush campaign got hold of President Jimmy Carter's debate briefing books.

Albosta was chairman of the House Post Office and Civil Service subcommittee when Laurence Barrett's 1983 book *Gambling with History* was published by Doubleday. The book reported remarks made by David Stockman that the Reagan-Bush campaign had obtained a "pilfered copy" of Jimmy Carter's debate briefing book before the 1980 presidential debate.

Stockman, a former member of Congress who was now director of the Office of Management and Budget, had helped prepare Reagan for the October 28 debate with Carter. Barrett's revelation was picked up by several newspapers and spurred Albosta to open an investigation. President Reagan also ordered a Justice Department probe.

The investigations were underway for almost a year, from mid–1983 until May 1984. The scope of the probes expanded from the debate briefing materials to a wide range of sensitive information about the Carter White House and campaign and eventually grew to include allegations about a secret intelligence network set up to monitor an October Surprise by Carter.

The press dubbed the affair "Debategate."

Stu Spencer and Art Teele had both been drawn into the probe. Art headed Blacks for Reagan in 1980. A volunteer, Thelma Duggin, sent Teele a memo about Carter's strategy to win the African American vote. It included budget details, target cities, and plans to send a "surrogate caravan" through black communities. Duggin's memo caught the investigators' attention because it described the information as coming "from a very reliable Carter aide." Art told the investigators he didn't know who the source was, and Duggin said it had come from a friend at the State Department.

Spencer's involvement stemmed from a memo Wayne Valis gave to the campaign regarding Carter's debate strategy. Valis, who was employed by the American Enterprise Institute, was a volunteer for my communications program as well as other campaign efforts. Spencer, along with other top campaign officials, was questioned about the memo. He said he didn't recall seeing it during the campaign.

Another of my volunteers, Dan Jones, had supplied a memo that ended up in the hands of the debate preparation team with the words "report from White House mole" handwritten on it. In a sworn affidavit, White House Chief of Staff James Baker said that to the best of his recollection the Carter briefing materials were given to him by Bill Casey, Reagan's 1980 campaign director. Margaret Tutwiler, who was Baker's aide in the 1980 campaign and followed him into the White House, backed up Baker's version.

Bill Casey denied being the source of the Carter briefing materials. Casey, a veteran of the Office of Strategic Services who ran spy networks in Europe during World War II, worked on Wall Street before becoming Reagan's campaign manager. Reagan appointed him CIA director after the election. The press office was on the same floor as Casey's in the 1980 campaign and we had several interactions. At the White House, Casey had an office two doors down the hall from mine before I joined the 1984 reelection campaign. Casey used his Old Executive Office Building hideaway frequently and I saw him in the hallways regularly, accompanied by a security detail even inside the secure building.

As the probes got underway, the *New York Times* published a story in 1983 about an effort by the Reagan-Bush campaign to counter an October Surprise by the Carter White House. The surprise was to be the pre-election release of the U.S. embassy hostages. According to the *Times* the effort was coordinated by Stefan Halper, a Reagan-Bush aide, who collected information from CIA insiders about the potential hostage release. Halper emphatically denied any involvement in gathering information from the Carter National Security Council or intelligence community. He called the *New York Times* report "untrue." Bill Casey also denied the existence of any intelligence operation.

The denials and counter-denials spawned media speculation that conservatives in the Reagan Administration were trying to use the Debategate and October Surprise investigations to force Jim Baker and David Gergen, both moderate Republicans, out of the White House.

I had a few dealings with Halper on the 1980 campaign. He was introduced to me along with his wife and father-in-law Ray Cline, whose career in intelligence began with the Office of Strategic Services and then continued with the Central Intelligence Agency. Cline was the chief intelligence analyst during the Cuban Missile Crisis and had accurately predicted the Sino-Soviet split.

The 1980 Reagan-Bush campaign did have an effort underway to detect any release of the hostages. Retired navy admiral Robert Garrick mobilized "watchers" at ports and military airbases to monitor flights and arrivals of naval vessels that might indicate the Carter White House had made a bargain with the Iranians. Another 1983 book, *The Reagans: A Political Portrait*, by longtime Reagan aide Peter Hannaford fueled the controversy. Hannaford wrote in the book that the Reagan-Bush campaign had learned in late September 1980 that the Carter White House was negotiating the release of the embassy hostages. When questioned by investigators, Hannaford said he didn't know the source of the information.

When Albosta's investigation wrapped up it failed to reach definite conclusions about how the Reagan team got hold of Carter's briefing book. The final report came out in May 1984, barely three months before Mondale's announcement that Gerry Ferraro would be his running mate. The report outlined a probable sequence of events and cast doubt on the truthfulness of many witnesses. It contained a section on the probe's October Surprise findings that was equally inconclusive.

The experience of the 1980 campaign investigations was fresh in everyone's minds, especially Art's and mine.

* * *

I thumped the transcript down on my desk and stared at it. How many other Reagan political appointees had been interviewed by these people? How many Cabinet departments and agencies might be combing their files for damaging documents about Ferraro and Zaccaro? How extensive was the paper trail of memos, scheduling notes in calendars, phone logs, and other evidence future investigators might find?

How many transcripts were still circulating?

Who had the tape?

I still had about 10 pages left to read, and although I didn't want to see what other surprises it contained, I kept reading. Toward the end there was a long passage in which the lead questioner explained the purpose of the interview:

_____ : Our taks [sic] is fine. Leet [sic] Atwater, who's a political director, and Ed Rollins, who's the campaign director and _____ who heads opposition research is as follows. And that's build the difinitive [sic] record, hand it to them. What they're going to do is pick the least and the most damaging things and they're going to go back in terms of the campaign time wind [sic] and make judgements. Because the key is you want to wear [sic] the little stuff and then keep hammering her more and more and more. And what we have to do is line all that stuff up first and I think you are culmulating [sic] the most valuable asset that we've got. And they've, of course, asked, I'm sure they told you when they talked to you over there, this whole project is going to be kept under real tight cloak and dagger and try to keep it close. So that the usage of these bullets that you have can be used in the most controlled possible fashion … you know there are no silver bullets in there all there are are dumb dumbs [sic] and there are things that help trip her, and then hopefully because of the enormous scrutiny and pressure to be placed on everybody, she's going to start making some mistakes and when that happens then we start wearing her out, tripping her and tripping her and tripping her. But if everybody runs out and says and says ok [sic], let me show you all the dirt we've got on Geraldine Ferraro, it shows up in one piece and then it's lost.

Cloak and dagger. Silver bullets. Dum-dums. Hammer her. Wear her out. Trip her up. It was typical political bluster, the kind of bravado you could hear in almost any campaign meeting, but in black type on white paper it looked damning. If it leaked the press pack would bay and howl over it like a freshly-killed caribou.

I walked three doors down the hall and handed the document to Art.

"We have a major problem," I said. "Roger Stone gave me this a few hours ago. You need to read it."

Art asked me a few questions I couldn't answer, wrinkled his ordinarily-smooth forehead, and plowed into it. About an hour later he came into my office.

"Do you suppose there's any significance to the fact that Lee Atwater is listed first when the interrogator talks about the campaign hierarchy?"

"I noticed that too," I said. "What do you make of the fact that they didn't list the head of opposition research?"

"The missing name is whoever's running it, is my guess," Teele said.

"What did you think of the transcript?"

"Clearly, it isn't the work of a professional stenographer. There's some useful information but we've got to put a stop to this freelancing."

"I thought about calling Greener to see what he knows," I said, "but I've come down against it. I don't think Greener would be part of this. Someone else at the RNC, maybe. Or maybe Atwater's operation. If so, we should let them own it. If it blows up, the less we know about it, the better."

"You give Rollins a heads-up and I'll talk to Spencer," Art said. "Maybe they can get to the bottom of it."

He handed me the transcript.

"Keep this in a safe place," he said. "I've got a meeting lined up for us at HUD tomorrow. Wear a good suit."

* * *

We rode in Art's Chrysler K-car to the Department of Housing and Urban Development. The K-car was key to Lee Iacocca's successful attempt at a comeback for the bankrupt company. There were K-cars all over Washington. The federal government had filled its fleets with the model in order to support Chrysler.

Art was recently divorced and his K-car was a bow to personal economy. Art extolled its virtues. It had innovative engineering, with a transverse engine and front-wheel drive, and it was inexpensive. The base model was $7,235. My car was a silver Mustang II I'd had since the late '70s. To me the K-car was boxy.

I asked Art how he'd come out in the divorce.

"It was very amicable. You can look at the divorce records and you won't see a thing about infidelity, spousal cruelty, abusive behavior. The only thing we accused each other of was incompatibility."

Art had a child, a boy.

"How'd you manage it without a custody fight?" I asked.

"We kept it very civil. I may want to run for office someday. It wasn't in anybody's interest to have a messy divorce."

"What's our tack with Pierce?"

"We need to keep the secretary above it all. We're not even going to see him. We'll handle it at the staff level."

We went to the Secretary's suite and met with his Chief of Staff and an assistant. After the pleasantries Teele took the lead.

"We've come across some information that your department may have been asked to look through the files for any HUD applications or grants from Ferraro's husband, John Zacarro, or his firm. You may have been asked in the name of the campaign. We're here to say that we do not want you to produce any files, and that if you were asked to do so, the people who asked were not authorized by us."

Eyebrows shot up. Pierce's aides were either surprised to hear about it or surprised to hear Art say it hadn't been authorized. We couldn't tell and we weren't there to dig for information.

"We don't want to involve Secretary Pierce or his office in anything to do with Ferraro and Zacarro," Teele said firmly. "That's the only reason we're here today."

They disclaimed any knowledge about requests for files but thanked us for the clarification. It's what I would have said in their position.

As we got up to leave I made a point.

"This might have gone through your regional office in New York," I said. "You should probably make sure they know about this too."

By the time we left it was cocktail hour. We went to the Hyatt across the street from headquarters. Like most hotel bars, the atmosphere was sterile. I preferred my bars local and independent. This place could have been in any city anywhere in the world the hotel chain operated.

For the first time that day Teele loosened his tie.

"What do you make of this?" he said. "Do you think it's a one-off or is there another team out there doing what we're doing?"

I shrugged.

"We won't know unless we start asking a lot of questions," I said, "and even then, we might not get straight answers."

"My feelings exactly. We'll waste a lot of time and call more attention to ourselves trying to find out."

"Do you think Baker's running it? Or he's got someone else on the campaign working on it and reporting directly to him?"

Art shook his head.

"Baker's too smart to get sideways with Nancy," he said. "This strikes me as more Atwater's style. He's trying to beat us to it, whatever it is, so he can take the credit with Deaver and Baker and, through them, Nancy."

It was plausible. I'd known Lee since 1981. He was extremely ambitious, anxious to impress.

"In the White House mess there's a staff table where anyone can sit," I said. "Lee made a habit of having breakfast or lunch at the table and talking about the latest books he'd read, usually serious stuff, politics, history. He always had pithy comments about them and pretty soon word spread that he was a voracious reader."

I paused to sip my drink.

"But he didn't actually read them," I continued. "His aide, Jim Pinkerton, read the books for him and scripted comments for Lee to memorize and use at the staff table. Lee's all about getting the credit."

Teele laughed.

"I wish I'd thought of that."

I told Art about the incident with the draft campaign plan and all the red ink on Atwater's critique of it.

"I doubt he wrote that for himself, either," I said. "He was pissed that he wasn't invited to those meetings."

"That might have made him feel very competitive toward you," Art smiled.

"There was another thing when I first came on board the campaign back in January," I said. "It was kind of weird. Lee came into my office and sat down and gave me a little sermon about loyalty. Then he said, 'Charlie Black and Paul Manafort and Roger Stone and I are 30-year guys. We're going to be around a long time. We remember our friends. We remember who's loyal to us.'"

"What did you say?"

"I told him I was loyal to Ronald Reagan and I was a team player, but I didn't plan to hang around Washington for 30 years."

Art snorted.

"The problem we have now is operational security," he said. "We've got to tighten it up. Make sure people don't start sending around a lot of memos.

Keep everything on plain white paper. Leave off the To and From and CC and BCC and all of it."

"And for God's sakes, no handwritten notes about secret moles or high-ranking sources!" I said. "So what do we do about Lee?"

"Like the saying goes. Keep your friends close and your enemies closer. We should try and figure out a way to include Lee in some of what we do, make him feel like he's a part of it."

We paid the tab in cash and left.

11

Our Man on the Hill

Reagan-Bush '84 Headquarters
Washington, D.C.
September 4–6, 1984

My radio was tuned to DC 101 for the morning commute. The German singer Nena (Gabriela Kerner) had a hit called "99 Luftballons" about a girl who releases 99 balloons that are mistakenly identified on radar and lead to a world war. It was the musician's contribution to the protest movement against Reagan's deployment of short-range nuclear weapons in Europe. An English version of the song, titled "99 Red Balloons," was playing on the radio. It became a #1 hit in the U.S. charts. I liked the tune and enjoyed listening to it while driving across Memorial Bridge on my way to Capitol Hill. Gabriela Kerner had the voice of an enchantress.

Clichés like "dog eat dog" could describe the morning traffic down the George Washington Parkway through Alexandria, Virginia's Old Town and across Memorial Bridge into the District, except the comparison was unfair to canines. The commuters who made the drive to work seem like a scene from *Mad Max*, wore Brooks Brothers outfits and had business cards with titles that were sometimes 10 or 15 words long, like "Special Assistant to the Deputy Under Secretary for Educational Research and Improvement." They were propelled by feral ambition and over-inflated egos to make sure another driver never, ever got one car ahead of them, coupled with raging insecurities that if they didn't get to the office before real or imagined rivals or an imperious boss whose business card only had two words on it, like "Deputy Secretary," they might be demoted.

It was a funny thing about Washington. The shorter your title, the greater your importance. Like "President" and "Vice President." Those four extra letters and the hyphen meant a lot of time attending state funerals for second- and third-rate leaders instead of running the free world.

My car was an aggressive-driver repellant. The rear quarter panel was smashed in and the tip of the front bumper was torn upward at an ugly angle that suggested in car-to-car encounters I might not budge for anybody no matter how many words were on their business card. I didn't bother to repair the Mustang after a taxi driven by a Russian émigré hit it in the middle of an intersection back in 1981.

The insurance payment came in when I was waiting for my paycheck from the White House Speechwriters Office to work its way through bureaucratic snafus that kept changing shape each time I asked about the hold-up, so I spent the insurance money on food, beer, cigarettes, and rent, more or less in that order. By the time my paychecks became regular I was much better acquainted with Washington traffic and knew it was a waste of money to repair a car. With smooth bodywork it was just a matter of time before I'd get hit again, whereas the mangled rusting mess struck fear into people whose cars were neatly detailed.

I bit down on my cigarette, turned up the volume on the radio, and pumped the accelerator to get into the tunnel which ran underground across the Mall and deposited me downslope of the Capitol a few blocks from headquarters. I was singing along to "Somebody's Been Using That Thing" on the radio and thumping the steering wheel to keep time when I pulled into the parking garage.

I paid for daily parking and turned the ignition key over to the attendant along with a couple of bucks. The homeless man who normally occupied the same spot of concrete to the right of the crosswalk was there, reciting his usual unending speech of intertwining topics connected by a vague theory. Or at least that was my impression of it from the three-minute snippets I caught each morning waiting at the crosswalk for the light to change.

"Cigarette?" I held out a Marlboro.

"Why, thank you!" he answered.

"Need a light?" I took my Normandy commemorative Zippo and flicked the top open. It was a White House souvenir from the trip and bore the presidential seal. He bent close and let me light it. I'd learned it was the only way to shut him up for a few seconds before he resumed the speech.

I was going to be doing plenty of listening soon enough. Morning meetings to coordinate campaign actions were daily affairs, attended by as many as 15 people. They were good reminders that there was more happening in the campaign than the Ferraro business.

Instead of the elevator I took the stairs and went up them two steps at a time. I hung my coat by the door and took a few minutes to collect my thoughts over a smoke and some coffee.

It was early September and Congress was back in session after the summer recess. Months earlier, Dick Wirthlin said something that stuck with me, and I thought of it again.

"Right now," he had said, "people are paying more attention to toothpaste commercials than they are to politics. That won't change until the end of summer."

With the Labor Day holiday over, that time had come. The voters were finally thinking about their political choices instead of their brand of toothpaste. Just like nine out of 10 dentists might recommend Crest, it was our job to make sure that Reagan and Bush got plenty of endorsements.

I counted a dozen faces in the seventh-floor conference room. Nofziger opened the meeting on a point of order. He went through the assignments to keep everyone coordinated, starting with the vice president's office. Mike Baroody, a deputy assistant to the president for public affairs, was responsible for keeping Chief of Staff James Baker and the Cabinet up to speed. Ken Khachigian, Kevin Hopkins, Jim Pinkerton and I were in charge of political statements and speeches. Jim Lake, his deputy John Buckley, and Roger Bolton were handling the press and radio news feeds done by our surrogates, called "actualities." Ken Duberstein, the former assistant to the president for legislative affairs, was the liaison between the campaign and our supporters on Capitol Hill.

The big item on the agenda today was Mondale's tax plan. In a gamble, the Mondale campaign had decided to "level" with the voters and tell them a tax increase was in store. Mondale charged that Reagan had a secret plan to raise taxes but wouldn't admit it, while he was telling it straight.

Treasury Secretary Don Regan had a news conference planned for 2 o'clock and Nofizger wanted him to attack Mondale's proposals. The Office of Management and Budget was on standby to analyze his plan. Nofziger wanted Regan to illustrate specific Mondale campaign promises and what they would cost individual taxpayers. OMB Director Stockman and White House Staff Secretary Richard Darman had signed off on the request. Jim Baker had called Regan to make him understand the importance of the campaign's request.

But Regan was difficult to work with, starting before the convention. He battled the White House senior staff over anything Reagan said about taxes, insisting it was his prerogative to approve statements about taxes, even in the president's speeches. Despite Baker's phone call, the treasury secretary wouldn't commit to going after Mondale's tax plan during his news conference.

Lyn brainstormed alternatives.

"If Regan is a no-go," he said, "we can have Bush insert some language in a speech and use Senator Howard Baker and Bob Dole as back-up."

"It's better if we have Regan do it," Mike Baroody said, "even if we have to wait a day to get it out."

John Buckley said that based on what Regan's aide, Chris Hicks, had told him, he was certain that the treasury secretary would do what we wanted.

"This problem is going to keep coming up," Baroody said, "until we tell the Cabinet secretaries that they will be on short notice for this type of exercise for the rest of the campaign and that no time exists for delays."

"Excellent idea," Lyn said. "Can you get Fuller to do this?"

Baroody nodded. Craig Fuller was Cabinet secretary. He was the best option short of having the president make an announcement in a Cabinet meeting. I envisioned something like "Hey, people, if you want to keep your jobs, don't drag your heels about doing what the campaign asks you to do!"

I knew the atmosphere in the White House and the Cabinet. They were already laying plans for the second term and didn't want anything said during the campaign to crimp them. Few members of the Cabinet had ever worked on a campaign, so they had little grasp of what it took to win a national election.

Earlier in the campaign there were lengthy, almost leisurely discussions of strategy. Now the tempo had changed. There was little strategizing in these sessions. It was all about action. Nofziger was focused on execution.

The meeting continued, covering the details of getting talking points on Mondale's tax plan to Senator Robert Dole and Congressman Del Latta, the ranking Republican on the House Budget Committee. Nofziger said that wherever Mondale or Ferraro campaigned, the Republican state chairs and Reagan-Bush state chairs in those states needed to attack them on taxes. If we had other local surrogates, they should be used too. Bill Greener took on coordinating the Republican officials and John Buckley said he would handle the Reagan-Bush state chairs.

Several senior economic officials were designated to make statements regarding the plan. Commerce Secretary Malcolm Baldrige was the cowboy in Reagan's Cabinet. He'd been the Professional Rodeo Cowboys Association Rodeo Man of the Year in 1981 and liked to ride horseback with Reagan. Alan Greenspan and former treasury secretaries Bill Simon and John Connally were also on tap.

Former presidents Richard Nixon and Gerald Ford were to be kept informed. Lyn took on coordinating statements about Mondale's tax plan with the U.S. Chamber of Commerce and Business Roundtable.

Lyn wrapped up the meeting.

"Report back to me between noon and 1 o'clock about where things stand," he said.

* * *

Important as it was to attack Mondale's tax plan, I had other problems on my mind.

The House Ethics Committee—formally known as the Committee on Standards of Official Conduct of the United States House of Representatives—was due to meet the following week, on September 12. There was a glitch regarding the Washington Legal Foundation complaint. Although it was filed on August 7, for some reason the filing wasn't recorded until August 16. By the committee's rules, nothing could be put on the agenda without 30 days' advance notice. The delay in "time-stamping" the complaint meant that it might not be taken up at the September 12 meeting and would have to wait until October.

Our goal wasn't to have the committee just consider the complaint. Our goal was to have the committee launch an investigation into Ferraro's compliance with the House financial disclosure rules. The closer we came to Election Day, the less likely it was that the committee would approve a probe.

September 12 was an all-or-nothing date for us. I had put my reputation on the line in Dallas when I briefed White House and campaign brass on the financial disclosure forms. There were clear violations of the rules. The facts were on our side, but it was the politics that worried me.

Several discussions were held between myself, Teele, and others on the campaign about how to get the committee to open an investigation. Art and I went out of our way to include Atwater in these deliberations. We hoped bringing him inside the operation would put an end to his freelancing.

Atwater favored having Floyd Spence, the ranking Republican on the committee, carry our case. Atwater had helped elect the South Carolina congressman. His congressional race featured Atwater's classic line about the opponent's electroshock therapy.

I argued against Spence on the grounds that the connection to Atwater was too well-known. If the campaign was believed to be influencing the Ethics Committee vote it would backfire on us. I didn't mind Spence getting our white papers on Ferraro's disclosure forms, but I didn't want anyone from the campaign to meet with Spence or brief him on our findings. Atwater had probably already given Spence the white papers in any case.

My preference was Barber Conable, a moderate Republican who was widely respected for his integrity on both sides of the aisle. Conable was a World War II veteran who fought at Iwo Jima. To avoid being reliant on big donors when he ran for Congress, Conable wouldn't take any campaign contribution above $50. He was a supporter of President Nixon until a White House tape instructing Chief of Staff H.R. Haldeman to obstruct the FBI investigation into Watergate was disclosed. When Conable called it a "smoking gun" a new phrase entered the political lexicon.

Conable was the perfect champion for our cause. No one would suspect him of pushing a probe for partisan purposes. In fact, the only way he *would* urge his colleagues to vote for an investigation would be if he genuinely believed it was warranted. That meant we first had to convince him our evidence was solid. I felt that proving our case to Conable was our best shot at getting the Ethics Committee to authorize an investigation.

While we went back and forth with Lee without resolving it, Stu Spencer lined up a meeting for us with Congressman Conable. It was set for 5 p.m., Thursday, September 6. That would leave ample time for Conable to study and consider the case for a probe before the September 12 committee meeting.

The morning meeting on September 5 again focused on Mondale's tax plan. We used the fourth-floor conference room, conveniently around the corner from my office. Atwater normally didn't attend this meeting, but today he joined the group. We went around the table with reports. Vice President Bush agreed to include an attack on the plan in his stump speeches. The Cabinet had been briefed. Baldrige was spinning reporters and had a news conference planned. Nofziger wanted Baldrige to follow up the news conference by issuing an in-depth statement critiquing the tax plan. Senators Bob Dole and Pete Domenici were also hitting Mondale's plan.

In going over the action plan for the day, Nofziger made an odd reference to Atwater as "a spy." He said it in a joking way, but I knew Lyn well enough to understand that he meant it. He was sending Lee a signal that if the meeting's details leaked to a reporter, he would be the prime suspect.

Kevin Hopkins suggested they should include a statement on how higher payroll taxes to pay for increased entitlement spending would hit lower-income families hardest.

"The Senate leadership does not want to say 'Social Security,' period!" Ed Allison objected.

Allison was chief of staff to Senator Paul Laxalt.

"Every time the GOP just says the words Social Security," he said, "the mail to the Senate from senior citizens goes up 20 percent!"

Allison explained that the Senate leadership had made a decision to "sit" on Social Security for the duration of the campaign. Hopkins agreed to revise his statement to focus on bracket creep and inflation and leave entitlements out of it.

"Let's get to work," Lyn said. "Give me progress reports between noon and one."

* * *

You could feel the new pace of work around the campaign. Phones rang constantly. Meetings broke up quicker. People moved faster in the hallways. They came into work earlier and left later and still looked like there wasn't enough time to get everything done.

My days began with Nofziger's morning meetings. After they concluded I would drop into Lyn's office privately to bring him up to speed on our Ferraro work. I also attended the campaign senior staff meetings, television advertising meetings, and participated in the Saturday conference call to coordinate campaign activities across a range of areas. Between all the meetings, I had the Ferraro investigations to manage.

On September 6, my day began with Lyn's morning meeting. I had a full day to get through before the late afternoon appointment with Barber Conable. After Nofziger's meeting wrapped up, Teele and I went straight into a meeting with Ed Allison. He gave us a sobering status report on the House Ethics Committee.

"As of this date, there's no agenda set for September 12," he said, "The time-stamp on the Washington Legal Foundation complaint is August 16. It's possible that Stokes will defer any action on it until after the election because of the congressional recess."

He meant Louis Stokes, an African American congressman from Cleveland, Ohio, who was chairman of the House Ethics Committee. House Speaker Tip O'Neill had taken Ferraro under his wing as his protégé and urged Mondale to pick Ferraro as his running mate. The view inside the room was that Stokes, out of deference to O'Neill, would do everything in his power to bury the complaint until after the election.

Ed Allison's sources on the Hill said Stokes was considering a compromise that would allow Ferraro to amend her financial disclosure forms without any official investigation or reprimand. Another option involved having the committee staff evaluate the complaint, and after finding sufficient grounds for an investigation, giving Ferraro 20 days to respond before launching an investigation. The second option amounted to running the clock past Election Day.

We didn't have very many counter-options available. A lawsuit to compel the committee to put the Washington Legal Foundation complaint on its calendar was a long shot, but it was worth exploring with our legal team.

The meeting broke up on a down note. Teele and I talked in his office afterward.

"What do you think our chances of success are?" he asked.

"I'm not sure we've got the right read on Stokes," I said. "He was chairman during ABSCAM. Look how that turned out."

ABSCAM was an FBI sting operation that started out in 1979 as an investigation into stolen artworks. The bureau set up a phony company called Abdul Enterprises, Inc., that grew into a wide-ranging corruption probe. The House Ethics Committee launched parallel investigations of members of Congress and the Senate. One Democratic senator and six members of Congress, five Democrats and one Republican, were ultimately convicted of crimes. Stokes had won praise from prosecutors for his integrity.

"He went after members of his own party," Art said. "He didn't cut them any slack."

"The evidence is on our side. If Stokes is as impartial with Ferraro as he was with ABSCAM we'll get an investigation going."

"The easiest way out for him is to run the clock." Art shook his head.

"That'll make O'Neill and Mondale happy, and the committee can still investigate after the election."

Our next meeting was with the campaign legal counsel, Ron Robertson and Bob Charrow. Ed Allison joined us. The group consensus was that O'Neill would pressure Stokes to refuse to place the Washington Legal Foundation on the agenda. Robertson and Charrow suggested a motion asking Stokes to recuse himself from participating in any aspect of the matter.

They pointed out that the Washington Legal Foundation had filed a complaint with the Federal Election Commission about Stokes and the Congressional Black Caucus violating election laws. The case had concluded three months earlier, on May 4, 1984, with the defendants acknowledging the violation and paying a fine. Their argument for recusal was that Stokes couldn't be impartial in considering the Washington Legal Foundation complaint.

Robertson suggested filing the motion on Monday, September 10, and following it up with a press conference. Art and I agreed that it probably couldn't hurt, although I still doubted that Stokes would cave to pressure from O'Neill.

"Why don't you write a memo to Lee about it?" Art said. "He would be the best one to suggest the idea to the Washington Legal Foundation."

Ron Robertson agreed.

I didn't like the feel of things. We still had five hours to go before seeing Conable, and we were already making contingency plans if we failed to make a compelling case for an investigation. If we didn't turn our attitudes around, we would go into Conable's office giving off an air of desperation instead of confidence. He would probably sense it.

* * *

I had an important appointment in the Senate basement at 1:30 with my barber. Yves Graux, a Belgian, and his wife Nancy ran Hair of Capitol Hill there. Before the Senate location, they worked in the White House barber shop. I started using their services in the West Wing in 1981. They had begun working in the White House under Carter, who got his own hair styled there but also opened the barber shop to staff. Jim Baker, who was no egalitarian, had other ideas. He believed that the only person who should use the West Wing barbershop was the president. Reagan's longtime barber was Milt Pitts, so Baker had the Graux's lease terminated. Yves and Nancy opened shop on Capitol Hill.

After I settled into the chair Yves asked how the campaign was going. I was always guarded in conversations in Washington. I'd overheard many confidential mutterings not intended for my ears at bars and restaurants. A barber shop on Capitol Hill was a perfect place to spread rumors.

"I'm hearing that the House Ethics Committee is going to authorize an investigation of Ferraro next week," I said. "That complaint from the Washington Legal Foundation is rock solid."

"Really?"

"That's what our experts say. If they don't, it will be because Tip O'Neill told them to forget about the law."

I really hoped someone was eavesdropping, preferably a Democratic Hill aide. I wanted word to get around that we expected O'Neill to play dirty. It might make the Democrats on the Ethics Committee just a little uncomfortable about playing along with the Speaker.

When I got back there was a sealed manila envelope on my desk. Inside was a copy of Ron Robertson's memo. The only thing I didn't like about it was that it was labeled "CONFIDENTIAL." The marking would draw prying eyes.

I buried myself in our briefing papers about Ferraro's disclosure statements and tax returns. They were written on plain white paper, with no attribution of authorship, no distribution list, not even a date. Our plan was to leave Conable copies at the end of our meeting. We needed to be at his office by 5 o'clock, and there were only a few hours left. There was nothing more important than concentrating on the facts of our case.

The next thing I knew Stu Spencer and Art Teele were standing at my door.

"Come on," Stu said. "We've got a car downstairs."

We took a campaign car to the Hill. The driver, Steve Watson, let us out at the curb. Capitol Hill police manned the magnetometers by the entrance to the Cannon House Office Building. As visitors, we needed to be screened to enter the building. The line was small. There were few people coming in at 5 o'clock. In just a few minutes the three of us were on our way to Congressman Conable's office.

The receptionist explained that the congressman hadn't returned from a meeting and ushered us into his office. Stu and Art took a seat, but I noticed some glass cases containing Native American artifacts. Archaeology had interested me as a child. I lived in Spain and was surrounded by Roman ruins and medieval castles. The National Archaeological Museum was one of my favorite museums in Madrid (the other was the Prado) and I used to spend hours prowling the collections. In the '60s, Greek Attic ware pottery was displayed on open shelves. The only security was the watchful eye of a lone unarmed guard.

I was absorbed in studying the stone tools and elaborately-carved pipe bowls when Conable entered the room. As we introduced ourselves Conable came over to me.

"I see you're looking at my collection," he said. "Are you interested in Indian relics?"

"I've been picking up arrowheads since I was a kid," I said. "These are museum-quality."

He explained how and where he'd acquired several of them before turning to business. Conable looked straight at Spencer.

"If you're here for the reason I think you are," he said in a pleasant but firm tone, "we can end this meeting right now."

Stu looked surprised by Conable's abruptness. Art's eyes fluttered once in my direction before engaging Conable.

"Congressman, we wouldn't waste your time if we didn't feel this was very important," he said evenly, "and we wouldn't ask you to do something that we didn't believe was warranted by the law."

Art launched into an outline of the legal grounds for an investigation. He ended on a high note.

"We're not asking you to compromise your integrity for the sake of the election," he said. "We've had numerous tax experts and accountants review their tax returns and financial disclosure requirements under the Ethics in Government Act, and there are serious discrepancies. We're just asking that you hear our findings."

Art turned to me. I could almost hear what he was thinking: "It's up to you, buddy. Don't blow it."

I explained to the congressman that there were serious omissions from Ferraro's disclosure forms. She had failed to list a $170,000 asset that was owed to her by her 1978 campaign committee. She had $61,000 in unreported income and didn't disclose it. Although required by law to do so, she had failed on her financial disclosure forms to report the sources of her husband's income.

Ferraro had claimed an exemption from the requirement to report her spouse's assets and income by falsely maintaining that their finances and business activities were separate. In fact, they had joint investments and assets. She was listed as an officer and a company director in many of his enterprises.

The couple's careers and income overlapped in other ways. They had a beach house in the Caribbean on St. Croix that was jointly owned. John Zaccaro had paid her half of the mortgage and real estate taxes. When she ran for Congress her campaign headquarters operated out of Zaccaro's offices. Her husband and the children's trusts gave her $110,000 in campaign loans.

"We've done a thorough analysis based on the information available to us," I said to the congressman. "Our conclusion is that there is a very strong case for an investigation."

Conable asked several detailed questions that showed he was listening closely. I answered in equal detail. I'd been living with the documents regarding Ferraro and Zaccaro's tax returns and her disclosure forms for almost six weeks. I knew them by rote. As Conable's questions petered out, I sensed the time was right to see if he was on board.

"I'd like to leave you with our analyses so your staff can go over them for corroboration," I said. "If we're off the mark they'll know. But I believe they'll find what we found."

Conable looked around the room and got out of his chair.

"Gentlemen," he said, "if what you say is true, we'd better not be seen together again until after the election."

12

Failure Is an Orphan

Reagan-Bush '84 Headquarters
Washington, D.C.
September 7–14, 1984

By mid–September Washington finally begins to shed its mantle of summer humidity and replace it with crisp and cool fall mornings. Inside headquarters, the campaign atmosphere was heating up.

Steve Watson caught up to me in the hall shortly after the Conable meeting.

"Spencer said you guys were getting thrown out," he said, "but then you turned it around. Way to go!"

He gave me a hearty slap on the back. It was flattering that Spencer gave me the credit, but it was also flustering. If he'd mentioned it to Steve, who else knew?

We had three different investigative groups working for us confidentially to ferret out leads about Ferraro and Zaccaro: the Guinea Chasers, Unitel, and the *Philadelphia Inquirer*. In addition to the investigators and investigative reporters, we had the campaign and RNC opposition research teams. Per our plan, we kept all these groups working separately from one another.

Besides the teams, we also had helpful singletons, individuals operating alone who either gave us leads or helped follow them. Dave McCormack was a fire protection consultant who helped us in tracking down building code violations on Zaccaro-managed properties and in understanding potential conflicts of interest between Ferraro's legislative activity and her husband's real estate business. Larry Hackman knew New York's archives like spelunkers know caves. Howard Bane gave me an introduction to an associate of his who helped significantly but wanted no credit. An attorney in New York named Jon Weinstein understood the legal milieu in which Zaccaro got his estate conservatorships and Gerry Ferraro's legal career flourished.

We had a lot going on. Combined with the reporters on the *Philadel-*

phia Inquirer, our investigative assets were impressive. On any given day we might have a dozen seasoned professionals delving into Ferraro and Zaccaro's lives.

Stu Spencer, Art Teele and I were the only ones who knew the big picture, and only Art and I knew the details.

I poured myself a cup of fresh coffee on the way to my office. Teele was waiting for me with a book in his hand.

"Have you read this thoroughly yet?"

He showed me the cover. It was *Gerry: A Woman Making History* by Rosemary Breslin and Joshua Hammer. Gloria Steinem had contributed an introduction. You couldn't ask for better feminist credentials than Gloria Steinem's endorsement.

"I've glanced at it. Is Rosemary Breslin by any chance related to Jimmy Breslin's daughter?"

"Good question," Art said. "I don't know."

Breslin wrote a column for the *New York Daily News*. He knew Queens politics and the Forest Hill neighborhood where Ferraro and Zaccaro lived. He'd written several recent columns defending her.

I picked up the book. It looked like a puff piece, quickly written to capitalize on her sudden prominence and the fact that she was virtually unknown to most people.

"Anything of interest in it?"

"She's always laying a predicate. Take a look at page 36."

I lit a cigarette and glanced over the page. It explained that after law school she'd applied to work as a prosecutor for District Attorney Frank Hogan of New York County. He had made a name for himself in high-profile Mafia and political corruption cases. Impressed by her credentials, Hogan interviewed Ferraro. When she got a call offering her the job, she said she couldn't start work until September, because she was getting married right after her bar exams in July and going to Europe for her honeymoon.

The book said that a few days later she got a second phone call retracting the offer. Ferraro attributed the blow to sexism. According to the book, Hogan's office supposedly told her it would be a waste of time training her as a prosecutor because she'd quit to have babies.

"I don't know if I'm following you," I said. "You think there's more to this?"

Art gave me a look I was getting to know well. It wasn't smug or self-congratulatory; it was just sheer confidence like he'd had a realization about something important and wanted to see if you shared the insight. The look was a moment of anticipation, like a teacher might have watching a student while waiting for the penny to drop.

"We've already found some mob connections. What if there are more and Hogan knew about them? He couldn't have someone in his office with Mafia ties. Or someone married to someone with Mafia ties."

He had my interest. There were some gaps in Ferraro's legal career that we'd wondered about. Despite her early ambition to be a prosecutor, after the Hogan rejection she went into private practice. It wasn't until the year of Hogan's death that she took a job as a prosecutor. Stricken with cancer, Hogan retired in December of 1973. The next month Ferraro was hired to prosecute sex crimes and domestic abuse in the Queens County District Attorney's Office run by her cousin, Nicholas Ferraro. Hogan died less than three months later.

"You think Hogan had something on her?" I asked.

"It would explain why she didn't become a prosecutor while he was still alive."

I took a drag and thought about it. It would have to be something serious if Ferraro was worried that Hogan would scuttle her chances in another DA's office. Or it might just be a coincidence.

"That could be hard to track down," I said. "We need a source who was close to Hogan at the time. Somebody who worked for him closely enough to know what the issue was."

"Maybe Ambrose can help," Art said. "There's another biography too, *My Name Is Geraldine Ferraro*. We need to read both of them."

I jotted down the title.

"Every time you see she's laying a predicate, that's where we need to dig. How many of those things do you smoke a day?"

"About a pack."

"It's a bad habit. Don't you have a child?"

"Ben. He's a year-and-a-half. I never smoke at home."

"You should quit."

"Maybe after the election."

Art laughed.

"Uh-huh, and the next election, and the one after that."

"You're almost as bad as Lisa," I said.

"The intern?"

"Volunteer. She saw the cupboard where I keep my pipe tobacco and the carton of Marlboros. She calls it my 'Cancer Closet.'"

"Is she any good?"

"She's smart. I have her watching the wires for anything on Ferraro."

The campaign subscribed to the wire services and received AP and UPI stories as they rolled off the ticker. We got the news stories as they broke.

Lisa Colgate was a student at Wheaton College and a Colgate heiress. But you wouldn't know it. She didn't have a shred of attitude or entitlement.

She was intelligent and hard-working, eager to apply herself wherever she was needed on the campaign.

She was also attractive, and if I hadn't been married I would have been tempted to invite her out. But even if I was single, it would still have violated one of my self-imposed rules that I learned in San Francisco one summer volunteering for the Mission Rebels in Action.

The Mission Rebels were community activists whose leadership included Samoans, African Americans, Latinos, and Caucasians. The Rebels were considered radicals by many other community groups, but they weren't militants like the Black Panthers, who they had rebuffed when the Panthers urged them to endorse violence. Their focus was on youth, and I was volunteering on a hot breakfast program that involved starting work at five a.m. to serve warm meals to summer school kids in the run-down Mission District. Edlow Powell, one of the Rebels' leaders, saw me eyeballing a willowy co-worker. Later that day he gave me some advice.

"Listen, brother," he said. "Don't shit where you eat. Women come and go, but you've got to keep a job. It's a lot harder to break up than it is to get together."

I would have stuck to Powell's advice even if I was single, but not many others on the campaign did. Most days the pheromones inside headquarters were thicker and sultrier than the summer humidity.

Some of the romances were wholesome. Penny Stirling and Rick Shelby, one of the campaign's political directors, fell genuinely in love.

Sherrie Sandy, an aide to Lake, came into my office one day and smiled at a photo of me standing outside a church holding an infant in a christening gown.

"Is this your nephew or godchild?" she asked.

I told her that was my son. She quickly stifled what I thought was a look of disappointment.

"He's so cute," she said, retreating out the door. Within a few weeks she too was involved in a deep relationship.

Roger Ailes, who was working with the Tuesday Team on the campaign advertising, was doggedly persistent in his pursuit of several young women working in the press office. They complained to Jim Lake, the press secretary, who in turn asked Doug Watts to have a talk with Ailes about his behavior.

And that's why, if I weren't married, I still wouldn't have asked Lisa out. She was smart and I planned to use her on as many projects as she could handle.

Achille Guest came from a prominent family with a tradition of government service, horse breeding and racing. Like Lisa, Achille was unpretentious, highly personable, very smart, capable of moving in multiple social circles, and eager to help. His father was a World War II veteran who served with the

OSS and later became ambassador to Ireland. Achille's mother was Princess Caroline Murat. He was in his early 20s and volunteering on the campaign.

Because of the volume of records we were amassing, both Achille and Lisa were saving me hours of work by doing preliminary analysis of the documents. I wanted to have a thorough grasp of all the information we acquired, but it would have been overwhelming. I needed people inside the campaign as well as the teams working outside, and I tried to put both of them on the payroll. Unfortunately, there was a kind of reverse discrimination at work. Because of their backgrounds, there was a perception they didn't need to be paid. The truth was that Lisa was like any typical college student and could have used the money while Achille was trying to start his career. Being on the staff was important, and they both deserved the validation.

Secrecy created some awkward misunderstandings about what people on the campaign thought I could deliver on Ferraro. Joe Kyrillos, a young campaign aide to Vice President Bush, came to my office almost daily asking for the latest research on her. Bush and Ferraro were scheduled to debate on October 12, and Joe's job was to make sure the vice president had all the information he needed.

After a few days of sending him off without anything more substantial than the daily news clippings, I decided I owed Kyrillos an explanation.

"The kind of research I'm doing is a little sensitive to be passing on to the vice president," I said. "What I can do is give you a 24-hour heads-up before one of our stories about Ferraro breaks so you can alert the vice president's office in advance."

Joe was smart. He got it without any need for elaboration. I was relieved. I didn't want Bush thinking the campaign was unresponsive to him or that Joe wasn't doing his job right. There would be advantages in Bush getting advance notice. It would show him the campaign was actively going after Ferraro, even if our work was largely invisible.

*   *   *

Don Alexander had something important to tell us that he didn't want to discuss over the phone. We took a cab to his offices at 1800 M Street and rode the elevator to the eighth floor. The meeting was scheduled for 4:30 but we arrived a few minutes early.

"Do you have any idea what this is about?" I asked Art.

"None at all. Your guess is as good as mine."

I didn't have a guess. Unless some new angle had come to light regarding the couple's tax returns, I couldn't imagine what Alexander wanted to talk about. I hoped he hadn't picked up bad news about the House Ethics Committee, which was due to meet the following day.

We didn't have to wait long. Alexander stayed behind his desk while we shook hands and took the chairs arranged in front of it. He got straight to the point.

"This is all confidential. Not a word of it goes anywhere. Don't spread it around the campaign. I've got an informant who was in a real estate transaction with John Zaccaro that broke the law. He wants to come forward, but only if there's an investigation underway first."

"Can you tell us more about it?" Art said.

Alexander shook his head.

"With all the press interest and reporters digging around he's getting nervous," Alexander said. "He wants to cooperate with authorities, but he doesn't want to instigate an investigation."

"I see," Art said. "He's got guilty knowledge, but he doesn't want to be the whistleblower, and he figures if he cooperates, he'll get off the hook."

"Exactly. So can you get an investigation going?"

Art and I exchanged glances. We were still wondering that ourselves. We couldn't tell Alexander about the Conable meeting. In any case, we didn't know what the committee would do tomorrow.

"Can you tell us anything specific about the transaction?" Art said.

"It involves making false statements to a bank," Alexander said, "but beyond that I can't divulge the details."

"So this is a real estate deal or a loan on something of value?" Art pressed.

The prosecutor in Art was coming out. He was trying to gently lead Alexander into giving away enough information for us to narrow down the list of Zaccaro properties that might be involved.

Alexander was an old Washington hand, one of the greybeards. He'd seen all the tricks.

"If you get an investigation opened," he repeated, "he'll come forward."

"We'll see what we can do," Art said. "We might have some good news on that soon."

We thanked Alexander for the meeting and reassured him that we would keep it in confidence.

"That wrapped up just in time for happy hour," Art said. "Want to get a drink?"

We walked to the Palm. It was a power-broker's haunt, with a clientele of lobbyists and lawyers and politicians. Journalists, too, wining and dining sources from the Administration or Capitol Hill. It was definitely not the kind of place where we would discuss anything sensitive.

The dining room was nearly empty at this hour, and the waiters, dressed in white shirts and dark, long bibs, lounged expectantly. The Palm was old school. The wait staff was almost entirely male, cigar and cigarette smoking were encouraged by free matches and ashtrays waiting on every tabletop, portions were gargantuan, and the drinks were not closely measured.

We ordered cocktails at the bar. The walls were covered with framed caricatures of Washington personalities, many of them autographed. Scattered between the political players were occasional celebrity portraits. I wondered how many of the political caricatures came down after an election and how long it took to replace the *ancien régime* with portraits of the new power elite.

"What do you think the Committee will do tomorrow?"

"I honestly don't know," Art said. "Have you heard anything?"

I shook my head.

"We still don't know if the complaint's on the agenda?"

"Ed Allison might know," I said, "but I haven't heard anything."

"I wonder if it will be enough if the committee does vote to investigate."

I lit a cigarette and weighed my choice of words.

"Supposing in the course of their investigation they got word of a criminal matter," I said. "Wouldn't they refer it to the proper authorities?"

"In due course," Teele said. "The question is how long that would take and then how long it would take to cut a deal for immunity."

"You think it could be too long?"

"You know the saying. If the mountain will not come to Muhammad, then Muhammad must go to the mountain."

"I'm not sure I follow."

"Our friend has to get his friend prepped and lawyered up so they can come in and get a deal quickly. If the committee opens an investigation."

We nursed our drinks.

"What are you going to do after the election?" Art asked.

"I'm not sure," I said, truthfully. "I only came to Washington to stay for a few months, and that was four years ago."

"Where's home?"

"I'm not sure about that either. I grew up in an Air Force family. We moved every three years. I was born in Panama and lived in Spain, mainly in the West in the States. Nevada, I suppose. I'd like to get back to Europe. What about you?"

"I'm not sure either. I'll probably practice law. I might go back to Miami."

"Miami's home?"

Art nodded.

"Ever thought of running for office?" I asked.

"Someday maybe. You?"

At the time my father committed suicide he'd gambled away all his money and faced legal problems. An audit where he worked uncovered what looked like embezzlement. On top of that, the IRS was after him for back taxes. No charges were filed before his death, but the news could easily become public if I were to go back to Nevada and run for office.

"I don't think so."

I told Art about a magazine a friend and I launched in London in 1980. It was already one of the top circulation gun magazines in Europe.

"I'd like to do a Spanish language version of that," I said. "Publish it in Madrid and Latin America."

"What's your wife think about that?"

"I think she's married to Washington," I said. "We met on the 1980 campaign. Every time I talk to her about what we do when the second term is over, she gives me a blank stare."

The bartender asked if we wanted another round but we declined. There were probably phone messages waiting for us back at headquarters and still time in the day.

In the cab, Art suggested we keep quiet about the purpose of our meeting with Don Alexander for the time being. If anyone asked, we'd just say he wanted to keep it confidential.

I wouldn't have wanted to talk it around the campaign even if he hadn't asked us to be discreet. Without knowing exactly what Alexander's insider knew, it was just a tantalizing crumb. Even if an investigation got underway, there was no guarantee Alexander's informant wouldn't get cold feet. I didn't want to raise expectations we didn't have the power to fulfill.

* * *

On Wednesday, September 12, I got to the office early. The House Committee on Standards of Official Conduct, i.e., the House Ethics Committee, was scheduled to consider the Washington Legal Foundation complaint and I wanted time to think before the rounds of meetings began.

The daily Reagan-Bush '84 news summary was waiting on my desk. I went to the coffeemaker and poured a cup and sat down to make a list. I was thinking about what to do if the Ethics Committee voted against investigating Ferraro's financial disclosures.

The idea behind the list was simple. If we failed to launch an ethics probe, the press would portray it as a victory for Ferraro and Mondale. The pressure would be on us to generate negative news about her as quickly as possible, and I wanted to have a list of actions ready.

The first item I wrote was "Nick Sands—where?" I made a note to contact an investigator on the Senate Judiciary Committee who handled organized crime to see if we could locate Sands. Finding him was key to the press being able to verify his story or at least get his side of it. I wrote down "Ambrose: how to use network" and "Spence—do we/don't we."

By now we had compiled enough matches between Ferraro campaign contributors and names in official organized crime reports to begin making sure the identifications were correct. I planned to propose putting the Guinea Chasers on the job. We didn't want to turn over a lead to the *Philadelphia*

Inquirer identifying the wrong person—someone who had the same name as a mobster—to the newspaper.

There was always the possibility—others on the campaign would say likelihood—that the committee either wouldn't consider the complaint because of its late filing or would dismiss the complaint outright. In that case, an op-ed in the *New York Times* explaining why a full investigation was warranted might increase the pressure. The meeting with Barber Conable had ended well, but I doubted I could persuade him to write such a column. It was one thing to argue our case in the closed committee session, but publishing an op-ed in the *Times* was another matter.

I jotted down "letter to NYT/op-ed by <u>Spence</u> on why full investigation" and took a sip of coffee.

Achille Guest was in New York, so I made a note to have him look into the location of Frank Hogan's archives. If we were going to search them for records of Ferraro's job application and the retracted offer, first we had to know where they were. We had been told Hogan's papers were archived at Columbia University, but I needed to know the details about which library and how we could access them.

Nofziger's morning Attack Meeting focused again on Mondale's tax plan. After the meeting, Mike Bayer mentioned to me that Roger Stone had gotten a call from someone named Barber offering information about Ferraro.

"Is that a first name or a last name?" I asked.

It would be a weird coincidence if we got an unsolicited tip about Ferraro from someone named Barber at the same time we were counting on Barber Conable to carry our case.

"Last name, I'm pretty sure."

We already had a heavy workload. In going through almost 1,000 pages of Ferraro's Federal Election Commission reports on campaign contributions and expenditures, we had identified dozens of names and addresses we suspected were linked to organized crime. Each one had to be closely scrutinized. There were thousands more pages of documents and records like the Hogan archives that we needed to review, and it all had to be done manually. I added the name "Barber" to the bottom of my list as one more lead to examine.

Everyone on the campaign with contacts on Capitol Hill had their ears to the ground trying to pick up advance word of the committee's decision. As the morning went by without any news, it seemed more and more likely we weren't going to get the result we wanted.

That afternoon, the House Committee on Standards of Official Conduct issued a three-paragraph statement:

> Whereas, a properly filed complaint has been put before the Committee on Standards of Official Conduct alleging violations of House Rule XLIV (Financial Disclosure) by Representative Geraldine A. Ferraro,

Now therefore be it Resolved, that the Committee determines pursuant to Committee Rule 10(b) that violations alleged in the complaint are within the jurisdiction of the Committee and merit further inquiry, and

Be it further Resolved, that this Committee conduct an inquiry pursuant to Committee Rule 11(a) to determine whether such violations have occurred, and that Representative Ferraro and the Washington Legal Foundation be immediately notified of this action.

The resolution was unanimous. All six Democrats and all six Republicans on the committee had voted to open an investigation. The mood around headquarters was jubilant, congratulatory.

Phase One of our Ferraro investigation, focusing on financial irregularities, was over. From now on it was up to the committee's investigators and staff to determine whether or not Geraldine Ferraro had complied with the rules regarding her financial disclosure statements. There was nothing the Reagan-Bush '84 campaign could do to affect the outcome. More importantly, there was nothing we should attempt to do to affect the outcome of the probe. The last thing we needed was to interfere with the Ethics Committee investigation for political purposes. It would backfire on us and play into Ferraro's hands.

We could now devote our full effort to Phase Two, Mafia connections.

* * *

On the morning of Thursday the 13th, newspaper headlines around the country reported that Geraldine Ferraro was under investigation. The same day, the *Wall Street Journal* ran a lengthy piece on the opinion pages by Jonathan Kwitny and Anthony M. De Stefano, reporters in the paper's New York bureau. The headline was "Rep. Ferraro and a Painful Legacy." The article opened with John Zaccaro's father, Philip Zaccaro, establishing his real estate business in what the paper called "a Mafia-dominated section of Manhattan." It went on to detail Philip Zaccaro's connections to Joseph and Salvatore Profaci, scions of a major organized crime family, and to Aniello Dellacroce, second-in-command in the Gambino syndicate.

The *Journal* article contained a bombshell. It revealed that a grand jury was investigating the 1982 sale of the building to Joseph LaForte, who had been identified in U.S. Senate organized crime reports as a subordinate of Dellacroce's in the Gambino family. The property at 232 Mulberry was Dellacroce's residence and P. Zaccaro Co., Inc., was his landlord. When the Zaccaro business sold the property in 1971, Gerry Ferraro was engaged as an attorney to close the sale between four buyers represented by Lawrence J. Latona. In 1982, Latona and the other owners sold the building to LaForte, who was at the time a known mobster. The *Wall Street Journal* couldn't determine the identities of the other sellers, and neither Geraldine Ferraro nor John Zaccaro would comment on the transaction.

The sale to LaForte had clearly come to the attention of someone. Don Alexander only needed one investigation for his insider informant to come forward. Now it looked like the tipster had choices.

Another Zaccaro associate identified in the article was Michael LaRosa, whose properties were managed by the family firm, P. Zaccaro Co., Inc. He had contributed $1,200 to Ferraro's congressional campaigns. She acknowledged knowing LaRosa as a "businessman in New York."

In fact, LaRosa had served time in federal prison in 1981 for arranging bribes from construction companies to labor unions. The paper reported the nicknames of the gangsters Mike "The Baker" LaRosa met with to arrange the payments: names like Funzi, Chin, and Tony Ducks. After his trial, LaRosa entered a plea bargain with prosecutors before the jury verdict was returned. He pleaded guilty to arranging the bribes and in exchange prosecutors agreed not to contend that he was a member of any organized crime family. However, an undercover FBI agent testified during LaRosa's trial that LaRosa was introduced to him as "the key liaison among New York's 'five families.'"

* * *

The following morning, September 14, the *Philadelphia Inquirer* ran a detailed story about financial irregularities in Ferraro's 1978 congressional campaign. In a series of complex transactions that included real estate sales, loans made to the campaign by Ferraro, her husband, and their children were repaid in a manner that appeared to violate federal election laws. We believed that publicizing as many of these oddities as we could uncover would spur the Federal Election Commission to investigate Ferraro's 1978 campaign funding. It would be up to their investigators to determine if there was wrongdoing.

In our analysis, it looked like some of the funds for the loan repayments could have been made with money contributed by vendors who had been hired by John Zaccaro to do work on the estates he managed as a court-appointed conservator.

In reviewing Ferraro's campaign contributions, I had noticed an interesting pattern. Many of the contractors that Zaccaro hired were also contributors to her congressional races. To us, these campaign contributions looked suspiciously like kickbacks from contractors. But we didn't have the investigative resources to interview all the contractors to see if there was a quid pro quo whereby they were given the contracts in exchange for the campaign contributions. Given all the leads we were finding, we had to prioritize rigidly. Without investigating more deeply to see if this was indeed the case, all we had was speculation. It was a mere possibility until someone could prove it. Without proof, I withheld notifying the *Inquirer* about our suspicions.

Later that day Lisa Colgate dropped off the midday update of the Reagan-Bush '84 news summary.

"You might want to take a look at the Reuters report," she said. "It's about Ferraro."

She handed me the one-page summary with a smile and continued on her rounds. The Reuters story featured a *Washington Post*/ABC poll published that morning that showed 50 percent of voters had a positive opinion of Geraldine Ferraro. Thirty-nine percent had negative opinions of her.

The number jumped out at me. Despite the Mondale-Ferraro campaign's efforts to quell the controversies surrounding her, Ferraro's negative rating had risen 10 percent since August 20. Today's date was Friday, September 14, which meant that the poll probably did not reflect the impact on public opinion of the Ethics Committee's decision to investigate her. The decision had only been issued Wednesday. For the poll to be published a day and a half later, most of the interviews would have been conducted before the news about the Ethics Committee probe was widespread.

Not even a month had passed since the GOP convention and Ferraro's negatives were soaring. I could see why Lisa was smiling.

13

Inquiring Minds

Reagan-Bush '84 Headquarters
Washington, D.C.
September 14–18, 1984

We gathered in my office on Monday morning. Art had his own copy of the *Philadelphia Inquirer* story. The Sunday, September 16, edition featured a page 3 article headlined "Questions about her family finances still handicap Ferraro's campaign."

The article began: "It was nearly four weeks since Geraldine A. Ferraro had sought to lay to rest questions about her political and personal finances at a nationally televised news conference. But the questions would not go away."

I couldn't have written a better lead paragraph if I'd done it myself.

The story was a wrap-up about the Ethics Committee vote, the *Wall Street Journal* article, and the controversy over her congressional campaign loans. For every questionable incident or acquaintance, the *Inquirer* story reported Ferraro's reactions.

"Listen to this," Art said. "She says, 'As I understand the committee's rules, receipt of the conservative group's complaint virtually obligated them to process it. I will cooperate fully with the committee…'"

Art chuckled.

"So that's her line," he said. "The committee had no discretion or they'd have tossed out this obviously politically motivated complaint. And get this about the *Journal* piece. It's an 'outrageous' smear because she's Italian-American."

"Why do you think the *Inquirer* ran this piece?" I said. "It doesn't break new ground, except for the correction on the pistol permit."

One paragraph in the *Inquirer* set the record straight. It noted the error in the *Journal* piece and said that Zaccaro provided a character reference for Salvatore Profaci, not his brother Joseph.

"You would be the one to notice the details about the gun," Art said. "Why do you think they ran it?"

"She's refusing to take calls or answer questions, according to them and

Kwitny. It's my guess they're pissed off by her stonewalling, so they're running the wrap-up in the Sunday paper for anyone who missed all the developments during the week."

"Precisely. They're telling her that stonewalling won't make it go away," Art said. "Where do you think we go from here?"

I took a drag on a cigarette, buying time to process my thoughts.

We had 18 different Mafia angles we were currently working. The list was three pages long. Mike Bayer's team had compiled a map of the Manhattan neighborhood where most of Zaccaro's business properties were located, overlaid with known organized crime properties. In many cases properties Zaccaro owned or managed were immediately adjacent to those of Mafia kingpins. In a handful of cases, the properties overlapped. At least figuratively, John Zaccaro had been rubbing shoulders with organized crime figures all his adult life.

I passed the list and map to Art.

"I think we give the *Inquirer* the mapping information and the rest of the campaign contribution leads we know are solid," I said. "What do you think about the Hogan story?"

"I'm not comfortable with giving them a rumor. Let's take a harder look at that 1958 case of construction kickbacks cited in the *Journal* article. If Hogan's office handled the prosecution, then we might have something."

I made a note to have Bayer check into it.

"I'm trying to locate Hogan's archives," I said. "I have a guy in New York right now to track them down."

Art was about to say something when Lee Atwater walked in. His eyes darted over the papers and notes we'd spread out on the credenza, trying to take it all in.

"I'm glad I found you guys together," Lee said. "I've got something for you."

"Here we are," Art said. "What is it?"

"There's a producer from NBC I've been talking with about Ferraro. I told them you could give them some background information about her finances."

Lee glanced at us, trying to gauge our reaction. I looked straight at Lee, trying to suppress the impulse to choke him.

"I'm sure all the press coverage last week has whetted their appetite," Art said, "but I don't think this kind of detailed story lends itself to television."

"How much do they know about us?" I said.

"You guys don't have to worry," Lee said nervously, "you're protected. You have my word. It will all be on background."

"I'm sure you've taken care of us, Lee," Art said nonchalantly.

Lee began to back into the hallway.

"Expect a call from NBC within a couple of days," he said.

Art nodded.

"Son of a bitch's set us up," he snarled as soon as Lee was out of earshot. "What do you say we go over to the Hyatt and get some coffee?"

As soon as we were out of the building I exploded.

"It's needless!" I fumed. "Every time the *Inquirer* or the *Journal* or the *New York Times* breaks a story, the network reporters on the campaign trail pick it up and ask their own questions and it ends up on television. I don't know about you, but I'm not talking to NBC. Unless it's fucking *60 Minutes* doing a definitive piece on where she buried Jimmy Hoffa, we don't need to work with TV producers!"

Art was steely. "We should tell Spencer that Lee's compromised us and we're not going to work with NBC."

"Nofziger and Rollins too."

We took an isolated table. I ordered a Bloody Mary and lit up. Art waited for the waitress to put some distance between us before speaking.

"We need a plan," he said calmly, "in case this blows up."

"I'll check in with Greener at the RNC to make sure he doesn't talk to NBC."

"I'll cover our legal team and Alexander," Art said, "anyone who did the financial analysis for us on the tax returns and ethics filings."

"I'll talk to Ambrose and Callahan."

"Does Lee know about them?"

"Not unless he's got my phone bugged," I said, "but if Lee has set us up and NBC starts a press feeding frenzy, I'll tell all our people not to say a thing if reporters get in contact with them."

"Why would the son of a bitch do it?" Art said. He meant it rhetorically, but I welcomed talking it through.

"The innocent explanation is that he has to have a piece of the action now that the story's red hot," I said. "That makes him either a control freak or an action junkie or both."

"And the sinister explanation is that he sees a chance to get rid of you and me and maybe even step into Ed Rollins' place as campaign manager," Art said.

"He's always talking about how the guy who starts out running an incumbent president's campaign is never the guy who's running it on Election Day," I said. "He knows if the story blows up big enough they'd force Ed to resign. Lee would love to take his place."

Lee was a walking dictionary of political statistics. If there was a Trivial Pursuit game dedicated to politics, Lee would be the champion, unless his adversary was Pinkerton. I suspected most of the statistics Lee spouted and sprinkled throughout his memos were supplied by Jim, just like the book reviews he gave at the White House staff mess. He always mentioned the grim statistics on campaign managers lasting until Election Day in the context of how Ed was about to make history, but I suspected Lee had one eye open to the main chance.

"Would he really risk the president's reelection just to advance his own career?" Art said.

"He's probably already drafted the memo to Baker about how the campaign can overcome the stumble and regain its footing by firing Rollins and Nofziger and you and me," I grumbled.

If Atwater had set us up, his next move was already planned. To get the campaign back on track he would urge Baker to bring in fresh management. I was only half-kidding when I said the draft memo to Baker had already been written.

We spent the rest of the day spreading the word about NBC. We couched it as a story we heard was in development but one we had no intention of cooperating with. Except with Spencer and Nofziger and Rollins, we left Lee's name out of it. I passed the news to our teams along with new assignments. No matter what kind of press storm might be brewing, the time left to dig into Ferraro's past was limited. We had to keep working.

When I got home that night Lotta Stromberg, our 18-year-old Swedish *au pair*, said she'd gotten a funny phone call that day.

"A man called and asked a lot of questions about you. He wanted to know what kind of work you did, things like that."

"Did he say who he was?"

"I asked him. He just said an old friend who'd lost touch with you."

"Did he leave a number?"

"No. But he kept asking questions, about Benner, whether you had other children…"

"He wanted to know about Benjamin?"

"Just if you had children, I guess. I told him I was your *au pair* when he asked if I was your wife." She giggled.

"He'll probably call back," I said, trying not to let my concern show. "If he does, tell him to call me at the office."

Lotta already seemed perturbed by the call and I didn't want to alarm her. But I didn't have any friends who wouldn't leave a message or a number. This was someone fishing for information.

I ruled out the *Philadelphia Inquirer.* If they wanted to check out who they were really working with on the Ferraro stories, they would have done it earlier. The same reasoning applied to Unitel and to Ambrose's gumshoes. I wouldn't have been surprised if any of them had tracked down my home phone number to do some due diligence on me. We'd asked around about the people we'd brought into our confidence on the Ferraro operation.

That left NBC. Lee said he had given our names to the producer he'd spoken with, and now NBC was gathering background information on us. I started to make a call to alert Art but decided it could wait until morning. I had a spirited toddler to play with, a jittery *au pair*, and a wife who was still at her desk in the White House.

There was another possibility, but I didn't want to think about it. Whether or not a Ferraro connection panned out, we were digging into lots of criminals' histories. Maybe they were doing some digging of their own in return.

14

Under the Microscope

Reagan-Bush '84 Headquarters
Washington, D.C.
September 19–24, 1984

Nofziger's morning Attack Meeting started later than usual on Wednesday, September 19. The 7:30 campaign strategy meeting had become a daily affair. It was followed almost immediately by a 9 o'clock senior staff meeting. Lyn's gathering didn't get started until 10:30 that day.

By the time I took my seat around the conference table I'd been in meetings all morning. One thing was certain. There was no way Lyn would end the meeting telling us to get him status reports between noon and 1 o'clock.

I wasn't in a very good mood. Every morning I got a copy of Rollins' schedule for the day. At 10:00 a.m. it showed an appointment: "NBC Interview w/Lee." My mood worsened when 10 minutes into Nofziger's meeting, Tucker Eskew brought an NBC camera crew and correspondent into the conference room. Eskew was an intern working in the press office. His job was to watch the evening news coverage and write a summary of its contents for the daily news digest.

Normally one of the senior press office staff would have accompanied a network television crew. Escorting a network television crew around headquarters was a heady departure from his usual duties for the 23-year-old. Tucker was a South Carolina native, and I detected the hand of Lee Atwater at work. Atwater would want someone he had leverage over to shepherd NBC around on what amounted to an ambush interview.

"This is Jamie Gangel," Tucker said, introducing the correspondent. "She's already interviewed Rollins, and they just need some B-roll for their story on the campaign."

"Fine with me if you want to shoot some footage," Lyn said. To anyone who knew him well, his face said the opposite. Lyn had been Reagan's press secretary for years, and he knew better than to make a scene in front of a network correspondent.

Gangel was an unknown to me. I'd spoken with Andrea Mitchell from NBC about the campaign a few months earlier and had dealt with dozens of other Washington correspondents since the 1980 campaign. One thing I'd learned was never trust an unknown reporter. I turned my notebook upside down on the table and folded my hands.

The lights came on and the cameraman started taping. He slowly panned his way around the conference table. A number of the participants went on talking, but I did my best to remain motionless and uninteresting. I liked photographing wildlife and knew that when a wild animal doesn't want to be seen it doesn't move. I used the same trick to keep the camera moving past me. I was relieved when the cameraman panned past me for someone more animated. At most I was on tape a few seconds.

When the meeting broke up I bolted for Art's office.

"NBC's in the building," I said. "Tucker Eskew just brought them into Nofziger's meeting."

Art gave me a look of disbelief and shook his head. Before he said anything a flustered-looking Rollins walked down the corridor toward Nofziger's office.

"He had an interview with them this morning," I said. "It was on his schedule."

"How did it go?"

"From the look of him, I'd say it went about as expected."

"Brace for the shit-storm," Art said.

A few minutes later Ed came back up the hallway to his office. I waited for him to pass and then went to see Nofziger.

"Johnny-boy, come in, sit down. If you're here to tell me to cancel the NBC interview I've already done it."

"They wanted you on camera too?"

"They did. But Ed just told me Jamie Gangel asked him if the campaign was behind Catholic bishops criticizing Ferraro and anti-abortion protestors at her rallies, so I canceled."

"Is that all they asked about?" I said.

"She also wanted to know if we're using surrogates to demand an investigation of Ferraro's financial disclosures."

"What did Ed say?"

"He denied it, of course."

"Who do you think leaked it?" I asked.

"Lee. Or maybe Baker, if Lee told Baker or Tutwiler about it."

In the first term, Chief of Staff James Baker and Lyn Nofziger had butted heads often. On one occasion, Baker misrepresented Reagan's position in a White House senior staff meeting. Nofziger confronted him, saying that was not the president's view on the topic. When Baker persisted, Lyn said the two of them should get up and go right to the Oval Office and ask Reagan. Baker backed down.

"I've just talked to Art," I said. "Neither of us has been contacted by NBC and we don't plan to talk to them if they do track us down."

We spent the rest of the day letting our teams know that NBC was definitely working on a story and to be extremely vigilant about anyone asking for information. We told Spencer the NBC crew had been in the building and to avoid anyone from NBC.

On September 20, UPI ran a wire story about protestors interrupting the rallies of Walter Mondale and Gerry Ferraro. President Reagan denounced the hecklers as "rude" and denied that his campaign was organizing them in any way.

The following evening, Jamie Gangel's piece was broadcast on the *NBC Nightly News*. Rollins and I watched it together in his office.

The big stories of the day featured the terrorist bombing of the U.S. embassy annex in Beirut, in which two Americans were killed and the U.S. and British ambassadors injured, and the exoneration of White House counselor Ed Meese after a six-month probe by Independent Counsel Jacob Stein. Gangel's report was fourth in the news line-up.

She said that Lyn and Ed were working to "have groups or individuals not officially connected to the campaign demand investigation of Geraldine Ferraro's finances" and had encouraged "criticism by the Catholic hierarchy" of her stance on abortion. She accused the campaign of orchestrating hecklers and anti-abortion protestors at Mondale and Ferraro campaign rallies. The thrust of her story was that Reagan-Bush '84 was running a dirty tricks operation.

None of Art's or my efforts had been reported by NBC. There was nothing about Ferraro's Mafia ties, nothing about the *Philadelphia Inquirer*, and nothing about Unitel or Ambrose's team.

Our operation had nothing to do with orchestrating hecklers and protestors at Mondale's and Ferraro's rallies. One youthful group of protestors styled themselves "Fritzbusters" after Walter Mondale's nickname and the hit movie *Ghostbusters* that had been released earlier in the summer of 1984. They referred to themselves as a "demoplasm removal service" and drew a lot of media attention with their chants of "If you think Fritz is really the pits, who're you gonna call? Fritzbusters!" Other hecklers were less inventive but active at most rallies. It didn't have the appearance of spontaneous activity.

For the moment, at least, we had dodged a bullet.

My relief lasted until the commercial break. Within minutes, Ed's telephone rang. Jim Baker was on the other end. Baker demanded that the campaign stop any activities it had going against Ferraro.

Ed hung up, visibly angry. He asked me to pick up on an extension and listen to the call while he dialed Atwater. Ed asked him point blank if he'd leaked the story to NBC. Lee denied it, and Ed didn't press him.

* * *

The following morning I wrote a memo for the file about Atwater's contacts with the NBC producer. The memo outlined the key events, including that Lee had offered our names as confidential sources for background information on Ferraro's finances. It noted that we had informed "campaign management" that we did not wish to be nor had we been contacted by NBC.

I didn't know how much this story might grow and I wanted it clear that we hadn't been involved in sourcing Gangel's reporting. From my office I could hear the telephone switchboards outside Ed's office on one end of the hallway and Jim Lake's at the other end. The ringing was non-stop, especially on the press office lines.

There was some good news that day. On September 22, the *Philadelphia Inquirer* reported that the New York Department of State had decided to conduct a review of Zaccaro's financial dealings as a conservator of Alice Phelan's estate. Zaccaro had been dismissed by the court after irregularities in his use of Phelan's funds were exposed. The inquiry was billed as routine, but there was no telling what the review might turn up.

Stu Spencer caught up to me in my office later in the day. He looked grim and tired.

"Take a few days off, go to the beach or something, lie low," he said. "Gather up all your files on Ferarro and take them with you. Don't leave anything behind. Whatever you do, don't talk to any reporters. If this thing gets worse, we may have to cut you loose. But don't worry. We'll take care of you after the election."

I understood Spencer's worries. Art and I might find ourselves the focus of a press stake-out any day now, especially if reporters found out we were overseeing an in-depth investigation of Ferraro. There might be television news crews on the sidewalk in front of my house tomorrow morning. Even if we said nothing or denied knowledge of any investigations, our faces would be on network television in connection with probing Ferraro. We could have been seen leaving Barber Conable's office by some observant congressional aide who might recognize us on the evening news and tip off the press to a connection between the Reagan campaign and Conable. The best thing for everyone was for us to make ourselves scarce and hope that the media's interest in the story blew over.

We didn't waste time in small talk. Somewhere I found a box. I collected my notebooks and files and phone logs and meeting notes and began packing them when Art dropped in.

"I see you got the word," he said.

"Yeah. Now we wait and see. Where're you headed?"

"Miami. Let's stay in touch."

He gave me a couple of numbers where I could reach him. One of them was at his mother's house.

We waited until twilight before taking the elevator, shook hands in the lobby, and walked out of the building separately in case any reporters were watching for the pair of us. Art went first. When no camera crew accosted him, I followed.

That weekend the Democrats tried to put the focus on our alleged dirty tricks. NBC's Sunday talk show *Meet the Press* featured Congressman Tony Coelho (D–California) as a guest. Coelho, chairman of the Democratic Congressional Campaign Committee, charged, "It's Nofziger and Rollins who are applauding the fact that they have been able to stop the message from getting out … they, off camera, or off the record, have bragged about it all over this town."

"Not only am I suggesting dirty tricks," Coelho continued, "but I'm suggesting that the people that were involved in the dirty tricks of the '72 campaign are re-involved in the '84 campaign. It's the same people."

Neither of the two correspondents who moderated the show, Marvin Kalb and Roger Mudd, challenged Coelho for proof of his assertions before they cut for a commercial break. When they came back on air, Marvin Kalb asked James Johnson, chairman of the Mondale campaign, if Reagan's age was an issue. Johnson said that he didn't think so.

The normally supportive *Wall Street Journal* ran an article by David Shribman and Rich Jaroslovsky speculating that the Mondale-Ferraro campaign could use the so-called dirty tricks issue to stir support for their otherwise lagging campaign.

On Sunday evening, ABC News reported that "Washington has been buzzing for days" over the charge that the Reagan campaign was organizing protestors. Mondale demanded that Reagan call for an end to the heckling. Jim Johnson called for an investigation into whether Reagan-Bush '84 was orchestrating the demonstrations. If NBC and CBS news reports hadn't been preempted by football games, their coverage would have been similar.

But overall the negative press coverage was muted. Gangel's story was overshadowed by the terrorist bombing in Beirut and the independent counsel's finding that Ed Meese had committed no criminal offenses. So far, it had failed to generate a media feeding frenzy. Atwater's leak looked like a dud.

Art called me from Miami.

"The *Philadelphia Inquirer* is holding tight," he said. "Did you see their coverage today?"

I hadn't. Art told me that the Sunday editions of the *New York Times* and the *Inquirer* reported that New York was going to reform the way conservators were chosen in the future to prevent the kind of improprieties that had come to light regarding Zaccaro's conservatorships.

"What are you hearing?" he asked.

"Not a thing," I said. "Nobody from the press has called me."

"It seems like they've just passed by Gangel's item about Ferraro's finances and are focusing on the protests and Catholic clergy," Art said.

"As long as the *Inquirer* doesn't run a story on us, we're okay. Bob Novak isn't going to say anything. Neither will the *New York Post*."

"It's not the *Inquirer* I'm worried about," Art said. "It's Fineman and Shackne. We talked to them about her financial disclosure statements and the tax returns."

Howard Fineman had agreed to keep our contacts on background. The same was true with Robert Schakne. In neither case had Art nor I tried to follow up and provide the journalists with more information.

"We're lucky Stu set those meetings up and not Atwater," I said, "or we'd be in deep shit right now."

"Unless there's a new development, I'm coming back tomorrow," Art said.

"Yeah, I'm going into the office too. So long as Atwater doesn't have another round in his chamber, this story's running out of steam."

I was thinking about the transcript Roger Stone had given me. If Atwater had a copy, or the original tape recording, why hadn't he leaked it yet? It would be red meat for the press pack, certain to provoke a major media feeding frenzy. The only theory I could come up with was that Lee had authorized the DelliBovi interview and was worried that if the transcript leaked it would implicate him in a real scandal.

On Monday the print media recapped the news from the weekend, especially Coelho's charges and Johnson's calls for an investigation. But the news coverage didn't advance the story: There were no new revelations.

When Art and I arrived at campaign headquarters John Buckley greeted us with a mischievous grin.

"Every reporter in town called me," he said. "Even the *Wall Street Journal* called today to see if there was a story in the NBC report. They all said the same thing. None of them had heard from anyone on our campaign peddling dirt on Ferraro. They just didn't believe Gangel's reporting could be true if they hadn't gotten called by us at least once!"

Buckley looked like he wanted to ask how we'd gotten our stories about Ferraro published but at the same time didn't want to know. The compartmented design of our operation and the decision not to hand-feed the Beltway press had paid off.

Ed Rollins told me he'd ordered Lee Atwater to investigate who was behind the protestors and heckling at Mondale and Ferraro's rallies. It was a good way to make Lee take ownership of the exculpation of Reagan-Bush '84 from Jamie Gangel's charges. The rumor going around headquarters was that Lee was having an affair with an NBC producer and loose pillow talk was the source of the leak. It wouldn't surprise me if Lee had started the rumor himself, to allay suspicions that the betrayal was deliberate. He had that kind of mind.

I preferred firing Lee.

In theory, Rollins had the authority to do it. But politics is a web of dependencies, and power is more illusory than it appears. Lee's supporters, who included Stu Spencer and Jim Baker, would intervene to protect him. If Rollins went ahead and fired Lee for the leak anyway, it could look like retribution and give credence to Gangel's charges that Rollins and Lyn Nofziger were behind the demonstrations. The instability in our campaign would become the story, preventing us from getting our campaign message out, at least until a replacement for Lee was chosen.

Then there was always the possibility that Lee wouldn't go quietly. If he was fired from the campaign, Lee could become a loose cannon and do even more damage than he'd already done. He might have compromising information on any number of people in the Administration or on the campaign and be willing to use it if he was forced off the team. If he was willing to risk the president's reelection to unseat his political rivals while being an insider, what would he be willing to do as an outsider? Burn down the campaign headquarters?

I took my mind off Lee's fate and composed some notes on the impact of the leak to NBC. I calculated that the complaint would lead to the press stopping their coverage of the protestors and instead give more time in their broadcasts to the candidates' messages. Mondale and Ferraro would be able to get their themes across. The charge that we were behind a dirty tricks operation would raise credibility questions among editors and journalists about the motive and veracity of any new damaging revelations about Ferraro and Zaccaro. News organizations would weigh fresh information more carefully before determining that they had crossed the news threshold that made a story worthy of publication or broadcast. Any new stories we did manage to get published would find a more skeptical audience among readers and viewers.

I summarized it in my notes for September 24 like this: "Should new stories appear regarding her and his background, they have inoculated against: (1) substance, (2) spread of information through other media outlets, and (3) credibility with audience."

All in all, Atwater's leak was a coup for Mondale and Ferraro.

*   *   *

I lit a Marlboro and thought about Rund's mid–August briefing. This was the break Ferraro needed to get off the defensive and start defining her candidacy. If she succeeded, by the end of the month she would be in a position to give the Mondale-Ferraro ticket the boost it needed to overtake our lead in October. Three debates would take place that month, one between Bush and Ferraro and two between Reagan and Mondale. If anything went wrong in the debates, it could be hard to recover the lead. Rund's projections that between 500,000 and one million more women voters would turn out in 1984 than in 1980 was ominous, especially if female voters now took a fresh and more supportive look at Ferraro's candidacy.

Before Lee's leak it seemed like we were on the way to a landslide. Now it looked like we might be in for a horserace.

Stu Spencer must have had similar intuitions. After congratulating us on staying out of the headlines, he got straight to the point.

"Have you guys got anything more on her in the pipeline?"

15

Mobbed Up?

Reagan-Bush '84 Headquarters
Washington, D.C.
September 25–October 4, 1984

We had plenty in the pipeline. The question was whether the *Philadelphia Inquirer* was still willing to work with us. The newspaper didn't reveal our role in the negative press coverage Ferraro had gotten from them, but that didn't mean our cover as rogue campaign employees hadn't been blown. Don Barlett was no fool. He had to suspect that we were fully authorized by the Reagan-Bush campaign to investigate Ferraro and to disclose any damaging information we found to the press.

And we had found lots of damaging information. A Republican National Committee opposition researcher had compiled a highly-detailed report on the nexus between known organized crime figures and Zaccaro and Ferraro. Mike Bayer had delivered the report to Art and me on September 18, just days before the NBC report on dirty tricks. It was one of the documents I carried out of the building when Stu said to clear out my files and maintain a low profile. I read it very closely over the weekend while we waited to see whether NBC's story would become a major problem for the campaign.

Art and I met with Stu Spencer to brief him on its contents and other leads we were following. Not only did John Zaccaro and Geraldine Ferraro have business associates or campaign contributors with organized crime connections, Zaccaro's father had organized crime connections. The mob ties ran at least two generations deep.

The question we wanted to resolve was whether Geraldine Ferraro's ties were coincidental or reflected deeper involvement. It would have been eccentric for a campaign contributor to list "organized crime" as his or her business. Without the kind of checking we were doing, Geraldine Ferraro could have accepted campaign contributions from individuals with ties to the Mafia and never known it. Similarly, John Zaccaro may have done business with organized crime figures without being aware of their activities.

The same could not be said of Zaccaro's father.

In the course of investigating Zaccaro's real estate business, we looked into Philip Zaccaro—the "P" in P. Zaccaro Co., Inc. In the 1930s, Philip established his real estate business in Manhattan's Little Italy. Fighting between rival gangs was out of control, so in 1931 Salvatore Maranzano gathered his followers for a meeting in the Bronx at which he anointed himself "capo de tutti capi," the overlord of all the Mafia crime families. Maranzano divided New York into five crime families, each with their own "capo" and territory.

Joseph Profaci was one of the Mafia Capos. He was also a silent business partner of Philip Zaccaro. In 1936, Profaci's younger brother, Salvatore, and Philip Zaccaro were partners in a company called Bowery and Spring Realty Corporation. The two men also set up the P.L.S. Clothing Manufacturing Company in Newburgh, New York. It was this company that Mafia boss Joseph Profaci invested in, a fact that was secret until it was revealed in 1959 by none other than Robert F. Kennedy, brother of future president John F. Kennedy, Jr. At the time, Bobby Kennedy was an attorney for a special Senate investigative committee on organized crime and labor racketeering.

Philip Zaccaro was reportedly a character witness for Salvatore Profaci when he applied for U.S. citizenship in 1943. Similarly, Zaccaro attested to Salvatore's good character when Profaci applied for a handgun permit from the New York Police Department.

Philip Zaccaro also had a pistol permit, but it was revoked by the police in 1957 following a meeting of top Mafia chieftains from around the country dubbed the Apalachin Conference. The conference took place at the rural estate of Pittsburgh mobster Joseph Barbara in Apalachin, New York. The police were tipped off to the mob meeting. Sixty-two leading organized crime figures, including Joe Profaci, were arrested there on November 14, 1957. The busts were widely reported in the newspapers. Philip Zaccaro lost his gun permit because he had vouched for one of the Profacis.

The initial announcement of the revocation of Joseph Profaci's gun permit came from the New York Police Department and included several other individuals attending the meeting. According to the first published reports, Philip Zaccaro had given a character reference to Mafia don Joseph Profaci, not his younger brother. Several days later three newspapers ran identically-worded corrections stating that Philip Zaccaro had affirmed the good character of Salvatore Profaci.

Our investigators were unable to determine which brother Philip Zaccaro helped get a gun license. By 1984, the New York Police Department had destroyed the records. But we did obtain a statement from Walter Arm, the deputy police commissioner who announced the 1957 gun license revocations. We wanted to know if he had inadvertently confused the two brothers.

"I knew there were two gangsters," he said, "Salvatore and Joseph Profaci. If I had made such an error I think I would have remembered it."

On July 9, 1954, Salvatore Profaci's yacht blew up in the waters off Asbury Park, New Jersey. The explosion appeared to be the result of a boating accident.

Joseph Profaci named a son Salvatore after his brother. According to a 1983 Senate hearing on organized crime, the son was now running the Colombo crime syndicate. The hearing report said that "Salvatore Profaci is considered to be the heir apparent to the position of 'boss' in the 'Colombo family.' Profaci aspires to regain the power and prestige the 'family' held when his father was alive."

It was this kind of research result which made us aware of the importance of maintaining secrecy in the Ferraro operation. By exposing campaign contributions from Mafia-related individuals to Ferraro's congressional race and business associates of John Zaccaro's with mob ties, we were digging into dangerous territory.

I knew what it was like to live in a place where criminals had influence over government officials. When I lived in Virginia City, Nevada, in the mid –1970s a local hood named Joe Conforte owned a nearby brothel called the Mustang Ranch. Conforte also owned a restaurant in the old mining town called The Cabin in the Sky. Joe Conforte had a number of Storey County officials in his pocket.

In response to a citizens' petition, a Storey County grand jury was convened for an investigation into Conforte's influence over local officials. After two years of work, the grand jury concluded that Conforte held "unusual influence and power" over local officials but found insufficient evidence to issue indictments.

Two people named by the grand jury were Sheriff Bob Del Carlo and District Attorney Virgil Bucchianieri. The district attorney was criticized by the grand jury for not pursuing a "vigorous prosecution" of an alleged murderer in a crime that took place at the Mustang Ranch.

In one of his ventures, Conforte decided to become a promoter for Argentinian boxer Oscar Bonavena. In his home country Bonavena was a hero, but in Nevada he chafed under Conforte's management. In what was believed to be an attempt to recover his passport, Bonavena jumped the fence at the Mustang Ranch. He only made it a few yards before Conforte's bodyguard, Willard Ross Brymer, shot and killed him.

Before the sheriff arrived, Bonavena was moved and a pistol planted on his body. If it was meant to persuade investigators that Bonavena was a threat, it was superfluous. He already had another gun on him. Both weapons were traced to Conforte's wife, Sally.

At the time the Mustang Ranch was like an armed compound. AR-15 military-style assault rifles were stocked in one of the brothel's buildings, which included a watchtower.

Bonavena was a national hero in Argentina. Thousands turned out for his funeral, including former Argentinian president Alejandro Lanusse.

There were rumors that Conforte had put out a $5,000 contract on Bonavena's life. A Los Angeles–based mobster known as Jimmy "The Weasel" Fratianno had allegedly been contacted by Conforte.

Bucchianieri declined to press murder charges, opting instead to allow Brymer to plead to the lesser offense of manslaughter. Brymer was sentenced to 18 months in prison for Bonavena's killing.

A group of concerned citizens considered the handling of the case a grave injustice, one of several instances of criminal wrongdoing on Conforte's properties that went unpunished. Maybe we'd been watching too many Clint Eastwood movies, but in a scene straight out of a Spaghetti Western we went to the Mustang Ranch and called out Conforte and his bodyguards. It was probably better for everybody that they refused to come out.

So we took revenge on one of Conforte's favorite cars. Like all pimps, Conforte owned expensive wheels. He had a Lincoln Mark IV Bugazzi, custom-built by George Barris, and it was parked right in front of us. It had reportedly cost more than $30,000 in the early 1970s. We didn't stick around to find out what it cost him to repair it.

We considered it a message to Conforte that no matter how many protectors he had in Storey County, he wasn't invincible. Conforte had his custom cars removed from the "ranch," and as far as we knew, no police report was ever filed about our visit.

To my mind, the power of the Mafia to corrupt elected officials, judges, and law enforcement officers was one of its most troubling aspects. While our investigations into Ferraro began as a way to defeat our campaign opponents, it had become a matter of keeping the White House free from Mafia influence. Whether or not Geraldine Ferraro realized it, her associations with organized crime figures made her vulnerable to blackmail.

* * *

In the course of investigating the leads we developed, Myles Ambrose found out that the name "John Zaccaro" was listed in the Department of Justice's investigative files. It was intriguing, but it could have been a different John Zaccaro. The only way to find out which John Zaccaro this was would be through someone with official access to the file.

That would mean asking someone in the FBI or Justice Department to pull the file and then divulge the information to us or to an intermediary. Teele and I had rejected out of hand involving Executive Branch departments or agencies in any way in our investigations. If we gained access to the information, it would expose the president to charges of abuse of power.

Another option was to tip off the *Philadelphia Inquirer* and let them try to establish the facts. If there was no active investigation underway, they might even succeed in getting some details through a Freedom of Information Act request.

Teele and I considered alerting the *Inquirer* problematic. We didn't know if this file pertained to Ferraro's husband or some other individual with the same name. We didn't even know for a fact that there was a file on a John Zaccaro. Ambrose had heard about it, but knowing the self-imposed constraints under which we operated, he stopped short and brought the matter of whether or not to take additional steps to confirm the file's existence to us.

So far, we hadn't given the *Inquirer* any leads that hadn't first been independently corroborated. On that basis alone, it seemed like a bad idea to pass the tip along to the newspaper. But there was another concern. The mere fact that we might seem to know what the Justice Department had in its investigative files would suggest that the campaign was at least using the Executive Branch to do a preliminary look for information on Ferraro and Zaccaro.

We didn't want to risk creating that misperception. Tantalizing as it was, we let the matter drop.

*   *   *

The more we learned about the Mafia connections of Geraldine Ferraro and John Zaccaro, the later I started arriving at work. My new morning ritual was to examine the Mustang's undercarriage before I drove away. I deliberately arrived at the parking garage late enough so that my car got stacked behind other parked cars instead of getting a spot on the wall, where it would sit unmoved all day. This way, the car had to be started and moved and re-parked several times during the day. If anyone put a bomb in it while I was at work, it wouldn't be me behind the wheel when it went off. Even when I left work late and a parking attendant said I could go get the car myself because it wasn't parked in, I asked for it to be driven up and tipped the attendant generously.

Philip Zaccaro wasn't the only member of the family with a questionable past. In 1960, John Zaccaro's uncle Frank Zaccaro was named in a 103-count indictment alleging that he'd taken kickbacks from contractors between 1954 and 1960. Frank Zaccaro was a managing agent for the New York City Real Estate Bureau.

The prosecuting attorney was D.A. Frank Hogan. Hogan told the *New York Times* that "each contractor had to kick back to Zaccaro to get any work from him. He received kickbacks on every single contract he had. He says the contractors offered the discounts to him, but the contractors all say he just put the bite on them."

In addition to managing properties for the Real Estate Bureau, Frank Zaccaro was a vice president of P. Zaccaro Co., Inc. The company was also named as a defendant in Hogan's indictment. Frank Zaccaro pleaded guilty to five counts of commercial bribery, made restitution for the kickbacks he'd received, and paid a $2,000 fine.

We suspected that this case was one of the reasons District Attorney Frank Hogan rescinded Gerry Ferraro's job offer when he learned that she was engaged to marry John Zaccaro. It wasn't sexism that made Hogan want to keep Ferraro out of his office. It was most likely legitimate concern that she would have a conflict of interest if his investigative attention turned again to P. Zaccaro Co., Inc.

One tip we received claimed that Hogan was prepared to prosecute Ferraro for perjuring herself in her job application, but the man who made the claim wouldn't go on the record. His reticence made me doubt that he had firsthand knowledge. I still didn't consider this enough information to turn over the lead to the *Inquirer*. I wanted to see if we could find ironclad confirmation of our suspicions in Hogan's archives.

Our top priority was Gerry Ferraro. Many mysteries surrounded her, and Frank Hogan's vanishing job offer was only one of them. After her father Dominic died suddenly when she was eight years old, Gerry was raised by her mother, Antonetta. Gerry was fond of saying that Antonetta only ate meat once a week to be able to afford to give her a good education. Her biographers depicted the family business as a nickel-and-dime store in Newburgh, New York, and the Ferraros as solidly blue-collar.

When the family store was sold a few years later, mother and daughter moved to Longfellow Avenue in the Bronx. Gerry went to Marymount Academy, a private all-girls boarding school. One of the yearbooks showed a photo of Geraldine Ferraro and John Zaccaro together. She was wearing what appeared to be an expensive fur coat. She went to Marymount Manhattan College, reportedly on a scholarship. We couldn't find any information about it. After her graduation from Fordham University School of Law, she received a baby blue convertible as a graduation gift and took the S.S. *Constitution* ocean liner on a trip to Europe.

Because we couldn't square her mother's meager means with the private schools and lavish presents, we started to wonder whether Gerry had a generous godfather. John Zaccaro's father partnered with the Profaci brothers to open a garment factory in Newburgh. It was plausible that the couple's families knew one another dating back to childhood. If they ran in the same social circles, it meant that Dominic Ferraro, Gerry's father, might also have Mafia connections.

We'd gotten rumors about Dominic Ferraro's nickel-and-dime store that suggested it was a front for other activities. But we hadn't gotten far digging into it. Art and I put a higher priority on activities undertaken by John Zaccaro and Gerry Ferraro as adults; children weren't responsible for what their parents did.

*   *   *

What was germane were Gerry's connections with organized crime figures. As dinner chairman of a 1979 fundraising event to retire debt from Ferraro's first congressional campaign, Nick Sands raised $300,000 for her. Sands was an official in a Carpenters Union local. He was brought into Ferraro's campaign by Carmine Parisi. He was Ferraro's campaign chairman and also a son of the Genovese family capo Camillo Parisi. The Ferraro campaign paid Carmine Parisi $4,800 for political consulting in July and August of 1978.

A few years after the campaign, Nick Sands was ambushed in his driveway and shot at nine times with a 9mm pistol. Despite being hit eight times, he survived the gangland-style shooting. We had found him hard to locate. After some effort, we discovered that Nick Sands was also known as Dominick Santiago. We located him under that name. Our plan was to turn the details over to the *Philadelphia Inquirer* at the appropriate time. I was particularly interested in how Ferraro would explain the presence of organized crime figures on her congressional campaign staff.

Joe LaForte, Sr., was one of Ferraro's campaign contributors and a business associate of Zaccaro's. He had been identified as a Gambino Mafia boss. In Dallas, Roy Cohn gave me some interesting leads about 23 Cleveland Place. In researching them we came across information that John Zaccaro had urged a Chinese investor to sell a property he owned at 23–25 Cleveland Place to Joe LaForte, Sr.

We found it when we started looking into a Ferraro campaign contributor named Edward Tse Chiu Chan. In 1982, Chan gave a maximum donation of $1,000 to Ferraro's congressional campaign. On a hunch, we had Ambrose and Unitel check the backgrounds of some of Ferraro's Chinese-American contributors. Our theory was that if many of her Italian-American donors had organized crime ties, perhaps some of her Chinese-American contributors might have ties to Asian crime syndicates known as the Triads. Edward Tse Chiu Chan turned out to be a former Hong Kong police detective who was rumored to be the head of organized crime in New York's Chinatown. Not only did Chan contribute to Ferraro's election, but he gave his address as 1 Mott Street. He listed his occupation as self-employed restaurateur.

We knew the 1 Mott Street property. It had stood out among many of the Zaccaro-owned or managed properties because of an unusual partnership structure that included Zaccaro's mother, Rose Zaccaro, as a co-owner. The partnership's name was FRAJO, and at various times interests in the property passed between Rose Zaccaro and Rosina Vacca. I had noticed this pattern on several Zaccaro and FRAJO properties and was surprised to discover that Rose Zaccaro and Rosina Vacca were the same person. Rosina Vacca was Rose Zaccaro's maiden name. When the ownership interests were transferred, the price of the properties often went up.

We consulted real estate experts and tax attorneys to try to determine why these transactions were taking place. There didn't appear to be any obvious explanation. I wondered if it could be money laundering.

Chan was believed to have links to a violent criminal youth gang known as the Ghost Shadows. They ran an extortion racket providing "protection" to the Chinese gambling clubs that proliferated on Mott Street. Their leader was Nicky Louie, a slender Hong Kong immigrant in his late 20s. Louie and the Ghost Shadows, who numbered about 50, had been written about extensively in the *Village Voice*. By 1977, police estimated that the Ghost Shadows' protection money exceeded $1 million annually.

Louie had been arrested numerous times on charges ranging from assault with metal pipes to murder and rape. But he had never been convicted. Each time witnesses either lost their recollection or failed to appear to testify against him.

The Ghost Shadows and rival Chinese gangs created a crime wave that extended far beyond New York's Chinatown. They expanded their protection racket to Chicago, Washington, Montgomery County in Maryland, and even Canada. The Canadian authorities were so alarmed they convened an unpublicized police summit involving law enforcement from more than a dozen American and Canadian municipalities in September of 1977.

In 1978, the New York City Police Department assigned a special task force of 20 officers to break the rackets. If estimates of the Ghost Shadows' membership were accurate, that was almost one officer for every two gang members. That summer Louie was playing a game of mah-jongg in the basement of the Gin Beck restaurant on Mott Street when a man with a .38 revolver shot him four times in the head and back.

Louie survived the assassination attempt. It was sobering to think that by taking a look into Eddie Chan, we might be digging into matters that could trigger retribution from a violent gang that operated not just in New York but also in the Washington, D.C., metropolitan area.

One of the buildings John Zaccaro managed, 68 Mott Street, had been reported to be an illegal Chinese gambling casino. The building was owned by the Soo Yuen Benevolent Association. Zaccaro issued a denial that said he had no knowledge of it being used as a casino or any gambling equipment that had been recently removed. Achille Guest looked into the property for me when he was in New York. Achille reported back that it looked like a traditional Chinese gambling club, just the sort the Ghost Shadows protected.

The address of 68 Mott Street was one block from Mulberry Street, where we had identified Zaccaro-managed properties leased by organized crime figures. The address of 248 Mulberry was listed as the residence of Michael Catalano, who law enforcement officials called a "soldier" in the Gambino crime family.

The whole area was riddled with organized crime figures.

There were 53 properties owned or managed by Zaccaro in close proximity to properties with organized crime ties. Of these, so far we had identified five properties owned or managed by Zaccaro or one of his partnerships that had a direct connection to organized crime figures.

Many properties neighboring Zaccaro's had interesting owners and tenants. The home of Peter Chin, a member of the Ghost Shadows, was 80 Mulberry Street. The house at 116 Mulberry belonged to Antony DeLutro, a Gambino member. Eugene Uricolb, a Genovese associate, lived at 122 Mulberry. The address of 65 Mott Street, right next door to the 68 Mott Street property Zaccaro managed that was suspected of being an illegal casino, was the home of David Wong. He was a member of the White Tigers, a rival gang to the Ghost Shadows.

Nicky Louie's propensity for violence was matched by other mobsters associated with the Zaccaros. Aniello Dellacroce had rented 232 Mulberry Street from P. Zaccaro Co., Inc., when John Zaccaro's father, Phillip, ran the business. Conveniently located across the street from the Ravenite Social Club, 232 Mulberry Street was reputedly the Gambino family crime headquarters. Dellacroce was close to Carlo Gambino and served as the don's underlord and enforcer. He often disguised himself as a priest and according to law enforcement officials had a reputation for liking to "peer into a victim's face, like some sort of dark angel at the moment of death."

Another name that showed up in Zaccaro property deals was Lawrence J. Latona. He was sometimes called a mortician, but in fact he ran a "body broker" business and functioned as an intermediary who would locate a mortuary service and arrange for the disposition of a body. We tried to find out more about Latona but came up blank. In an Organized Crime and Illicit Narcotics report of July 1964, issued by the Senate Government Operations Committee, we found a reference to a "Joe Latona" in a section on Gambino crime family associates of Anthony Mirra, a known narcotics trafficker. We had no way to determine whether Lawrence J. Latona and Joe Latona were the same individual.

Lawrence Latona, however, had also been identified as connected to organized crime. In 1982, Latona sold 232 Mulberry to Joseph LaForte, Sr. Latona and three other buyers had acquired the property in 1971 from P.

Zaccaro Co., Inc. The attorney who represented the buyers was Geraldine Ferraro. A grand jury was probing the 1982 sale of the property. One of the mysteries of both the 1971 sale and the 1982 sale was the identity of the other individuals associated with Latona in buying the property from Aniello Dellacroce, an organized crime figure, then holding it for a decade before selling it to another organized crime figure.

In Senate hearings, LaForte Sr. had been identified as one of Aniello Dellacroce's underlings. In 1983, the New York Police Department identified him as a captain in the Gambino family. Latona was listed as the managing agent for one of LaForte Sr.'s properties, 247 Mulberry Street. The ground floor of the building housed the Ravenite Social Club. Latona was one of the original incorporators of the club in 1942.

It seemed plausible that Latona and his mysterious co-owners were straw purchasers, but without knowing who the other people were there was no way for us to investigate the matter. Why Latona would engage Gerry Ferraro to represent him in the purchase of 232 Mulberry, a property owned by her husband, was an intriguing question. But it was just one among many intriguing questions.

Stu Spencer seemed bemused when Teele and I finished our rundown on the Mafia ties.

"There's one more thing," Art said. "Don Alexander says he had a witness who wants to come forward if an investigation gets underway. He was in business with Zaccaro on a real estate deal."

"Okay," Stu said, "keep it up. And don't get caught."

* * *

I wasn't looking forward to the call I had to make.

After rearranging the papers on my desk, I picked up the phone and listened for the dial tone. I put the phone down and lit a cigarette.

Don Barlett and I had been talking regularly, so Art and I decided I should be the one to see whether our working agreement was still intact after the NBC story. Just because the *Philadelphia Inquirer* hadn't disclosed our role in helping source their reporting on Ferraro and Zaccaro didn't mean Jamie Gangel's charges hadn't harmed the relationship. The reporters might have felt they were being used by us as part of a broader dirty tricks operation. They had probably been as worried as we were that the relationship between the paper and the campaign would be exposed by another leak, bringing their journalistic integrity under attack by the Democrats. They might stop working with us just to prevent further risk to the paper's reputation.

Whatever the fallout might be, I had to know. I let the cigarette dangle on the edge of my ashtray, a purloined souvenir from the Keble College bar at Oxford University, and dialed Barlett's line. There was reserve in his voice when he answered.

"I wanted to call and let you know that we don't have anything to do with protestors and anti-abortion activists," I began. "Someone else on the campaign may be doing that, but it isn't us."

I knew what I was saying went counter to Atwater's so-called investigation, at the end of which he'd announced to the *New York Times*, "I've thoroughly investigated this campaign from top to bottom. This campaign is as clean as a hound's tooth."

My concern was re-affirming our credibility with the *Inquirer*, not Atwater's. I couldn't guarantee there wouldn't be another story tomorrow depicting Atwater as the hand behind the heckling.

"I hope this didn't create any trouble for you at the newspaper," I said.

"It did raise some questions about whether we should be cooperating with you," Barlett said. "We had a few discussions. There's some editorial resistance we'll have to overcome if we keep working together."

"Well, that's understandable."

"How about you? Did it cause you any trouble inside the campaign?"

"No. We've been very secretive about our relationship. No one around here knows we're working with you, or it would have been all over the networks by now. Art and I are fine."

In one way, Atwater's leak had turned out to our advantage. The fact that we hadn't been exposed by the press digging around for proof of a dirty tricks operation lent credence to our cover that the campaign brass didn't know what we were doing. Because we clearly weren't part of the activities Jamie Gangel uncovered, it was at least slightly plausible that Art and I really were lone cowboys acting of our own volition.

Don asked if we had come across anything new. I thought about mentioning the Hogan story. Instinct told me to hold back. This wasn't the time to push what might be nothing more than rumor on him. The next lead we gave to the *Inquirer* had to be solid. We chatted for a while about the campaign and by the time we hung up we'd agreed to keep the channel open.

* * *

Fate intervened on our behalf. On October 4 the *Philadelphia Inquirer* published a lengthy article on Zaccaro under the headline "Report links Zaccaro to loan probe." District Attorney Robert Morgenthau of Manhattan had convened a grand jury to hear testimony about an unusual loan made by the Port Authority of New York and New Jersey credit union. The loan involved a real estate transaction in which John Zaccaro acted as co-broker with a man named Ronald Harnisch, the credit union's counsel. The $4.9 million deal for an apartment building in Manhattan was partly financed with a loan from the credit union, even though none of the participants in the transaction were credit union members. Zaccaro and Harnisch were reported to have earned a $100,000 commission for brokering the transaction.

If any of the top editors at the *Inquirer* had doubts about the legitimacy of scrutinizing Zaccaro and Ferraro's finances, Morgenthau's summons for Zaccaro to appear before the grand jury dispelled them. The article not only covered the credit union loan but also went on to report the latest developments in Zaccaro's handling of the Alice Phelan estate from which his company had borrowed a total of $175,000 before he was removed as conservator.

There was another call I needed to make before the week ended. I'd asked Roger Stone for his phone logs from late summer so that I could try to find that phone call from someone named Barber. Sure enough, a message had been left from a man named Cliff Barber. Roger recalled returning Barber's call but got the impression that he was a blow-hard. He claimed to have important information about Ferraro but wouldn't discuss it on the telephone.

I decided to give Mr. Barber another try. I dialed his number in upstate New York and reached him at his office. Just as he'd done with Stone months earlier, he told me he had information about Ferraro's family ties to the Mafia. When I asked for more detail he said he would not discuss it over the phone.

"My secretary has had death threats, I've been threatened, so I'm not going to go into this unless you're serious," he said. "I'm willing to talk about it—in person."

I asked if he could come to Washington but he said work was pressing and he couldn't get away on short notice. I vacillated for a moment, trying to decide whether Roger was right about Barber being a crank. I'd dealt with quite a few of the latter while working at Reagan's political action committee, Citizens for the Republic, and later on the 1980 campaign. Most of the cranks sent lengthy letters outlining world-class conspiracies, while some of them showed up in the lobby of campaign headquarters insisting they had messages the candidate had to see for himself. Barber didn't strike me as a nut case. To the contrary, he sounded like a reasonable guy who knew something interesting and had been threatened not to talk about it.

In his position, I wouldn't take the risk of being secretly recorded or wiretapped either. I would want to know someone else wasn't listening in on the line.

We made a date to meet early in the coming week for lunch at the Thayer Hotel at West Point. When I told Art about it, to my surprise he didn't question my decision. I expected lots of questions about why this wouldn't turn out to be a waste of time and money.

"Leave the flight arrangements to me," he said. "What do you think about inviting the *Inquirer* to send along some reporters?"

"I don't get the feeling he'll want to talk to reporters," I said. "He's pretty serious about the death threats."

Barber had told me on the phone that he'd gotten a message that he'd be "blown up at five p.m." on the same day any newspaper ran a story about Ferraro's parents.

"Making it public makes him safer," Art said, "so long as it's on background and his name doesn't come up. Maybe we can get the reporters to come, and after we've met maybe we can convince him to talk to them."

I saw the beauty of Art's idea. It would reaffirm our credibility with the *Inquirer* and speed up publication of the story, assuming that Barber had enough facts to make a story. It was also a risk. If Barber's leads weren't solid, we would be wasting the reporters' time and travel budget.

"I'll call Barlett," I sighed, "They can take a nearby table and watch the meeting. Even if Barber won't talk to them, at least they'll know we have a real source."

"Don't overpromise," Teele said. "Make sure they understand we can't guarantee anything. And ask them to book a room at the hotel so we'll have a private place to talk if it does work out."

16

Debate Disaster

Reagan-Bush '84 Headquarters
Washington, D.C.
October 5–October 9, 1984

The first presidential debate was scheduled for October 7 at the Kentucky Center for the Arts in Louisville. The topic was domestic policy. ABC's Barbara Walters was chosen to be the moderator.

For weeks debate preparation sessions had been underway with Reagan at Camp David and the White House. David Stockman, a former congressman from Michigan who Reagan had made head of the Office of Management and Budget, played the role of Walter Mondale. Stu Spencer attended many of the debate practice sessions alongside Reagan, but the debate preparation was largely in the hands of Chief of Staff Jim Baker and Staff Secretary Richard Darman.

I had reason to doubt Darman's political acumen. In 1983, as the White House began to shift its attention to the coming election year, I was asked to design a series of presidential appearances and policy actions around the themes of a report by the National Commission on Excellence in Education. The report took an alarmist tone about the state of American education and made sweeping policy prescriptions. Unlike most advisory commission reports, this one attracted network news coverage, thanks in part to a provocative press release about the commission's stark findings that Tony Blankley and I co-wrote when we worked together at the U.S. Department of Education.

Tony and I also developed proposals for presidential events and policy actions to follow up on the report's dire findings about the state of American schools. To ensure consistency with Reagan's existing education policy, we reviewed his record on education as governor of California and his public statements and radio broadcasts dating back to the 1970s. We found that many of the ideas Reagan had supported through the years were completely consistent with the reform agenda Tony and I proposed.

Richard Darman (left), Ronald Reagan and Jim Baker at Camp David preparing for first debate with Walter Mondale, October 6, 1984 (courtesy Ronald Reagan Presidential Library).

Nancy Reagan and Stu Spencer at Camp David taking a break from debate preparations, October 6, 1984 (courtesy Ronald Reagan Presidential Library).

Steve Studdert, then head of the Presidential Advance Office, submitted the proposals to Mike Deaver. He was eager to shore up Reagan's standing on education. In 1983, as the recession faded, the issue of education had risen in prominence in White House polls. More voters disapproved of Reagan's education policies, which included dismantling the Department of Education, than approved of them.

Deaver adopted most of our suggestions and planning for the presidential events got underway. But when it came to the policy agenda, Darman objected that without major new spending Reagan's education initiatives would lack credibility. Darman had evidently convinced Baker and possibly Stockman to back new federal spending on education. Word got back to me that we should include up to $1 billion in spending for new programs—almost a 10 percent increase over the president's proposed education budget!

To me it made no sense to try to buy credibility, given that many of the reforms we advocated were administrative and managerial and required little or no new federal funding. Moreover, any budget increase would only open a competition with the Democrats who controlled Congress to see who could spend the most on education. A $1 billion increase would quickly turn into a $3 billion appropriation, with the political credit going to Senator Ted Kennedy and Speaker Tip O'Neill. It would be just another example of Washington throwing money at a problem instead of undertaking serious reforms.

After conferring with Anne Graham, my boss at the Education Department's Office of Legislation and Public Affairs, we decided to torpedo Darman's proposal.

One of Reagan's favorite newspapers was the conservative weekly *Human Events*. I spent about two hours on the phone with Allan Ryskind, the newspaper's editor. Ryskind was the son of screenwriter Morrie Ryskind, who had co-written many of the Marx Brothers movies. Morrie Ryskind and Ronald Reagan knew each other from Reagan's Hollywood days. Baker and Darman so disliked *Human Events*' influence on Reagan that they tried to keep him from seeing it. He got around them by ordering multiple copies for the White House.

Ryskind asked good questions and took copious notes as I walked him through the complex financing of public education in America, making the case that the reforms Reagan was about to announce required no new funding. I filled him in on Darman's $1 billion proposal and why it was unnecessary. I gave Ryskind many concrete examples, the kind of anecdotes I knew Reagan liked from my work in the White House Speechwriting Office early in his first term. Everything I told Ryskind was on background. He agreed to keep my name out of his article.

Ryskind ran a detailed front-page story the day before Reagan was set to deliver the first major speech in Deaver's education reform initiative.

Misty Church, one of the presidential speechwriting research aides and fact-checkers, called my office early the next morning and left word it was urgent that she reach me.

Misty was a former colleague, and I knew if she said it was urgent, she meant it. I called her back immediately.

"The president completely re-wrote his speech overnight," she said a little breathlessly. "We're going nuts over here. No one knows where he got the information from and I have to verify it. I figured if anyone might be able to help it's you."

She started going through the facts and numbers Reagan had put into the speech one by one and it was only a matter of minutes before I realized he'd incorporated the *Human Events* article almost in its entirety. I gave Misty the official source for each fact in the article, knowing that once she'd annotated the speech with the sources no one in the White House could object to it. Reagan gave the speech he wanted to give, no doubt with Darman clucking from the sidelines that without more spending the initiative would never work.

Over the next six weeks, Reagan made numerous appearances at educational events and schools and proposed a series of reforms. At the end of the education initiative, his standing in the polls had been reversed. More voters approved of his education policy than disapproved of it. In a June 28, 1983, letter to members of the Cabinet, Deaver said, "One of the most successful efforts we have had to date is the recent turnaround in polling results and in the media on education. These results were in part due to a comprehensive plan for Presidential travel to, and participation in, high profile education forums."

I now hoped Darman's advice on the upcoming presidential debate was better than his judgment on the education initiative. He had met with Lee Atwater and Ed Rollins several times at campaign headquarters and clearly thought of himself as a political strategist, although he had no actual experience working on a political campaign. Like some others I'd come across in the White House, he imagined himself an expert in everything but wasn't able to grasp his own limits.

Our own polling and the *Washington Post*/ABC poll showed Reagan ahead in at least 48 states the week before the debate, including Mondale's home state of Minnesota. By October 5, the tone of the campaign press coverage was almost triumphalist for Reagan. The *Post* predicted that Reagan might be heading for "an electoral college landslide." Even staunch liberal columnists like Mark Shields and Tom Wicker conceded that the domestic policy debate represented Mondale's last chance to make a breakthrough and prevent a Democratic rout on Election Day.

President Reagan spent Saturday, October 6, at Camp David in last-minute preparations for the 90-minute domestic policy debate with Walter Mondale. Aside from an interruption to broadcast his regular Saturday

Onboard Air Force 1, President Reagan congratulating me on the success of the White House education initiative after his appearance at Shawnee Mission High School, Shawnee, Kansas, June 29, 1983. My moustache was stained with cigarette smoke (courtesy Ronald Reagan Presidential Library).

five-minute radio address, the practice session consumed the day. The following day the Reagans returned to the White House. That afternoon, some 500 White House and campaign staffers gathered on the South Lawn to give them a send-off to Louisville. Accompanied by key White House and campaign staff, Ronald and Nancy Reagan flew to Kentucky for the first showdown with Walter Mondale.

At the Hyatt Regency Hotel, the Reagans were scheduled to have a private dinner with Mike Deaver and one or two other close aides before the debate. Jim Baker and Richard Darman weren't included in the dinner but were scheduled to briefly join the group before the debate started. Both men fluttered around outside the room throughout the dinner, waiting to be beckoned inside.

When they were ushered into the room, Baker and Darman inadvertently made a huge mistake by using their few minutes of time with Reagan to talk about debate strategy.

Only those who were really close to the president knew that despite his confidence as a public speaker, three kinds of events made him nervous: press conferences, State of the Union addresses, and debates. Reagan was most effective in these kinds of speaking engagements when he had a little quiet time with a few close advisors, including Nancy, before they took place. Instead of last-minute kibitzing, the goal of those close to Reagan was to create a relaxed atmosphere.

Deaver accomplished this with humor. One time he passed Reagan a private note written on his personal stationary, with "Michael K. Deaver" at the top, saying, "Show them what an old fart can do." Everyone cracked up, and Reagan started the news conference in a light-hearted mood.

But Baker and Darman were never Reagan intimates. They neither knew nor understood the man. So instead of leaving the room in the tranquil mood they found it, they heightened Reagan's anxiety by turning the conversation to the debate.

Many of Reagan's close advisors already thought he had been over-coached. Darman and Stockman had given Reagan books of notes that were inches thick, layered in details and numbers about government programs and spending. Reagan was also expected to have command of similarly-thick notebooks outlining Mondale's record and vulnerabilities. Stockman, whom Reagan once called a "hard-headed son of a bitch," had pummeled Reagan when Stockman played the role of his opponent, Walter Mondale.

When Reagan took the stage shortly before 9 p.m. Eastern time, he was over-prepared, saturated in the minutiae of government programs, and lacking in confidence due to the grueling debate practice sessions. The result was an awkward performance that culminated at the end of 100 minutes (the debate ran long) with a rambling, inchoate closing statement.

Media polls taken during and immediately after the debate showed that the question of who won was a toss-up. Presidential pollster Dick Wirthlin tracked viewers' responses throughout the debate. His polling showed that the number of those who thought Reagan won the debate dropped from 49 percent to 41 percent after Reagan's closing remarks, ending in a near-tie with Mondale.

Publicly, our team kept a stiff upper lip for the first few days after the debate. Campaign chairman Paul Laxalt called the debate "a wash" and dismissed Reagan's performance as due to "a heavy debate that did not lend itself to humor." Jim Baker said that simply by agreeing to debate Mondale, Reagan "put to rest all these charges that he's somehow out of touch, that he's not accessible, that he lives in a show-business cocoon." Deaver explained the clumsy closing statement by saying Reagan tried to talk extemporaneously in the final moments of the debate and didn't have prepared remarks. Campaign press secretary James Lake said laconically, that "We would have liked a better close."

Behind the scenes it was a different story. The first debate was a disaster, and everyone on Reagan's team knew it. Laxalt was furious at Baker and his team for botching the debate preparation. Nancy Reagan was even more irate. The truth was Reagan had prepared a closing statement. Darman included it in the briefing books. Inexplicably, somehow the debate prep team never got around to letting Reagan practice the closing statement. When he got on stage at Louisville, it was like an actor trying to deliver his lines without the benefit of rehearsal.

The detail-laden, wonkish debate strategy devised by Baker, Darman and Stockman had played into Mondale's strengths. The former vice president put Reagan on the defensive almost immediately, and Reagan struggled in a morass of numbers and statistics to refute Mondale's charges. If the foreign policy debate, scheduled for two weeks later on October 21, went as badly, it would change the course of the campaign.

Reagan was depressed. He blamed himself for letting the team down.

Spencer and Laxalt demanded that planning for the foreign policy debate be taken away from Baker and Darman. The president agreed, and responsibility for debate preparation shifted to the campaign team.

In the reshuffling of responsibilities, Darman concluded that he was in danger of being fired from his job at the White House. He wasn't far off the mark. Aside from Chief of Staff Baker, Darman had few supporters in the White House. Nancy Reagan would have been happy to see him go. The same was true of Laxalt, who complained privately that the Baker-Darman-Stockman debate sessions had "brutalized" the president.

Darman took preemptive action. He threatened to disclose confidential matters if he was fired. The implication was that he would depict Reagan as muddled and too old to serve a second presidential term if he were made the scapegoat for the debate fiasco. The threat worked. Darman kept his job, at least for the time being, even if the ploy meant he would no longer be trusted by Reagan's inner circle.

There were only five days between the first presidential debate and the vice-presidential debate between George H.W. Bush and Geraldine Ferraro. It was the next major event in the campaign. Expectations were high that Bush would dominate the debate, which was bad for our campaign. Any stumbles by Bush would be magnified and give further momentum to the Mondale-Ferraro ticket.

* * *

The aftermath of the first presidential debate created plenty of drama around campaign headquarters and the White House, but Art Teele and I didn't have time to hang around and see how it worked out. The Monday after the debate we met at the Butler Aviation terminal at Washington National Airport. It was Columbus Day, and we were on our own voyage of discovery to see what Cliff Barber had to offer us.

Teele had chartered a twin-engine prop plane to fly us to West Point. When we were airborne I asked why he'd decided to hire the private plane.

"I don't want a record of us flying commercially," he said. "If Barber's afraid of Mafia retaliation, we should be too."

It was a clear fall day and beautiful weather for flying. Except for our thoughts, there was no turbulence between Washington and New York. The plane flew along the Hudson as we passed the city. The Twin Towers gleamed in the strong autumn light. As our pilot followed the river north toward West Point the urban landscape gave way to forested rolling hills along the riverbanks. From the air, the trees seemed daubed in splashes of red and gold. The scenery was bucolic.

We took a car to the U.S. Military Academy at West Point. I briefed Teele on what I'd learned about Barber.

"This guy is far from a nutcase," I said. "You ever wondered about who has the keys to Fort Knox? Well, Barber has the keys to the second-largest bullion depository in the United States. He's responsible for 60 million ounces of gold. That's about $25 billion worth."

"How could we have overlooked him for so long?" Art asked.

"He didn't make a big deal out of his credentials when he called Roger," I said. "He really doesn't want to draw attention to himself."

I told Art that Barber was a military veteran who had been active in the local Republican Party. Reagan had appointed him superintendent of the U.S. Bullion Depository at West Point.

The Thayer Hotel was an impressive gothic building on West Point's grounds overlooking the Hudson River. In 1981, Reagan had ordered that the hotel be used for the U.S. hostages who had been held in Iran for 444 days. After their release on January 20, the day Reagan was sworn in as president, the 53 hostages were flown to Germany for medical check-ups. Former president Jimmy Carter greeted them, but they were also swarmed by U.S. congressional delegations, known as CODELS, eager to share the limelight and stage photo ops with the newly-freed diplomats.

When the White House learned that the senators and congressmen were using official U.S. airplanes for their travel while the hostages and their families were being shunted off onto chartered aircraft, top aides were outraged. Reagan wanted the diplomats to have time to be with their families after the long ordeal, and he wanted them to be treated like honored U.S. employees instead of second-class citizens to the members of Congress.

The White House ordered the CODELS onto the charter jets and put the freed hostages and their families on official aircraft for the flight back to the United States. They landed at an Air National Guard base in Newburgh and were bussed to West Point, where they spent several days in seclusion with their families at the Thayer Hotel before traveling on to Washington. I had received an invitation from the president to attend the White House reception for the freed diplomats, who drew a crowd estimated at more than 200,000 people along Pennsylvania Avenue. The hostages' homecoming made an indelible impression on me.

I wondered what it would be like to spend a long weekend at the Thayer during the peak of the fall color. We arrived a few minutes before our scheduled 12:30 lunch meeting with Barber. We walked in and sized up the restaurant. There was a decent-sized crowd. We took our table and glanced around. The reporters from the *Philadelphia Inquirer* were seated two tables away, close enough to watch and probably overhear most of our conversation with Barber.

Promptly at 12:30, a middle-aged man dressed in a gray suit came toward our table. I'd given Barber our descriptions. As the only black guy and white guy dining together, we were easy to spot.

We introduced ourselves, shook hands, and sized up the menu and each other. After the waitress took our order Barber opened one side of his coat and flashed the revolver in his shoulder holster. I quickly sized up the cylinder and determined it was large caliber, probably a .357 Magnum. I didn't know whether to feel worried or relieved that he felt carrying a piece inside the Thayer Hotel was a suitable precaution. From where the *Inquirer* guys were seated the view must have been interesting.

Barber wanted to know how badly the debate had hurt Reagan's standing. We told him about the shake-up in the debate preparation team and what we knew about the polling: that Reagan's lead over Mondale was holding, but that we couldn't afford a repeat performance. Ordinarily we wouldn't have been that candid, but we were looking for candor from him and wanted to establish trust.

Over lunch, Barber laid out an amazing story about Geraldine Ferraro's parents and childhood.

"They didn't run a nickel-and-dime store like she says," he began. "It was actually a night club and a burlesque joint. The nickel-and-dime store was just a sideline business in the same building, maybe a front for the gambling operation."

Teele and I stared at one another. Ferraro's biographies had no mention of a night club, much less illegal gambling. We'd never even heard a rumor about a burlesque club.

"Are you sure about this?" Art said.

"It was called the Roxy. They used to advertise the place," Barber said. "Go to the morgue of the local newspaper in Newburgh. You can find the ads there."

Barber leaned over the table like someone with a secret to spill.

"It wasn't her parents' business alone," he said. "They had a partner. A gangster named Mike DeVasto. They ran an illegal gambling operation out of the club. They were bookies."

I literally sat back in my seat. My thoughts went straight to evidence to back up the story.

"How do we verify that?" I asked.

"It's not hard," Barber said. "There's a bar in Newburgh called Scully's. If you go there around 5 o'clock, you'll run into Frannie De Vasto. He's a regular. He usually rolls in there around five for his daily pop. He's Mike's son. Buy him a drink or two, he'll talk all about the good old days."

"How did you find out about this?" Art asked.

"There's more," Barber went on. "Her mother and father have arrest records. They were busted for numbers running in 1944. You can find the arrest records in the county courthouse."

"Numbers running?" Art was bemused.

Barber nodded.

"Was there a trial?"

"No. The day before the trial, her father died of a heart attack. At least that's what the doctor's report said. When he died, the prosecutor dropped the charges against the widow."

I shook my head. Geraldine Ferraro would have been eight or nine years old at the time. I wondered whether she knew her parents had been arrested or whether she'd been sheltered from their legal troubles. Surely a precocious kid would have known something was wrong. Then again, it was conceivable that they'd concealed it from her.

"So you tracked down this information yourself and asked a lot of questions," I said, "and that's when the death threats started?"

It was a guess, but Barber confirmed it. Of course it didn't mean the Mafia was threatening him. It could just be overzealous Democrats hoping to intimidate him. At least that's what I told myself.

"I'm sorry it's taken us so long to get back to you," I said. "Your first call to the campaign sort of fell between the cracks."

This line was Art's cue to pitch Barber on meeting with the reporters from the *Inquirer.* He gave it his best shot. Art explained that we'd been working with the newspaper on a confidential basis for months. He told him we could guarantee that the *Inquirer* wouldn't use his name and that they would independently verify everything he'd told us before running a story. Barber was clearly annoyed that we'd invited reporters to the meeting without telling him, but I sensed that his reticence had more to do with the potential for his involvement to leak out through the inevitable chatter among journalists in a newsroom. He was taking no chances. I couldn't blame him. In his position, I would have done the same.

Art finished by thanking him profusely for the help he'd given us.

"I know you didn't have to stick your neck out like this," he said, "and I appreciate the risks you've taken."

Barber wouldn't budge.

"I've given you the information," he said. "It's up to you to get it in the papers."

We said our goodbyes and went with the *Inquirer* team to the room they'd reserved. We gave them Barber's story in full detail. Art explained that we'd pitched him to meet directly with them but Barber was too cagey. Art emphasized the death threats.

They were disappointed. Newburgh was only about an hour up Highway 87 from West Point, but the *Inquirer* reporters were non-committal about heading north to check out Scully's bar and the arrest records at the county courthouse. They thanked us for trying to set up the interview with Barber, but I had the feeling they weren't going to follow up on the story.

As we headed back to the airport we traded notes.

"Barber struck me as very credible," Art said. "I think he really is worried about those threats."

"What I like best is that we don't have to trust his credibility," I said. "He's shown us exactly how to document his story. Now we just have to get someone to do it."

"What do you think of the *Inquirer's* reaction?"

"I don't think we can leave it to them. I'm going to get Ambrose and his Guinea Chasers to work on it as soon as we get back. And I think we need to call the *Post.*"

"The *Washington Post?*" Art was incredulous.

"No, no. The *New York Post.*"

I had in mind two reporters that Roy Cohn had recommended at the *New York Post*, Guy Hawtin and Jeff Wells. This was the kind of story they'd eat up. They'd be in Newburgh tomorrow morning checking out Barber's leads.

"I'm with you on that. The sooner we get all this out in the press, the better off we'll all be."

"How do you figure?"

"Threats are only effective before the information's public," he said. "Once it's public knowledge, they'll back off."

"What about retaliation?"

"They won't risk it. It will all be too high profile. We're doing Barber a favor by getting the facts out."

"Why don't you fill in Stu when we get back so I can get straight onto Ambrose and the *Post.*"

We didn't talk a lot on the flight back home. Neither of us had expected the bombshell Barber tossed in our laps. If what he said could be proven, it meant that both Zaccaro's and Ferraro's parents had ties to organized crime. Given their ongoing business dealings with and campaign contributions from organized crime figures, the Mafia might have a way to put pressure on the White House if the Mondale-Ferraro ticket won. In the worst case, it might have an open door. The election was now less than a month away, and it felt as if the full responsibility for uncovering the truth was squarely on our shoulders.

We went directly from National Airport to campaign headquarters so I could make my calls. Guy Hawtin was effusively grateful for the lead. Ambrose said he'd mobilize his people. I wanted to have confirmation of Barber's facts and not leave it up to journalists to do our fact-checking for us. If the *Philadelphia Inquirer* or the *New York Post* passed on the story, we might have to use other means to make it public.

Before I left that night I stopped by Roger Stone's office to let him know that the meeting with Barber went well. I didn't go into details. The last thing we needed were rumors about Ferraro's parents floating around Washington.

The Heartland Special

I didn't have any more time to worry further about the Ferraro operation. I had to pack my bags and fly to Ohio. I was going to take a train trip through the fields and small towns of farm country. The pressure was on the campaign to make sure that Mondale couldn't capitalize on his newfound momentum from the first debate, and we were counting on a whistle stop train tour to restore Reagan's edge over Mondale.

Since September, the White House had been working on a whistle stop tour modeled after Harry Truman's 1948 campaign. Don Clarey, Special Assistant to President Reagan for Cabinet Affairs, had been enthusiastically pushing the idea in memos and conversation with Steve Studdert, the former head of the Presidential Advance Office who became a consultant to the White House after 1982. The 1948 presidential contest was the election that produced the famous "Dewey Beats Truman" headline. Truman stumped the country, speaking from the back of a train car called the Ferdinand Magellan.

The Ferdinand Magellan was an historic train car kept at the Gold Coast Railroad Museum in Fort Lauderdale, Florida. It was custom-built for President Franklin Delano Roosevelt, fully-armored, and weighed 286,000 pounds. It was the heaviest passenger railcar ever built in America. The interior was preserved exactly as it had been in FDR's day, including the president's special railroad wheelchair.

Truman gave more than 200 speeches from the brass-railed rear platform of the car. Winston Churchill used it in 1946 to travel to Westminster College in Fulton, Missouri, to give his famous "Iron Curtain" speech. The night before the speech Churchill still hadn't decided on the metaphor he wanted to use to describe the growing impact of Communism on Eastern Europe. When he looked up at the curtain between his sleeping berth and the car's passageway, inspiration hit. The curtains of the Ferdinand Magellan became the "Iron Curtain" that descended across the continent of Europe.

The Ferdinand Magellan was in excellent condition but the proposal for a modern whistle-stop tour had its skeptics. The Secret Service worried about how to secure miles of train tracks from hidden explosives. They raised concerns about how near the tracks along the proposed route ran through residential areas and the potential for children trying to see the president's train to be killed on the tracks. They worried about the manpower required to secure nine different crossings so that no one could smash into the train and potentially derail it.

Instead of speaking from the back of the railroad car like Truman did, the Secret Service proposed that Reagan speak from an armored flatbed so he wouldn't be exposed to as large a crowd—and potential snipers. Some White House aides worried that the cost of the whistle stop tour would seem extravagantly high.

But Steve Studdert wasn't deterred. He summed it up in his September 25 "Ohio Railroad Survey" memo to Bill Henkel, Special Assistant to the President and Director of Presidential Advance. Studdert wrote:

> "This is a fantastic series of events. There is a certain romance about American railroads that can be captured: I love this event notion.
>
> Based on the number of crossings, the population base, and for example the large turnouts for any steam train that passes through, it would not surprise me to see a total turnout of a million or more. There will be crowds at ALL communities.
>
> This will be a monumental task for the Secret Service, and the most complex advance of this campaign for us. But I believe the potential impact fully warrants the effort. This potentially is one hell of a day.

Henkel was sufficiently persuaded to take a look on the ground. At 5:15 a.m. on September 29, vans carrying the pre-advance team left the West Basement of the White House en route to Andrews Air Force Base. The team flew to Wright Patterson Air Force Base in Ohio on a C-20 aircraft. Bill Henkel, Charles Bakaly, Jim Hooley and Karen Groomes were there from the Presidential Advance Office. There were three Secret Service representatives, an Air Force One advance officer, a military aide, two members of the White House Communications Agency, and an advance officer for the presidential helicopter. They toured over a half-dozen sites in the next 12 hours.

On October 2, Henkel sent a memo to Mike Deaver proposing the whistle stop tour through Ohio for October 12, 1984. By the time of the first presidential debate, the trip was in its final planning stages.

There were plenty of reasons to scuttle the idea, but after the Louisville debate there was one overriding reason to go through with it. If we could pull it off, it was precisely the sort of event that might restore Reagan's morale. It was in the country's heartland. The train would pass through a series of small towns where presidential visits were so rare that they might occur only once in a lifetime. The crowds would be proud and excited to see a president, especially on an historic train car.

My job was similar to what it had been at Normandy. Steve Hart was again in charge of press for the trip, and I was there to handle one of the sites where Reagan would speak. Then I would hop on the train and back up Steve throughout the day by handling the White House press pool that traveled with the president.

I picked up a rental car at the airport and drove to downtown Dayton. My event site was the Old Montgomery County Courthouse mall. President Reagan's first public remarks in Ohio would take place there. My hotel was conveniently nearby. I checked in and went to the staff office. John Gartland was the lead White House advance man for the site, and we would have to work in close coordination to make the event a success. I picked up my copy of the draft presidential schedule and messages and went to inspect the construction of the press platform and familiarize myself with the site layout.

That afternoon there was a countdown meeting.

The news we got was sobering. Protestors planned to gather at 8:00 a.m. at the federal building for a "Rally Against Reagan." A group calling itself the "Ad-Hoc Committee to Rally Against Reagan" was organizing the protest. A flyer listed their grievances as the number of unemployed in the Dayton area, federal budget cuts on spending for senior citizens and health care, the nuclear arms race and the "war in Central America," failure to pass the Equal Rights Amendment, "attacks on the rights of blacks and other minorities," destruction of the environment, and "assaults on unions." The bottom of the flyer said: "Vote Mondale/Ferraro."

We were used to protestors, but in this case a lawsuit had been filed in federal court demanding that they have access to the rally site at the courthouse square and be within view of the press covering Reagan's speech. The protestors wanted the judge not just to uphold their First Amendment rights but also to guarantee that the press would be able to see and hear them clearly.

Gartland said he was due in court on Thursday, the day before Reagan's arrival in Ohio, to present a plan to accommodate the protestors that would be acceptable to the judge.

I took in what this meant. I might establish the location for the press platform, stanchioned off to keep the public from intruding on it, with dedicated access through the square so that the press could enter and leave separately from the crowd that we expected the president to draw. This was standard operating procedure. I would of course coordinate the media's requirements with the requirements of the Secret Service and the White House staff advance so that everyone could move smoothly on the day of the event and perform their respective jobs. But all of that planning would mean noth-

ing if a federal judge decided to re-shape the layout of the event to conform
to the protest organizers' demands.

I spoke privately with Gartland after the countdown meeting.

"Given the number of people you expect and the size of the square, this
is going to be a very crowded event," I said. "Getting the White House travel
press from the platform to the train won't be easy if I don't have a dedicated,
clear pathway for them to move after the speech is over."

John reassured me he understood the problem. He had started in advance during the Nixon Administration and was clearly a pro. But I needed
to be certain Gartland would make a strong case if the judge demanded more
space for the protestors at the expense of the media.

"I've seen it happen before at a large rally," I went on. "The president
finishes speaking and starts off the stage, and the crowd starts moving. If the
rope lines for the press chute aren't far enough apart, the crowd just starts
going right over the ropes to save time in getting out. The next thing, the press
can't get through, and then either the president's delayed in leaving or they
miss the train and we lose the coverage. Either way, we both know that's not
how we want to start the day."

John got the message. He said all the right things to me. Hopefully, he
would lay out the case for the judge.

"You know there's one other issue the judge needs to be aware of," I said.
"When the public starts mingling with the White House travel press, that's
how we get another Hinckley."

Gartland had been through the same Secret Service seminars on John
Hinckley's assassination attempt that I had. Hinckley had infiltrated the
White House press pool waiting outside the Washington Hilton to cover
Reagan's departure. As Reagan left the hotel and started to get into his lim-
ousine, Hinckley fired from the cluster of journalists. In a mere 1.4 seconds,
he shot and wounded President Reagan, Press Secretary James Brady, Secret
Service agent Timothy McCarthy, and Washington, D.C., policeman Thomas
Delahanty.

After the assassination attempt, White House security procedures were
tightened to prevent a similar intrusion into the press. But if I couldn't move
the press from the rally to the train in a controlled way so that the public
couldn't swarm them, there was a serious risk of an intruder getting into a
group of reporters and making it onto the train.

That wasn't happening on my watch.

On the day Hinckley tried to assassinate Reagan, Howard Bane and I
were having lunch on Capitol Hill. When Howard heard the sirens he said
"something big" must have happened. When I got back to my office I got the
news and went straight to Nofziger's office at the White House. A small crowd
was gathered there, waiting for the latest news from the hospital. It was there

I learned that Reagan's wound was serious. For a while it seemed like the beginning of another national nightmare.

For the next 12 days my wife was assigned to work at George Washington University Hospital screening visitors to the president's hospital room. For the most part the job consisted of blocking them. From Supreme Court justices to senators and representatives, Washington's political class jockeyed to see Reagan. Almost all were turned away. Every morning I dropped her off and picked her up in the evening. It seemed unreal that less than three months into Reagan's presidency it had come so near to ending.

All the press covering the whistle stop tour would be given credentials to use as a press pass. They wore their passes around their necks so they were always visible. The press who formed the pool that got closest to the president were accompanied by me and a Secret Service agent. The reporters who were traveling on the train were also accompanied by White House staff and the Secret Service. Security was assured only if the press movements were designed so that outsiders couldn't mingle with them.

* * *

Thursday morning I got up leisurely, ate a decent breakfast in the hotel restaurant, and concluded there was no point trying to finesse the arrangements for the press until the court case was resolved.

I decided to tour the Dayton Arcade. It was one of the city's architectural landmarks, a glass dome 70 feet high and 90 feet in diameter that spanned an open space between five historic buildings. It was built between 1902 and 1904 and housed boutiques, restaurants and specialty shops, many of them featuring food.

When I lived in Madrid and London I'd seen lots of glass domes, rotundas, and covered markets but this was one of the best. I couldn't believe the city of Dayton had managed to preserve such a jewel through the heyday of urban renewal, when so many of America's best landmarks were torn down at the behest of city planners and developers instead of being preserved.

After lunch I called Art at campaign headquarters.

"How's it going back inside the Beltway?" I asked.

"Very ugly. Have you seen today's news summary?"

"No, there are no copies out here. What's it say?"

"Safire's column is headlined 'Farewell to Hubris.' He says Mondale quote 'creamed' Reagan in the debate. He says at the end Reagan looked like quote 'an old fighter on the ropes.'"

Bill Safire was a former Nixon speechwriter whose column in the *New York Times* was must-reading.

"Safire tells it like it is," I said. "He's not a partisan hack. You've got to give him that."

"Listen to this one," Art said. "Can the old man hack it for another four years? That dirty question, once only a whisper, is now out in the open as a central feature of the campaign ... even the huge lead President Reagan has built up is not entirely secure unless he can somehow trump the issue."

"Who wrote that?"

"Joseph Kraft."

Kraft was a respected journalist whose syndicated column ran in more than 200 newspapers. In the 1960 campaign he'd been a speechwriter for John F. Kennedy, but when it came to his reporting, he was scrupulously objective.

"Anybody else jumping on the age issue?"

"It's been percolating all week, but now it's hit critical mass. The *Wall Street Journal* ran a piece 'The Fitness Issue' on Tuesday, and the *New York Times* has one today headlined 'Reagan's Health: How Issue Emerged.' Tip O'Neill's jumped on it, Tony Coelho's talking about the age issue, David Broder's done a column on it. It's the new conventional wisdom."

Barely two weeks ago, when Mondale's campaign chairman Jim Johnson and Tony Coelho were asked about Reagan's age in a television interview, they downplayed its importance. The tide had clearly turned.

At 73, Reagan was the oldest incumbent president ever to run for reelection. Our campaign polling still showed Reagan with a comfortable lead over Mondale in both the Electoral College and the popular vote. But if the voters developed doubts about his ability to finish a second four-year term in office, the lead would narrow or even disappear.

"This puts the pressure on Bush," I said. "He has to come across as someone our voters would find acceptable if Reagan can't complete his second term."

Bush and Ferraro were scheduled to face off in the vice-presidential debate at the Philadelphia Civic Center tonight.

"The *Washington Times* editorial board agrees with you," Art said. "How are things going out there?"

"The train trip should be spectacular. The weather forecast for tomorrow is good, we'll get big crowds, and there's a lot of excitement here. What I'm worried about is the downtown rally that kicks it all off."

I explained the court case and how my planning was on hold pending the judge's decision.

"Maybe we should start tying them up with litigation," Art said. "I think I'll have a talk with Ron Robertson about it. Heard anything from the *Philadelphia Inquirer*?"

"I haven't spoken to them, and I don't have any messages from them either. I think they're giving Barber's story a pass."

"Good thing the *New York Post* is on it."

I rang off and went to the staff office to see if I had any new messages.

*   *   *

John Gartland was absent for most of that night's countdown meeting. We went over the details for the whistle stop tour, now dubbed the "Heartland Express," and the planning for Reagan's stops at small towns throughout the day. After the downtown rally, Reagan would board the train for a series of short speeches in Sidney, Lima, Ottawa, Deshler, and Perrysburg, Ohio.

Air Force One was due to land in a little more than 18 hours. Normally every detail would have been decided on at this point in a presidential trip. But the lawsuit was holding us up. Gartland was still in the courthouse, and until he emerged we couldn't finalize the details of the rally.

Finally, at about 9 p.m., Gartland got in touch with me. The judge had ordered that the protestors be given access to the rally in a place where they would be visible from the press platform. For the safety of the public and the protestors, this required creating an area separated by ropes and stanchions with sufficient space between the rally-goers and the demonstrators so that nobody could easily throw a punch over the rope-line. Police would patrol the gap to keep the two groups separated.

To create the protest zone the judge demanded, Gartland needed to find some space elsewhere in the zones we'd mapped out for the public attending the rally and the press platform and dedicated access points. John told me we would have to shrink the chute through which the press would get to and leave the platform area.

"Just leave me enough space so people won't be tempted to step over the rope and crowd the chute before the press can get there from the motorcade and then get to the train," I said, "otherwise it's going to be a royal cluster fuck."

"I'll do the best I can," Gartland said, "but I had to give the judge my word we'll comply with his order. It's my neck on the line."

I didn't like the sound of that. Gartland's plan called for the layout of the rally site to be cordoned off with 55-gallon drums and demarcated with ropes. To keep the crowd from collapsing the rope lines, the metal drums would be filled with water later that night. I asked some of the workers around the site when the drums were scheduled to be filled, went to dinner, watched the debate between Gerry Ferraro and George Bush on the television in my hotel room, and then caught a few hours of sleep.

At two a.m. I got up, threw on some clothes, and went to the courthouse square. Just as I guessed, the area for the press to access the platform had been shortened to only a few feet wide. The press would almost have to walk single file to get through it. It needed to be at least six feet wide, preferably eight. The space in front of the platform, where reporters generally stood to witness the event, had also shrunk overnight.

It was a completely unworkable layout. The reporters wouldn't have room, which would cause them to try to wedge their way onto the platform, which was usually filled with photographers and television crews. A number of spaces were always reserved for the television networks and the wire service photographers, but if local news reporters started crowding their way onto the platform the reserved spaces would be overrun, and when the travel press arrived with the presidential motorcade, they would have no place to set up.

I knew Gartland didn't have any choice. He had to follow the judge's orders. But I had a choice. The 55-gallon drums hadn't been filled yet. I paced off the room I needed in front of the press platform and moved the first drum. I did the same with the next corner and then moved the drums in between until I had an adequate zone for the media.

Then I worked my way down the entry and exit, rolling the empty drums to make a wide enough space so that the press would have easy access and the crowd wouldn't be tempted to infringe on the chute. About a half hour later, the crew arrived to start filling the drums all around the rally site.

I didn't want to take any chances that Gartland would come to inspect the site a final time before the drums were filled and rearrange my handiwork. I found a supervisor and asked him to fill the drums around the press area first. I told him we expected people to arrive early to mark out their space close to the president to watch the speech and that it was imperative these drums were filled first so nobody could move them. He was happy to oblige and a little impressed that one of the White House team was up at two in the morning to make sure everything was right.

I got back to my room at about three and set the alarm for five. Two hours' sleep was better than nothing. I'd learned a long time ago to grab shut-eye when I could. When I got up for the second time, I dressed in a suit and tie, got some breakfast and coffee, and headed to the rally site to make sure my barrels were still where I'd put them.

John Gartland was already there. He looked at me like I'd taken his car for a joyride and returned it covered in muck. I prepared myself for a blistering.

"I'm getting too old for this game," he said. "I can't stay up until three in the morning anymore."

"I don't think the judge will be out here with his measuring tape," I said. "Nobody will ever notice."

"Yeah, but I'm the one he'll hold in contempt."

I braced for the rest, but that was all he said about it.

It was barely dawn, but people were already staking out spaces closest to the podium. The president wasn't scheduled to speak for hours, but the crowd was building. John and I turned our attention to going over the movements of press, White House staff, dignitaries, and the president. We had a final schedule, and we needed to know its details intimately. It had to work in synchrony for the event to be a success.

I lit a Marlboro while we waited. It seemed forever before we got word that Air Force One had landed at Wright-Patterson Air Force Base. Reagan was greeted there by General Earl O'Loughlin and his wife Shirlee, Colonel Charles Fox and his wife Sharon, and Congressman Bob McEwen and his wife Elizabeth. Another Ohio congressman, Mike DeWine, rode with the presidential motorcade to Dayton.

So did half the White House, it seemed. James Baker was there, along with Dick Darman, Margaret Tutwiler, and John Rogers. Ed Rollins and Lee Atwater had both come for the train trip, along with Ken Khachigian. Mike Deaver and Bill Henkel were there, along with the president's doctor, the military aide, Jim Hooley as the lead advance man, Dave Fischer, the president's personal aide, White House Press Secretary Larry Speakes, Admiral Poindexter from the National Security Council, Kathy Osborne, the president's personal secretary, and Mark Weinberg from the White House Press Office. Steve Hart, my close colleague and friend, was with the travel press.

The "Heartland Express" whistle stop tour was likely to be a once-in-a-lifetime experience not only for Ohio but also for the White House staff. I imagined the competition to get a seat in the motorcade had been fierce. Early in the campaign, I'd handled the media when Reagan toured a Ford factory in Ohio. Deaver was the only member of the White House senior staff who'd come along for that event.

It took just under half an hour for the motorcade to get to the Old Montgomery County Courthouse mall from Wright-Patterson. Reagan was greeted offstage by former Ohio governor James Rhodes and Stuart Northrop, president of the Huffy Corporation.

I met the motorcade and directed Mark and Steve and the travel press to the pathway leading to the press platform. As they always do when they're separated from the president, even briefly, the press got nervous. They hustled down the chute so they could set up in time to cover the president's remarks.

The band struck up "Ruffles and Flourishes" followed by "Hail to the Chief" and the crowd was electrified. But I wasn't. Reagan looked tired, gray, almost listless.

The plan called for former Ohio governor Rhodes to introduce the president with brief remarks. Instead, he droned on interminably, as if he'd forgotten who was running for reelection. The crowd began to get bored, and then restless, and all the while Reagan listened through it patiently. It did nothing to enliven his mood. I thought we missed a trick in not having an old-fashioned hook on hand to yank the ex-governor off the stage, vaudeville-style.

When Rhodes finally relinquished the podium, Reagan delivered his stump speech. It lasted about 10 minutes, every second of it agonizing to me.

Over the years I'd been present when Reagan spoke dozens and dozens of times. This was one of the most lackluster deliveries I'd ever heard from Ronald Reagan. It was flat, almost monotone, as if he was reading it instead of delivering his speech with the usual Reagan timing, style, and impact. The crowd still applauded wildly. Many of them had arrived before dawn, but you wouldn't have known it from their enthusiasm.

At least Reagan had energized them.

I reminded myself that seeing a president is a unique event for most people. I was judging Reagan's performance with the jaundiced eye of a longtime observer—the same point of view the press accompanying Reagan would have. If his spirits didn't pick up during the day, tomorrow's stories would be about a tired-seeming Reagan going through the motions in Ohio.

From the stage Reagan went to a holding room in Dayton's Union Station for the day's first photo op with local dignitaries. After he boarded the Ferdinand Magellan (re-christened "U.S. Car One" in the presidential schedule in a similar vein to Air Force One and the presidential helicopter, Marine One) the president placed a telephone call to astronaut Robert Crippen, commander of the crew onboard the Space Shuttle *Challenger*. It wasn't the first time Reagan had greeted Crippen onboard a space shuttle. When the first space shuttle flight took place in 1981, NASA relayed a message from Reagan to the crew of the *Columbia*. Crippen piloted the spacecraft. In remarks broadcast to the crowd outside the train station, Reagan said making a call to the *Challenger* was like talking on an old-fashioned party-line. I wondered how many people in the audience understood the reference.

Steve Hart and I ushered the press pool and travel press through the access route and onto the train. I breathed a sigh of relief when we got them settled in the press cars. Only a handful of rope-line jumpers got into the chute. It was relatively easy to keep them separate from the press.

*   *   *

An hour down the line from Dayton was our first stop, a small town called Sidney. I wanted to shut my eyes and get some sleep but I couldn't. We were in vast expanses of farmland, but everywhere there were people. Mile after mile, people lined the tracks, sometimes in groups no bigger than one or two families, sometimes in crowds, to catch a glimpse of the president on the historic train. Many carried campaign placards; others waved flags or just cheered the train. The atmosphere was festive, the mood catching.

When we pulled into Sidney the crowd numbered in the thousands, sandwiched into an open area near the depot. Red, white and blue bunting was everywhere. I escorted the press pool to their viewing area. A few minutes later, the band played "Ruffles & Flourishes" and "Hail to the Chief" and the audience went wild.

President Reagan speaking during the Heartland Special Whistle Stop Tour through Ohio, October 12, 1984. Barely visible at lower left, I look toward the camera and press platform in order to ship exposed film for the wire services (courtesy Ronald Reagan Presidential Library).

When Reagan gave his 10-minute stump speech my ears perked up. Small changes had been made since he'd given it in Dayton. There was no doubt they were improvements. Then I noticed Ken Khachigian, scribbling on a text of the speech as the president spoke. Khachigian was at work again as Reagan's chief speechwriter. He was taking notes based on the audience reaction to the president's lines. My guess was that he was refining the speech between stops to make it more effective, like a scriptwriter tweaking an actor's lines between takes.

After the speech Reagan went back onto U.S. Car One for another photo op with local figures. Roger Stone, who was on the train, had helped cull the lists of requests for a photo with the president to those most worthy of the privilege and, not coincidentally, most valuable to the reelection effort.

From Sidney the train traveled an hour and 20 minutes to Lima, Ohio. The pattern repeated itself. The band struck up and the crowd erupted in cheers. Reagan spoke for 10 minutes. I listened closely. The speech was sharper; it hit on the laugh lines and high notes with greater precision than before. Still, Khachigian kept taking notes. As we traveled down the tracks between whistle stops, he was inside polishing Reagan's lines on an IBM Selectric typewriter.

The stop at Lima concluded with the usual photo op. The next town was
Ottawa, a little less than an hour away. Along the tracks people waited to wave
hello and see the train pass and try to catch a glimpse of the president. In Ottawa, instead of speaking from a dais near the train, Reagan spoke from the
back of the Ferdinand Magellan. I escorted the press pool to the rear of the
train, positioning the reporters between the crowd and the president. Behind
me, I heard someone sobbing.

For a second I had a feeling of déjà vu. The previous October, I handled the press advance for Ronald and Nancy Reagan's trip to Camp Lejeune,
North Carolina, to attend a memorial service for the 241 Marines, sailors,
and army personnel killed in the Beirut airport barracks bombing. There was
sobbing behind me on that day from the families of the soldiers who had died
in Lebanon.

This crying was different.

I turned around and saw a small boy, no more than five or six years old.
He was upset that the influx of people blocked his view of the president. His
parents were trying to console him but he wasn't having it. The family had
probably been waiting for hours to have this close-up position in the crowd,
and we had bombed in right in front of them.

I wanted to ask the parents if I could put their son on my shoulders and

**Ronald Reagan and Ken Khachigian during the Whistle Stop Tour fine-tuning
the president's stump speech, October 12, 1984 (courtesy Ronald Reagan Presidential Library).**

give him a really good view. But then I thought about all the problems that might ensue. First and foremost was my radio. My earpiece would likely get dislodged with a little boy on my shoulders. Even if it didn't, my ability to raise my hand to talk into my microphone would be impaired if I was hanging onto the kid. Then there was the Secret Service pool agent. I didn't know how he'd respond to me bringing a child into the secure area. The last thing I wanted to do was to bring the kid over only to have to put him right back with his parents.

Then there was one final factor. As staff, we're trained not to take the spotlight off the president. I first learned the lesson from Khachigian, who lectured us that we should never, ever take credit for anything in one of the president's speeches, especially if it's a particularly memorable or newsworthy line. Of course, some speechwriters didn't pay much attention to this. The press always seemed to know which lines they'd written.

We got a similar lecture when it came to presidential advance work. We went out of our way to keep as low a profile as possible during a presidential event. A White House advance man with a little boy on his shoulders might make an irresistible photograph or television shot for the evening news, which meant I couldn't do it.

The next best thing was to implore the reporters to make a little room for the family to be able to see the speech. They did their best to clear a view, and the boy quieted down. This time Reagan's delivery was perfect. I'd noticed that with each stop he seemed to have more energy, more vigor in his speeches and better timing with his delivery. I couldn't see Khachigian from where I was, but I imagined he must be satisfied with the changes he'd made.

When we wrapped up at Ottawa the press agency photographers needed to ship film so that it could get processed in time to make the first-run newspapers. I hated shipping film. I always feared somehow dropping a roll or two and being responsible for losing the photos that might otherwise have appeared in hundreds of newspapers the next day. And I didn't like having to wander around looking for the shipping service, wondering if I'd get left behind by the motorcade or, in this instance, the train if it took too long to find the courier.

As the pool was escorted back onto the train, I took the precious canisters and waded my way through the crowd toward the press platform. Reagan was tied up in another photo op for five minutes, just enough time for me to get to the platform, hand off the film, and get back onboard U.S. Car One before it pulled out of the station.

I spotted a courier waving frantically to get my attention. I passed the canisters to him and he gave me a shipping receipt to hand to the photographers. I actually had several minutes to spare getting back through the crowd

to the train. The transfer had gone off without a hitch, but I still hated shipping film.

It was now late in the day. We had a little over half an hour to get to
Deshler, the next to last stop. The major challenge during the ride was keeping my eyes open. That lack of sleep was catching up and the rhythm of the
train rocking its way down the tracks was hypnotic. When we pulled into
Deshler I took the press pool to the back of the train and Reagan spoke again
from the rear platform of the Ferdinand Magellan. This time, his delivery was
just as energetic as before, but to my ear something new had been added. It
was a hint of nostalgia, as if a unique and magical day was wrapping up, and
he and the crowd knew it. It was like a subtle taste in a complex wine, and I
don't know if anyone else detected it, but it was there.

Reagan seemed to be lingering longer at the end of each whistle stop
speech to soak up the atmosphere and adulation from his supporters. Most of
the day's handshakes and photos with local dignitaries and supporters took
longer than the allotted five minutes. The accumulation of small delays meant
we were running late. By the time we pulled away from Deshler it was well
after 6 o'clock.

The approach of dusk didn't dissuade the crowds lining the tracks between towns. The trip from Deshler to Perrysburg, our final stop, took about
30 minutes. It was almost dark when the train began braking and we pulled
into the station.

Someone yelled, "Fire!" on one of the press cars and a journalist came
running up the aisle in a panic. I whipped my head around and saw the orange glow of flames on the glass windows. Somebody else yelled, "Fire!" and
there were cries of "Where, where?" Steve Hart and I exchanged glances and
raced down the corridor to calm the reporters.

One of the advance team at Perrysburg thought it would be a good idea
to light the tracks approaching the station with torches. Steve and I had been
briefed on this old-fashioned touch, but we hadn't given the press a heads-up.
Everyone thought it would be a nice surprise. Instead it was an unpleasant
adrenalin rush. We explained that it was harmless and apologized for causing
the confusion.

At Perrysburg, the crowd seemed to like the torchlight. The president
gave his final 10-minute stump speech of the day and five-minute photo op
with local Republican leaders. But instead of getting directly into the presidential motorcade and leaving for the airport, he sent Bill Henkel and Jim
Hooley to assemble about a dozen of us from the advance team in the vintage
rail car next to the Ferdinand Magellan.

Ronald Reagan came into the car, closely followed by Mike Deaver. Reagan was brimming with energy and Deaver was beaming. Henkel introduced
us as the ones who were responsible for organizing the day's events.

"Well, I want to thank you all very much," Reagan said, "Believe me, I know that things like this don't just happen."

The official photographer tried to get a group photo. While he was shooting, Henkel introduced one of the team.

"Mr. President, this is Terry Baxter," Bill said. "You remember him, he's the one who had the fight in New Jersey."

Baxter was one of the best advance men, mild-mannered and diligent. But on a recent event in New Jersey, a local Republican official had hounded him with request after request for special treatment for his VIPs. Terry was patient, and he tried to accommodate any request within reason, but when the man tracked him down at a restaurant where he was trying to have a quiet dinner and threw a brand-new set of demands at him, Baxter lost it and punched him hard. Terry ended up briefly in jail until the White House persuaded the man to drop the charges.

Reagan looked at Baxter.

"Well," he smiled, "are you still the champ?"

Baxter flashed a bashful grin and nodded "yes" as the room erupted with laughter.

Reagan thanked us all again, and then we scrambled for our spots in the motorcade. Reagan still had a few more photo ops, this time with Roger Schmorr and his team from the Gold Coast Railroad Museum, who had overseen the handling of the vintage rail cars as well as the train crew and railroad officials who had made the day possible.

It took the motorcade about 25 minutes to reach the Toledo Express Airport. The photo agency photographers gave me more film canisters to ship. We waited until Air Force One was wheels up before starting the drive back to Perrysburg.

The crowds had melted away, but kids and families were out souvenir hunting. I had a bunch of unused press passes that said "The Heartland Special, the President's Ohio Whistle Stop" and listed all the towns on the route. I gave one family a bunch of the leftover passes commemorating the trip.

We were exhausted. With the president gone and the day's events done, fatigue hit hard. I had to find a courier and ship the film again, the third time that day. Some of the team planned to return to Dayton by train. They loosened their ties, some changed to casual clothes, and they started hitting the beer. A breezy conversation got underway with Roger Schmorr and his crew, and I regretted the fact that I had an early morning flight.

A smaller group of us drove back to Dayton. I fell asleep quickly but woke up when I felt the wheels of our rental car jerk. Our driver was as tired as I was, so I tried to help him stay awake by keeping up a conversation. Patchy ground fog settled around us, and we swerved off the road several times. We were beyond fatigue now, grown bone-weary. It was nearly three a.m. when we finally got back to Dayton. I had been awake the better part of 24 hours.

When I got to my hotel room, I was asleep before my head touched the pillow. The next morning I packed and headed to the airport. It was an early morning flight and breakfast would be served on the plane. The only problem was my rental car.

The lights had been left on and it wouldn't start. An African American phone company technician who was pulling lines out of the railroad station stopped working when he saw me trying to start the car. He tried to help me with a jump start, but we just couldn't get it to turn over.

Even at this early hour, there were a few customers drifting in and out of the porn shop between the hotel and the train station. I decided I didn't want to spend another day in Dayton. I got a cab to the airport and I told the rental company where I'd left their car.

At the airport I picked up some local newspapers to sample the coverage. The official estimate of the crowd size for the Heartland Special was a quarter of a million people. The pictures were great. The whistle stop tour reinforced the themes and feel of the campaign's television advertising, and the Reagan who returned to Washington wasn't the same disheartened candidate he'd been when he arrived in Ohio.

The date was October 13.

I jotted some notes on the flight back to National Airport. Reagan and Deaver were "sky-high" at the end of the day. "We knew he had his legs back for the rest of the campaign," I wrote in my notes. It was a tremendous success. My only regret was not being able to pick up that little boy so he could have a clear view of the president.

18

Arrested and Booked

Mason Hill Drive
Alexandria, Virginia
October 14, 1984

Sunday was a rare day off. With the election less than three weeks away, most of us were at campaign headquarters seven days a week. After the week I'd had, catching up on rest wasn't optional. Benjamin, my son, had other ideas. His method for seeing whether I was done with a nap was to gently pry open an eyelid, look into my pupil, and ask whether I was awake. No matter how exhausted I felt, I could never resist getting up and playing with him.

One of his favorite pastimes was running around the house pushing his toy, Bucky the Wonder Horse, until he was panting and red in the face. Actually riding Bucky never appealed to Ben. It was too slow. In his mind, Bucky was meant for the racetrack.

Later, while Ben took his nap, I perused the *Washington Post* and *New York Times*. Vice President Bush's post-debate press coverage was taking an ominous turn. At a campaign event the day after the debate with Ferraro, Bush boasted to an official from the International Longshoreman's Association that he had "tried to kick a little ass" in their encounter.

Normally I would brush it off as an odd statement coming from the usually taciturn George Bush. If it weren't for a slew of similar statements coming from the Bush camp, I could have dismissed it as Bush trying to talk like he thought longshoremen did on the docks.

A few days earlier, on Air Force Two on her way to a Columbus Day parade in New York, Barbara Bush complained to the Associated Press' Terence Hunt about the Ferraro camp's sniping at the Bush clan over their preppy mannerisms and upper-class status.

When Hunt said Barbara and George "weren't exactly paupers," Barbara shot back that they had never tried to downplay their fortune, unlike that "four million dollar.... I can't say it, it rhymes with rich."

A few days later, Pete Teeley, Bush's press secretary, told reporters that Ferraro came across as "too bitchy." I knew Teeley from the 1980 campaign and considered him a professional. In my mind there was no way he would make a comment like that on the record unless it was what the vice president—or Barbara Bush—wanted him to say.

Either way, the last thing I needed was for the Bushes to keep saying demeaning things about Geraldine Ferraro. For months we'd kept the campaign staff, including our state and county people, on a tight leash when it came to criticizing her. If the Bushes kept dishing out sophomoric insults, they would provoke an outpouring of sympathy for Ferraro from the press. What made it even worse was that public polls again showed Reagan and Bush with a comfortable lead over the Mondale-Ferraro ticket. The crude comments looked like we were kicking Ferraro when she was down.

Nancy Reagan had wanted us to take the gloves off with Ferraro, and we had. If Hawtin and Wells came through with their article on her parents' arrest records in the *New York Post*, Ferraro was about to have a very bad week. In fact, we had put her squarely in the sights of a shit bazooka just when the Bush team started spouting off.

Everything we had done in our operation was fact-based, researched, verified, and accomplished in such a way as to keep an arm's length between the hard-hitting news stories and Reagan-Bush '84 and the White House. Now the Bushes were jeopardizing the whole thing.

The next morning I registered my complaint with Lyn Nofziger before the morning Attack Meeting started.

"Somebody needs to get to Vic Gold and have him tell Bush to lay off the offensive language with Ferraro," I said. "This goes against everything we've told everyone else on this campaign. If they keep it up we won't be able to hold back all of our team and we'll spend the rest of the campaign apologizing for calling the lady a bitch and worse."

Vic Gold represented the vice president's office and often attended Nofziger's meeting, but he wasn't present that Monday. Gold was a speechwriter and political advisor to Bush and our best means to get a message through to the vice president quickly. Nofziger said he would make the call.

Whether or not Gold ever talked to Bush about the issue, the spate of name-calling stopped. It was just in time.

On October 18, Guy Hawtin and Jeff Wells' article, "The Ferraros of Newburgh," appeared in the *New York Post*. We got two copies of the paper so Art and I could read it simultaneously.

The article was several thousand words long, a rare example of in-depth reporting for the newspaper. It opened with a quote from Ferraro's acceptance speech at the Democratic National Convention: "I stand here before you to proclaim tonight: America is the land where dreams can come true for all our citizens. The promise of our country is that the rules are fair. If you work hard, and play by the rules, you can earn your share of America's blessings."

Then the article went on to paint a picture of Newburgh and Ferraro's early environment as a "far cry from the American dream," a place where "murdered mobsters by the score littered surrounding byways. And doctors were always available to certify that last night's bullet was this morning's heart attack. Newburgh was a glittering sin city, its speakeasies, whore houses, horse parlors and nightclubs were the most sophisticated on the East Coast."

Hawtin and Wells pulled no punches in their reportage: "And its most fashionable nightspot—The Roxy at Mill St. and West Parmenter—was run by Dominic Ferraro, father of today's Democratic vice presidential candidate."

The reporters had done their homework. They found an old newspaper advertisement for the Roxy which featured "eight dancing girls." They characterized Mike De Vasto as Dominic Ferraro's boss, a man who controlled most of the rum-smuggling on the Hudson River during Prohibition. They even tracked down De Vasto's son, Frannie, who told the reporters that Dominic Ferraro had come to his father for "protection" because he was "being harassed."

Mike De Vasto had made a reputation as someone to be respected. A local mobster named Dominick "The Gap" Petrillo was hired by Dominick Laviano to kill De Vasto, according to the article. Laviano had connections. He was a friend of notorious gangster Charles "Lucky" Luciano. When Petrillo showed up at the Roxy, De Vasto challenged him to a duel at Newburgh's baseball diamond. "Petrillo never showed," the *Post* reported, and De Vasto subsequently turned a bedroom in his mansion into an armored vault, presumably so he could sleep easily at night in case Petrillo showed up.

The article chronicled the budding business relationship between De Vasto and Dominic Ferraro, which culminated in 1933 with Ferraro buying the Roxy from De Vasto. Two years later Geraldine Ferraro was born. De Vasto, according to Frannie, had problems with the IRS and was incarcerated with the infamous Al Capone.

On April 6, 1944, the police raided Dominic Ferraro's home and business and arrested Dominic and his wife, Antonetta, on two separate charges of illegal gambling operations. The indictment called Gerry Ferraro's parents "common gamblers." The *New York Post* covered the incidents in detail, including the fact that Dominic was released on $1,000 bail and Geraldine's mother, Antonetta, on $500 bail. The sums were a large amount of money in 1944. At the time, the average price for a new car was $800.

Dominic Ferarro never had his day in court. On May 29, the day his trial was scheduled to begin, he was pronounced dead.

The *New York Post* story reported several conflicting versions of his final hours. In Geraldine Ferraro's biographies, a police officer found Dominic

Ferraro in his car by the roadside, too weak to drive himself home. The police officer phoned Antonetta, who in turn called a doctor and got a cab to bring her husband home.

An initial death notice stated that at 6:40 a.m. Dominic Ferraro was found dead in his own bed. That notice was changed after undertaker Dominick Coloni clarified that Dominic Ferraro became ill around midnight and Dr. Eric Steinthal subsequently attended to him for approximately three and a half hours. Although an emergency room was available about a block from the Ferraro residence, no attempt seems to have been made to transport him there.

After Antonetta Ferraro's husband's untimely death, the local district attorney dropped the criminal charges against her.

The article was political dynamite. Everything Cliff Barber told us at the Thayer Hotel turned out to be not only true but verifiable. Nothing in the article hinted at sources from the Reagan-Bush campaign. Cliff Barber's name wasn't mentioned at all.

"I can't believe we almost missed this tip," Art said, folding the paper. "I wonder how the *Philadelphia Inquirer* feels today about passing on the story."

"They'll be playing catch-up."

"So will a lot of others," Art said. "This has the potential to open the floodgates."

We had been patiently collecting and verifying information about organized crime figures with links to Ferraro's congressional campaigns. With the news about her parents' arrest records made public, these connections suddenly had new relevance.

"I don't see any harm in sharing some of the information we've got with the *New York Post*," I said.

"By now the *Inquirer* knows we went straight to them with Barber's leads," Art agreed. "They know our relationship is no longer exclusive, so we might as well see how interested the *Post* is."

We discussed it with Stu Spencer. Rupert Murdoch, the owner of the *New York Post*, had a reputation as a conservative with close ties to the Republican Party. Along with Roy Cohn, who was an attorney for the media mogul, Murdoch had met with Reagan in the White House. The primary reason we'd decided to work with the *Philadelphia Inquirer* was to avoid the appearance that damaging information about Ferraro was being fed to a friendly news organization. With the *Post*, it would be readily assumed that the paper was getting tips from the campaign or the White House.

There were only two weeks left in the campaign. We didn't want to do anything to revive the "Reagan campaign dirty tricks" storyline Atwater's leak had spawned. At the same time, we didn't know how Reagan would perform in the second presidential debate, due to take place on Sunday, October 21.

The debate practice sessions had been completely revamped to avoid a repeat of the first debate's disasters, but if Reagan stumbled again in his delivery, the age issue would become even more prominent.

We could easily sit back and wait to see what the press found on their own if they followed up on the Mafia angle. But we had Mondale and Ferraro on the defensive, and we wanted to keep them there until Election Day. Working with the *Post* was a calculated risk, but one worth taking.

We kept that decision between me, Art, Stu and Lyn.

A reporter on Ferraro's campaign plane had told one of our press office staff that Ferraro cried when she read about her mother's arrest. I told Lyn about our trip to West Point and how lunch with Cliff Barber had resulted in Guy Hawtin and Jeff Well's article in the *Post*. Lyn was effusive.

She may have broken down on her airplane, but on the campaign trail in Columbia, Missouri, Geraldine Ferraro was angry. She told reporters that she had spoken to her mother about the story but didn't ask her if it was true. She then said, "I will not ask" to emphasize that she had no intention of providing the press with more information about her parents' checkered past. *Newsday* ran a story about her mood under the headline "Story About Parents Irks Ferraro." The following day she made headlines about the story again when she banned a *New York Post* correspondent from traveling on her campaign plane and said that Rupert Murdoch was not worthy of wiping her mother's shoes.

Ferraro's behavior played into our hands. Her reactions had made a one-day story a three-day story. Banning its reporter only whetted the *Post*'s appetite for more revelations. Either she or her campaign strategists must have sensed she was losing control.

From a political perspective, exposing her parents' past was a success. But I had qualms about it. Given her age in 1944, Gerry Ferraro might have known little or nothing about her mother's and father's legal troubles. It was conceivable, even likely, that she'd been shielded from the truth. The first time she learned about it might have been when she picked up the newspaper story we'd helped plant. Her decision to go to law school, her subsequent work as a prosecutor, and her successful bid for a seat in Congress suggested someone playing by the rules but unable to escape the baggage from her past.

"Do you think that we are visiting the sins of the fathers and the mothers on the son and the daughter?" I asked Art over drinks that evening. "Could it be that the first generation was mobbed up, but the second generation's been trying to play straight?"

"That thought has occurred to me," he said, "but there are an awful lot of Mafia connections in this generation for it all to be coincidental."

"If it's the milieu they grew up with, then sure, you're going to run into these people from time to time, do business with them, take a campaign contribution, whatever. Knowing someone in the mob doesn't make you part of the mob."

"Is your conscience getting to you?"

"I don't know." I lit a Marlboro. "I guess it's the ambiguity. There's no way we can really know the truth. All we can do is dig up facts."

"Don't forget that Roy Cohn is convinced they're connected," Art said, "as well as a lot of other people we've talked to. If you go by the evidence, they've at least got a lot to explain."

"To Ferraro, it must have felt like a low-blow," I said. "We probably shattered the image she had of her mother. And think how shitty her mother must feel having this come out when her daughter's been given the chance to become vice president. No matter how you look at it, that's nasty."

"I can't say I disagree with you," Art said, "but it's up to the voters to decide if it means anything. They have a right to know before they vote."

"Do you think Tip O'Neill knew about any of this when he pushed her candidacy?"

"I hadn't thought about that."

"You'd think the Speaker would want to make sure his candidate for vice president didn't have any scandals in her background. He's from Boston, for Chrissake, he should know all about unions, politicians, and the mob. Would you have just taken her word for it, or would you have checked her out before you endorsed her?"

"It would be interesting to know who his campaign contributors are," Art said. "Maybe the Speaker's got some wise guys in his own closet."

"No skeleton left unturned. I guess that's our motto."

We clinked glasses.

*   *   *

The next day, the *New York Post* ran a new Ferraro story in the Saturday newspaper. It was headlined "Gangland-Style Hit Victim Was Booster for Ferraro." Guy Hawtin and Jeff Wells shared the byline with a reporter named Jack Peritz. A veteran reporter, Peritz covered Queens and frequently wrote about crime and corruption.

The article featured Nick Sands, a.k.a. Dominick Santiago, who helped raise $300,000 for Ferraro's 1978 congressional campaign. The lead paragraph reported that Sands had been shot nine times in a "gangland-style attempted rubout" and been a fundraiser for two of Ferraro's congressional races.

The *Post* went into depth on Sands' background. It went into detail on how Dominick Santiago came to work for Ferraro and on his previous indictment on labor racketeering charges for embezzling from the Independent Local 8108 of the Brotherhood of Carpenters. In addition to the union funds, Santiago was charged with dipping into the union's pension funds. He was convicted in 1975, three years before Ferarro hired him under the name Nicholas Mario Sands to be a fundraiser for her first congressional race, and served time in prison.

So far, the story covered what we had found out and the *Philadelphia Inquirer* had reported in the summer. But the *Post* was great at adding colorful details to its reporting. We hadn't known that Santiago was shot when he was walking from his house to his chauffeur-driven car or that his wife Lucy's quick action in having the chauffeur take her husband to St. John's Hospital had saved his life.

Not be outdone in its weekend news coverage, the *Philadelphia Inquirer* printed a lengthy article chronicling John Zaccaro's links to various organized crime figures. It opened with John Zaccaro reportedly pressuring the investor who owned 23 Cleveland Place to sell the building to Joseph LaForte, Sr., a Gambino crime family boss. This was the same building Roy Cohn brought to my attention at the GOP convention in Dallas two months earlier.

The owner, a Chinese-American doctor named Yat Tung Tse, was described by the *Inquirer* as a "beleaguered small real estate investor" when Zaccaro pushed him to sell his property to "Joe the Cat" LaForte, whom the paper called "a major figure in the Gambino crime family." Zaccaro sent a note to Tse, telling him, "You must take this offer because I will never get another buyer like this." According to the paper, Zaccaro's letter to Dr. Tse was written a month after LaForte was indicted and pleaded guilty on tax charges. Three months later he was sentenced to six months in a federal penitentiary.

Then the article segued to the property at 232 Mulberry, owned by the Zaccaro real estate ownership company Frajo Associates, Inc. The *Inquirer* identified Aniello Dellacroce as one of the building's tenants. The newspaper called Dellacroce "one of the most powerful organized crime figures in the nation." It noted that in sentencing Dellacroce to three years in jail for tax evasion in 1973, U.S. Judge Arnold Bauman called Dellacroce "a top hoodlum, a danger to society, a menace to the community, a parasite who lives off the life blood of his people."

The article even reprised the press coverage from July regarding Zaccaro's lease of a warehouse at 200 Lafayette Street to BO-NA-TE Distributors, which it called "the largest printer and disseminator of pornographic material in the country."

In closing, the *Inquirer* devoted another thousand words or more to the "Little Italy" neighborhood and John Zaccaro's father's ties to Joseph and Salvatore Profaci. The paper reported Philip Zaccaro's business venture with Salvatore Profaci, whom U.S. District Judge Irving Kaufman labeled "a notorious member of the underworld, the perfect example of the trinity of crime, business and politics that threaten the economy of the country."

It was a lengthy wrap-up of the high-profile connections between John

Zaccaro, his father Philip, and major organized crime figures. James Asher got the byline, but a note at the end of the long article credited six other reporters as well.

The *Inquirer* had devoted major investigative reporting assets in its scrutiny of the Democratic vice-presidential candidate and her spouse. No other newspaper in the country was as diligent in pursuing the story. Art and I felt vindicated in our choice of the *Inquirer* as the best newspaper to share our investigative leads.

When the Associated Press wire service ran a piece based on the *Inquirer*'s reporting the story mushroomed. The *Times of London* covered it on the front page with a headline blaring "Ferraro's Past Linked with the Mafia."

We had one of our researchers tally the newspaper coverage. On the weekend of October 20–21, it was a front-page story in the *Philadelphia Inquirer, Miami Herald, St. Paul Pioneer Press, San Jose Mercury News, Dallas Times Herald, Seattle Times, Atlanta Constitution,* and *Houston Post.* The Associated Press version of the story appeared in the *Pasadena Star-News, Lexington Herald-Leader,* and *Omaha World-Herald.* A Florida paper, the *Bradenton Herald,* ran the Zaccaro story on page 3. *Newsday* ran its own in-depth piece on Nick Sands, headlined "2 Ferraro Backers Had Organized Crime Ties," on page 5 of the Sunday paper.

We were especially interested in the newspaper coverage because October 20–21 was the weekend of the second presidential debate. There was no doubt in our minds that given the combined circulation of these newspapers a sizeable portion of the viewing audience would be wondering whether Walter Mondale had chosen a running mate whose Mafia connections would trail her into the White House.

Our press survey indicated even more newspapers expected to run stories on the organized crime ties in Monday's newspaper. The *Los Angeles Herald-Examiner, St. Petersburg Times, Newsday, Greensboro Daily News, St. Louis Globe-Democrat, Charlotte Observer, Cincinnati Enquirer, Milwaukee Journal,* and *Pittsburgh Post-Gazette* all said they "would likely" run the story the morning after the presidential debate.

*   *   *

The second presidential debate, featuring defense and foreign policy, took place the night of October 21 at the Municipal Auditorium in Kansas City, Kansas. Instead of Jim Baker leading the preparation for the second showdown with Mondale, Roger Ailes had taken charge. Ailes was a television producer. While Darman, Stockman and Baker had crammed Reagan with numbers and statistics to ready him for the first debate, Ailes concentrated on Reagan's performance on live television and emphasized connecting with the audience beyond the camera lens. While the Darman and Baker team might have successfully coached a high school debate team to victory, Ailes wanted a knock-out performance that would make a lasting impression in living rooms across America.

Once again, I watched the debate like most other Americans, from the couch in my living room. From the start it was clear that Reagan was on his game. He answered questions fully and frequently turned the tables on Mondale. Once or twice he corrected or clarified minor misstatements he'd made in a previous response, such as one about having a CIA officer stationed in Nicaragua when he meant elsewhere in Central America. It came up during an exchange with Mondale about a controversial CIA training manual for U.S.-funded contra rebels that included the use of political assassination as a tactic.

More than halfway through the debate, panelist Henry Trewhitt, the diplomatic correspondent for the *Baltimore Sun*, bluntly raised the age issue.

"Mr. President," Trewhitt began, "I want to raise an issue that I think has been lurking out there for two or three weeks and cast it specifically in national security terms. You are already the oldest president in history. And some of your staff say you were tired after your most recent encounter with Mr. Mondale..."

Tired, I thought? That's an understatement. The man I had seen 10 days ago in Ohio was flattened, not fatigued.

Trewhitt went on.

"I recall that President Kennedy had to go for days with very little sleep during the Cuban Missile Crisis. Is there any doubt in your mind that you would be able to function in such circumstances?"

"Not at all, Mr. Trewhitt," Reagan replied, "and I want you to know that also I will not make age an issue of this campaign. I am not going to exploit, for political purposes, my opponent's youth and inexperience."

The audience in the Municipal Auditorium convulsed with laughter. Even Walter Mondale couldn't suppress a chuckle. What Baker and Darman had failed to achieve with hundreds of pages of fact-crammed briefing books, Roger Ailes had helped Reagan pull off with a one-line joke.

To gauge the spin, I watched the post-debate commentary by journalists and the interviews with politicians and campaign staff they interviewed. Geraldine Ferraro was notably absent. Ordinarily, the vice-presidential candidate would have been all over the airwaves hitting at the opponent's weak spots in the debate and amplifying Mondale's strengths. Polling shows that this kind of post-debate spin influences voters' perceptions of who won and who lost the debate. Polls done immediately after the debate often have very different results than polls taken three days later. For political campaigns, the job is to drive home perceptions that your candidate was the winner for at least several days following the debate.

Washington Post journalist David Broder, who had covered every pres-

Ronald Reagan and Walter Mondale at second presidential debate, Municipal Auditorium, Kansas City, Missouri, October 21, 1984 (courtesy Ronald Reagan Presidential Library).

idential campaign since Adlai Stevenson ran against Dwight Eisenhower in 1956, wrote the next morning, "It may well be that the biggest barrier to Reagan's reelection was swept away at that moment."

Broder was known as "the Dean of the Washington press corps." His verdict was sure to resonate with political correspondents across the country. I had just finished digesting the good news when Art came into my office.

"Did you notice Ferraro canceled her debate appearances?"

"I sure didn't see her anywhere on the tube," I said. "Did she really cancel?"

"That's the word. After the article about her mother and the other Mafia stories she probably didn't want to face questions."

"Maybe she thought she'd be a distraction to getting across Mondale's message," I guessed.

"She's right about that," Art smiled.

That same day Geraldine Ferraro tried again to squelch the Mafia stories. She explained to reporters that she believed Sands was a respected member of the community when she hired him as a campaign fundraiser. She complained that the mob stories were taking a toll on her candidacy. It was an emotional interview, in which she was described as angry and had "wept in frustration."

The barrage of negative publicity continued. On October 23, the *Los Angeles Times* ran a story on page 6A about Nick Sands and ties between Ferraro and Mafia figures that was eight column-inches in length. Two other newspapers focused on her husband, John Zaccaro.

The *New York Times* reported that the Manhattan district attorney had convened a grand jury probe into the Port Authority Credit Union loan involving Zaccaro. The *New York Post* featured an article about Harold Farrell, a former business partner of Zaccaro's who had been disbarred for bribing state officials on behalf of Mafia-connected clients.

The media momentum had now become self-sustaining. We really didn't need to add any more fuel to the fire. Back in July, journalists had been as cautious about covering America's first female vice-presidential candidate on a major party ticket as we were about critiquing her qualifications. But the cumulative weight of the facts we had uncovered, working mainly with the *Philadelphia Inquirer* and then the *New York Post*, made it impossible for the media to dismiss Ferraro and Zacarro's Mafia links and the multiple investigations underway.

It looked like Art and I could coast until Election Day, but that was because no one told us that the President's Commission on Organized Crime was holding hearings that same day in New York.

19

Eddie Chan, the Inside Man

Federal Hall, Lower Manhattan
New York, New York
October 23, 1984

On October 23, the President's Commission on Organized Crime dropped a bombshell in a public hearing covered by the press. Staff investigator David Williams revealed that in early 1983, "a high-level Triad leader in Hong Kong identified Eddie Chan as an organized crime leader and gang leader in the United States." Williams said that Chan "controls the activities of New York Chinese criminal groups through his influence as a leader of the On Leong Tong."

The Triads were Chinese secret societies, some of which also were organized crime groups. The On Leong Tong was a benevolent association or social club with a membership primarily composed of merchants and businessmen. It was not uncommon to find overlapping memberships between criminal Triads and the benevolent associations. What made this a bombshell was that Eddie Chan was a respected banker and politically well-connected in New York and Washington.

The two-day hearings at Federal Hall were the commission's first to feature witnesses testifying under subpoena. Because the commission initially lacked subpoena powers, its ability to call witnesses was severely limited. But in the spring of 1984 Congress gave the commission subpoena powers, and the dramatic public hearings in New York resulted.

The President's Commission on Organized Crime was a blue-ribbon panel established by Executive Order in July of 1983. Its 20 members included not only experts on organized crime but also Senate Judiciary Committee Chairman Strom Thurmond (R–South Carolina) and House Judiciary Committee Chairman Peter Rodino (D–New Jersey). For the past year the commission had worked in relative obscurity, holding hearings and drafting a report on the financing of organized crime activities. By coincidence, the commission's chairman was federal judge Irving Kaufman—the same judge who presided over the Apalachin Conference trials of dozens of Mafiosi a quarter of a century earlier in his career. It was the raid that cost John Zaccaro's father, Philip, his pistol license.

Kaufman was determined that the New York hearings would draw attention to the commission's work and heighten public awareness of organized crime and its inner workings. The topic for the two days of hearings in New York was Asian organized crime. To generate publicity, Kaufman had U.S. attorney general William French Smith attend the October 22 press conference to announce the hearings and stay for the first day of testimony about Asian crime syndicates, including the Chinese Triads. But having a big name at the hearings wasn't Judge Kaufman's only tactic for getting press coverage.

Naming names was also what Kaufman had in mind, and none of them got as much press attention as Edward Tse Chiu Chan, a.k.a. Eddie Chan, a.k.a. Chan Tse-Chiu.

Eddie Chan was a former Hong Kong police detective who immigrated to the United States in 1975 and became a naturalized citizen. Over eight years, Chan rose to prominence in New York. He was a director of United Orient Bank, owner of several restaurants and a funeral parlor, and past president of the On Leong Tong. He liked to flash his wealth by wearing an expensive Rolex. He was 53 years old, married, and had seven children.

With his square jaw and neck like a tree trunk that ran straight down from his jawline to his shoulders, Chan cut an imposing figure. He resembled Odd Job in *Goldfinger* and looked every inch the tough Hong Kong detective he'd been back in the "Five Dragons" era. It was a period when corrupt cops "controlled vice, gambling, the distribution of heroin and extortion throughout the British Crown Colony," according to staff investigator Williams. I certainly wouldn't want to have run into him in a police interview room.

According to Williams, Eddie Chan had ordered an ambush of Nicky Louie's Ghost Shadow gang loyalists in Chicago. Williams said Chan directed rival gang members to "violently neutralize the threat." The ambush involved a gun battle between gang members firing from inside a building into Nicky Louie's car.

Chan was also among the Ferraro contributors who had drawn our attention earlier that summer. In 1982 he gave $1,000 to Ferraro's congressional campaign. He listed his occupation as restaurant owner and gave as his address 1 Mott Street—the property John Zaccaro managed and co-owned through the partnership Frajo Associates. After we came across a 1983 New York Police Department report that said the On Leong Tong was "in control of all of Mott and Bayard Streets, including the gambling houses," our antennae were up for anything involving Edward Tse Chiu Chan. But we hardly expected anything like this.

One of the revelations made by the commission was that Chan was the CEO of the Continental King Lung Group, a firm that operated in 22 cities around the world and three cities in the United States. Williams testified that there was an active fraud investigation into the company that involved a "bucketing scheme" whereby the firm told investors they'd made a purchase of commodities when no purchases had in fact been made. Four of the cities where Chan's company operated were London, Vancouver, Singapore and Hong Kong.

A second commission witness, Special Agent John Feehan of the Drug Enforcement Administration, said that Chan used the Ghost Shadows as his enforcers until the falling out with Nicky Louie. According to Feehan, the Ghost Shadows were "involved in the importation of heroin and sale and distribution of cocaine."

Feehan described the treatment of an informant by a Chinese organized crime group in the late 1970s. He said the snitch was "dispatched in a Triad fashion. He was cut hundreds of times with a razor blade and hung from a meat hook." He said that because most gang members like the Ghost Shadows now wore bullet-proof jackets, "the only way to do it is to walk up to the person you are going to kill and put the gun to his head and this is the way usually most of the murders take place now."

"Eddie Chan inducted one of the Ghost Shadows into his particular Triad as a lieutenant," Feehan testified. "It was a reward ... it took place after the attempted assassination of Nicky Louie in Chicago."

Not long after the testimony in New York there was a commotion in the hallway outside my office. Mike Sotirhos, the chairman of the campaign's Ethnic Voters Division, was scurrying between the corner offices of Lee Atwater at one end of the corridor and Ed Rollins at the other.

I didn't know Sotirhos or have much to do with the Ethnic Voters Division. Earlier in the campaign we'd been in some meetings together, and he struck me as an affable and intelligent guy. Something had him flustered.

Art popped into my office. He had the look about him of a man who had just sprung into action.

"Have you heard about Eddie Chan?" he asked.

"It just gets better and better, doesn't it?"

"Then you haven't heard."

He took a seat and shifted into a low voice.

"He's our national director of Chinese-American voter registration," Art said. "He's been in the building."

I got a similar feeling to the one I'd had when Tucker Eskew escorted Jamie Gangel and her television crew into Nofziger's morning meeting. The dominant emotion was betrayal; the physical feeling was an almost bodily awareness of vulnerability; and the mental state was acute alertness like prey must feel when it hears a twig snap in the woods.

"Holy shit."

All I could think about was the security of our operation. Chan had probably been squired around the offices by Sotirhos as he was introduced to campaign management. I hadn't noticed Chan, and I generally didn't leave sensitive papers on my desk, but if I were popping into Stu Spencer's office or Lyn Nofziger's I could have left some notes out in the open. I had no way of controlling what other people put on my desk when I was away. For that matter, I could have been on a phone call about Ferraro with my back turned to the corridor when Chan and Sotirhos walked past. If Chan had to wait a few moments outside Rollins' office before going in, there was no way to know what he might have overheard.

I lit a Marlboro.

"We need to think about damage control," Art said. "How's it going to look when it comes out that Chan is working for us?"

My mind was still on security. There had long been rumors of a Chinese-Gambino heroin trafficking connection. Maybe this was it.

What if Chan thought the president's reelection committee and the Commission on Organized Crime were somehow connected? How long would it take for the Ghost Shadows to make the trip from New York to Washington? And when they got here, what would they do?

"The first thing we need to do is to take a look at Sotirhos' files on Chan," Art said. "I'll take care of that. Meanwhile, keep it quiet. The press hasn't caught on yet."

Art came up with 18 pages of correspondence on Chan dating back to May. He had first come across Sotirhos' radar screen after a $1,500 a plate fundraising dinner in Washington that Sotirhos attended. He was impressed that Eddie Chan had bought an entire table for $15,000 and sent a letter to Alfred Hong in New York telling him that "Mr. Chan is very interested in politics" and asking that Hong follow up directly with Chan about getting him involved in the campaign.

Alfred Hong was president of the New York Republican Party's Heritage Groups Council. If Chan won his approval, it would give him entrée to New York's elected GOP officials.

Predictably, the next letter in the file was to Sotirhos from Congressman Bill Green endorsing Eddie Chan to head up the Reagan-Bush voter registration drive among Chinese-Americans. The New York Republican called Chan "a most competent individual, one whom I would wholeheartedly recommend."

"I know him personally," Green wrote, "and firmly believe that his will be a significant contribution to the Republican Party, the Reagan-Bush Committee, and to the Chinese population."

Someone, however, must have objected to Chan's presence on the

Reagan-Bush campaign. About 10 days later Chan wrote to Sotirhos, whom he addressed as "Michael," thanking him for hosting Chan and his wife for dinner in his home.

"As per our discussions," Chan wrote, "I hope that any one individual's obstacles will not hinder our support for the reelection of the president. I am fully prepared to throw the extensive network of the Chinese Welfare Council into the registration of new voters and the reelection of our president."

Chan invited Sotirhos to visit and view his antique collection when Sotirhos was in New York. I wondered if the opposition to Chan's involvement stemmed from the usual petty squabbling over political spoils or indicated more serious concerns. If so, there was nothing in Sotirhos' files to reflect it. Within a week, Chan began sending "Michael" regular reports of his voter registration activity.

In early August, Alfred Hong wrote to Senator Alfonse D'Amato of New York, urging him to give his support to Chan's bid to become national director of Chinese-American voter registration. Hong said Chan had already signed up "more than a thousand" Chinese-American volunteers for Reagan and called him "an eloquent supporter of the president." He told D'Amato that Chan was chairman of the National Chinese Welfare Council and immediate past president of the "On Leung Chinese Merchants Association" and "heads two business organizations with member organizations in all the cities with heavy concentrations of Chinese-Americans."

"Through this network," Hong wrote, "he can provide substantial campaign support."

The word "network" jumped out at me. It took on an entirely different meaning after the commission's revelations.

Hong closed his letter by noting that Congressman Green had already "given Mr. Chan a solid endorsement" and told the senator that "it would be a wise political move to inform Michael that you approve of Mr. Chan's appointment."

D'Amato's letter followed in mid–September. The senator called Chan "a distinguished leader in the Chinese-American community with widespread following throughout the U.S." He lifted a paragraph almost verbatim from Hong's letter about Chan using the On Leong Tong and the Chinese Welfare Council in "swinging voters into the Reagan-Bush column in the cities with large concentrations of Chinese-Americans."

"I wholeheartedly approve of his selection," D'Amato wrote.

Sotirhos forwarded the endorsements from Senator D'Amato and Congressman Green to Anna Chennault, National Chairman of Chinese-Americans for Reagan-Bush. Chennault, who had just returned from Europe, gave her approval on September 28. Sometime during the process Chan contributed $1,000 to the Reagan-Bush campaign.

On October 3, Sotirhos wrote to Chan to inform him of his appointment as "Director of Voter Registration for Chinese-Americans for Reagan-Bush '84." Sotirhos sent Roger Stone a copy of the letter.

Three weeks later, the President's Commission on Organized Crime identified Chan as an organized crime leader who used the On Leong Tong and the Ghost Shadows to further his criminal enterprises. I felt a twinge of sympathy for the Mondale campaign. This must have been what it felt like when one of our revelations about Zaccaro or Ferraro was disclosed in the press.

"We have two problems," Art said. "the first is that the campaign now has an organized crime boss as a contributor and a campaign official. Somebody else can worry about cleaning that mess up. The second problem is that you and I have had him on our list of questionable Ferraro associates for months, and he may have been digging around in our own backyard. How much exposure do we have?"

"Roger was on the chop circuit for the letter appointing Chan," I said. "He's probably been lobbied to give it his approval. I still don't know the full story on that transcript."

By chop circuit, I meant that Stone was copied on many of the letters and that usually indicated he had a role in signing off on the decision to appoint Chan. Minimally, it meant he was to be kept in the loop and probably could have vetoed the choice if he wished.

Art's brow wrinkled. In the months we'd worked together, he was usually a very cool character. Most of the guys I'd worked with before would have flown off the handle at Atwater for the NBC leak. Some of them would have done a lot worse than a display of temper.

But Art had handled it cerebrally. We shared the same kind of temperament. Neither of us was volatile. It took a lot to rattle him. I could see he was bothered.

"I sent Achille to check out one of the illegal gambling operations," I continued. "I've got a couple of informants in New York City. That's where the Hogan tip came from. Then there's Barber. Ambrose and his Guinea Chasers. Bill Callahan and Unitel. Roy Cohn…"

"So we have to assume word's been circulating in New York Republican circles that we're up to something involving Ferarro and organized crime," Art said pensively, "and now Eddie Chan is inside New York Republican Party circles."

"Hold on a minute," I said. "Was there a paper in that file listing Chan's business holdings?"

Art thumbed through it and pulled out a document on United Orient Bank letterhead.

"This?"

"That's it."

It was a brief resume. It gave Chan's address as 10 Waterside Plaza, 29 K, New York, New York 10010. The resume said he was born in 1931 in Canton China and educated at Kuo Min University. It identified him as a U.S. citizen and listed him as vice chairman of the United Orient Bank, chairman of the National Chinese Welfare Council, and chairman of Chinese Help in National Affairs.

Four businesses were listed. Chan was president of Ng Fook Funeral, Inc., chairman of the Sung Sing Theater, and chairman of two Chinese restaurants—the Grand Fortune and China Royal. The addresses of the business were included in the resume.

"Look what's missing." I handed the paper to Teele. He studied it for a moment.

"Mott Street. None of these businesses are on Mott Street."

"Exactly. In the 1982 contribution to her campaign, he lists his occupation as restaurant owner and gives his address as 1 Mott Street, the Frajo property. The only restaurant listed there is Hunan Gardens. He's kept his connection to Zaccaro off the resume!"

"Or there's something else about that Mott Street business that he wants to keep hidden," Art said. "Is Hunan Gardens a Ghost Shadows hangout? He's got to have somewhere to meet with those guys if they're his enforcers. My guess is it isn't in the boardroom of the United Orient Bank."

"The Sung Sing Theater rings a bell," I said, reaching for a file of *Village Voice* articles from 1977 about New York's Chinatown and its violent youth gangs. "Here it is."

I shoved a page in Art's direction. It showed a photo of the Sung Sing, although in the photo the sign read "Sun Sing." The caption was unambiguous: "Sun Sing Theater: scene of shootout."

The articles were extensive pieces of investigative reporting by Mark Jacobson, and the photography was credited to Sylvia Plachy. Jacobson detailed the relationships between the Kuomintang Chinese nationalist party that ruled Taiwan, the On Leong Tong, and Chinese youth gangs including the Ghost Shadows. Jacobson's theory was that the Kuomintang was moving its investments and influence from Hong Kong to New York and other major cities because the Crown Colony's days of independence from Beijing were dwindling. He cited the opening of the United Orient Bank as an example of this shift.

"What do we need to do?" Art said.

"Someone else can figure out how to spin this if the press find out about Chan's role in the campaign. I'm going to give a little thought to how these pieces might add up."

"Good luck with that. I'll see you in the morning."

*   *   *

A passage in the *Village Voice* about the heroin trade had intrigued me since I first came across it in one of Jacobson's articles, "Nicky Louie's Mean Streets: Tongs Strike Back in Chinatown." It read: "The connection—which is believed to be kept running by a manager of an On Leong restaurant who is also believed to be the only Chinese ever admitted to the Carlo Gambino crime family—works well. While most of the country is flooded with Mexican smack, in New York the percentage of Golden Triangle poppy runs high."

Jacobson attributed the information to Drug Enforcement Agency sources. There had been longstanding rumors of a Gambino-Triad connection, but this was the clearest and most detailed depiction of the connection I'd come across.

My interest in the Triads wasn't new. Four years earlier, when I was living in London publishing a start-up magazine with an Oxford buddy, I'd read Richard Deacon's book about the Chinese secret service and developed an interest in the relationships between Chinese businesses, crime groups, and Chinese espionage. When I came across an Australian author's book on the Triads while browsing a London bookshop, I devoured it. I had no idea at the time that the information might prove useful in a presidential campaign.

I called Myles Ambrose and asked him to use his network to check on Chan's whereabouts. There was a reference in the commission testimony to the fact that Chan had been invited to appear but had not shown up and was now "wanted for questioning." I didn't like the idea that Chan or his enforcers might show up at any moment at headquarters, or in the parking garage, or at my house. It was unlawful to carry a gun in Washington, D.C., without a permit, but it was also against my moral code to be a sitting duck.

I mentally reviewed the tradecraft we had used in the investigations into Ferraro, especially as it concerned Art and me. A handful of people in New York knew my name as the one to call with information about Ferraro and organized crime. Most were trusted insiders and a few were people like Cliff Barber whom I didn't know well but decided to take a chance on. Some were reporters. There was always a risk that confidential information would slip out.

Instead of keeping a desk calendar or wall calendar I carried a pocket calendar. I always took it with me, even when going to the bathroom. Nobody could snoop through my appointments, contacts, and phone numbers without picking my pocket or mugging me. Sensitive files were never left in my office overnight. The most sensitive information was on plain white paper, and names of sources were kept separate from the information they imparted.

None of that meant that someone I had trusted couldn't have tipped off Ferraro, Zaccaro, or Eddie Chan that we were scrutinizing their businesses, their lifestyle, their incomes, their ancestors, their associates, and associates of their associates. It was always possible that someone who seemed trustworthy was playing both sides of the fence. Eddie Chan was Exhibit A in that regard.

The campaign grew quieter while I brooded, staffers packed up their things and ladies freshened their appearances before going out to meet friends for a drink on the way home while harried aides made one last phone call to try to close the loop on some vital business before calling it a night.

I called home and said not to wait up for me.

When it was late and there were only a handful of people still in the building, I took out some large sheets of paper and taped them over the window that overlooked the street. Then I spread out my files and notes. Using a felt tip pen, I began jotting names and dates, street addresses and companies, under headers like "Gambino" and "Genovese," "Colombo" and "On Leong Tong."

I scoured the files. Whenever I found ties between Ferraro campaign contributors or Zaccaro business associates and the headers, I began drawing connecting lines. I expanded the diagrams to include Chinese gangs like the Ghost Shadows and put separate boxes in for the odd real estate transactions whose purpose still eluded us.

Many of the transactions involved a handful of the same people. The name Jeannette Juskovitz came up frequently. So did an attorney named Murray Mickenberg. Haskel Jacobs also appeared in the transactions. In addition to Frajo, companies like Atlanta Associates Inc. and China-Mott Associates were involved with back-and-forth changes of ownership.

There appeared to be transactions between shell companies, often with the same place of business listed (usually an attorney's office) and a revolving roster of corporate officers amounting to about half a dozen of the same people. Jeannette Juskovitz was a corporate officer of several of the companies.

The names of the companies caught my interest. The Gambino crime family was said to have operations in Atlanta, Georgia. Was "Atlanta Associates Inc." a reference to stockholders or real estate investors in Atlanta? The name "China-Mott Associates" could have been a reference to the On Leong Tong. Did the names reflect silent owners of the companies, or were they chosen for some other reason?

Frajo we understood: The name was a contraction of Philip Zaccaro's two sons' first names, Frank and John. Had the practice of using a derivation of meaningful names become a habit, and if so, were the Atlanta Associates and China-Mott Associates also a kind of family connection?

I knew I wasn't going to find the answers tonight but I kept jotting connections and questions on the charts. Pretty soon they expanded beyond the window to the wall. I wrote out what we knew about Ferraro's parents and Zaccaro's parents and their known criminal ties. Around nine I took down the charts and locked them away and went to the Dubliner on F Street. The bar and restaurant was just 10 years old but was already a Capitol Hill fixture with live music and an even livelier pick-up scene. The dark wood interior reminded me of some of my favorite English pubs, although management was proud to point out that it was designed to be an authentic Irish pub.

I took a seat at the bar and ordered a bacon blue cheese burger and a pint of Harp lager. While I waited for the food I lit a cigarette and pondered what I was doing. If I wasn't going to identify anything but more questions, what was the point? I took a drag and flicked off the ash.

Maybe the whole exercise was just my way of soothing my nerves. As if, by gathering all the facts and really getting a command of the information we had, I could regain a sense of control. Truth was, finding out that Eddie Chan had been invited to our headquarters, and no more than a foot from the entrance to my office, had made me determined to discover everything I could to level the playing field with my adversaries. For months we'd worried about leaks when what we really needed to worry about was what Art preminisced in Dallas. Our own team was the greatest threat to us.

Should Mike Sotirhos have known better? And what about Anna Chennault, the first lady of Republican Chinese-American politics? She was the widow of Major General Claire Chennault, commander of the famed Flying Tigers, American pilots who volunteered to fight against the Japanese from bases in China. He also led the Republic of China Air Force in World War II. The couple became deeply involved in politics after the war, forming what was called the "China Lobby" and working closely with the nationalist Chinese Kuomintang government in Taiwan.

After the war, General Chennault created an aircraft company called Civil Air Transport. It later became known as Air America and was closely identified with the CIA. For years there were rumors that after Chennault's death in 1958 Air America was used to transport opium from Asia's Golden Triangle in order to surreptitiously fund anti-communist guerrilla movements. Similar rumors plagued us now, only this time the allegations involved aircraft supplying arms and equipment to the Contra rebels in Nicaragua being used to transport drugs back into the United States. I wasn't inclined to credit the rumors and considered them to be Soviet disinformation, spread by Western dupes and left-wing opponents of the Reagan Administration's Central American policy.

But I might be wrong. I was halfway through the hamburger when I began scribbling notes on a napkin. How exactly had Chan come to Sotirhos' attention? Did anyone make introductions? Was it casual or calculated? How extensive were Chan's political contacts in the U.S. and Taiwan? Was he really just a crooked cop turned millionaire-gangster-banker? Or was Chan doing somebody's bidding, and if so, who?

I ordered another Harp and wondered again why I'd gotten a job in politics. All around me what looked like carefree people my age were having a good time, and here I was slogging my way through my second presidential campaign worried about things that for others existed only in movies and thrillers. Like most of my contemporaries on the campaign and in the Administration, I had responsibilities far out of proportion to my age.

While most people in their 20s were preoccupied with having fun, we worked in jobs without clear boundaries between personal and professional life. Working in the White House meant that everything you did reflected on the president. If someone cut you off in traffic and you gave them the finger, you'd better hope no one recognized you as a White House aide. Misbehavior wasn't compatible with representing the president, and just because it happened on your own time didn't provide an excuse. You were never really off the clock working on a presidential campaign or at a White House or senior departmental job. I sometimes felt like I'd traded in my 20s to make Ronald Reagan's 70s a better decade for him, and I suspected I hadn't gotten the better end of that deal.

I paid the bill, stuffed the receipt and napkin into my coat pocket, and scraped my barstool back from the rail. The crowd was intoxicated with music and beer and I reluctantly trudged back to the NACO building. When I got to my office, I hung my jacket, took off my tie, rolled up my shirt sleeves and put up the charts for a long look.

I added a new section on the Kuomintang and re-read Jacobson's articles from the *Village Voice*. The first article, "Nicky Louie Gets Busted," was published in July of 1977. The second story, "Nationalist Chinese Agents Are Taking Over Chinatown," ran on the front page of the August 8, 1977, edition. Given the lead time to report and write these pieces, Jacobson had to have been on the story for months before they were printed.

Eddie Chan had only arrived in the United States in 1975. That meant that the substantial changes in Chinatown that Jacobson was reporting were near-contemporaneous events to Eddie Chan's arrival on the scene. While Jacobson never mentioned Chan, and his only mention of the United Orient Bank involved plans for it to open soon, it was highly likely that Chan's arrival in the United States and the gang violence and drug trafficking Jacobson chronicled weren't coincidental.

I added a new section to the charts involving Triads, Golden Triangle smuggling, Claire and Anna Chennault, and Eddie Chan. I used a red felt tip marker to highlight known organized crime figures, put question marks near everything speculative, and started writing items for further investigation on a separate sheet of paper.

Long after midnight I tried to find a phone number for the Triad expert whose book I'd read in London. I tracked down his publisher in Australia, but given the time difference I decided not to make the call. I wanted to talk to him off the record, but it would have been dicey. If I told him I worked for the Reagan-Bush campaign, he would probably mention it to somebody. The fact that I'd called might even find its way into the hands of a reporter, and when it comes to newspaper publishing, I knew the distance from Australia to the United States was very short. I would have had to go to a phone booth and lie to him about who I was and come up with a cover story about why I was interested in Triads. Anyway, most of what he knew was probably in the book.

Around three I decided to call it a night. I rolled up the charts and took them home with me.

After a few hours' rest, I showered and shaved and headed into work early. I wanted to go over the charts again with fresh eyeballs. I taped them to the windows and left briefly to get a cup of coffee.

When I returned Art and Stu were standing in my office, backs to the door, staring at the maze of scribblings, lines, question marks, and double-underlining on some of the names. As I was approaching I could hear Stu talking.

"We've got to take this down before some reporter sees it," he said to Art.

"Sorry, guys," I said, "I thought I'd be the only one here this early."

Stu eyeballed me. I think he was trying to figure out if I'd gone over the edge.

"Did you work all night?"

"I quit around three."

"What did you figure out?"

I looked at the charts and thought about it. If there was a Gambino-Triad drug connection, it might be right in front of our eyes. I had hoped a pattern would pop out at me and things would become clear. But it was elusive.

"We've got more questions than answers," I said.

"We'll get this down before somebody else starts asking questions," Art said.

But instead of helping me take them down, Art gazed at my markings. He looked at me thoughtfully.

"You missed your calling," he said. "You should have been in the CIA."

He didn't know how close I'd come when he said that. In 1983, CIA Director Bill Casey had his chief recruiter call to invite me to come to the agency for an interview. We'd just moved into a new house, our first child was due in weeks, and my wife was reluctant about my working in what she perceived to be a dangerous job. I told the recruiter I wasn't interested in a job change at that time, and Casey sent a nice letter saying I was welcome to contact him again if I changed my mind.

I stifled a laugh. Getting in the Mafia's knickers was about as dangerous as life gets. We took the charts down. I folded and put them in my briefcase.

When I picked up my copy of the morning Reagan-Bush '84 news, I saw that the *New York Times* was noncommittal about the Chan revelations. The paper's headline was "A Chinatown Merchant Portrayed as Crime Boss."

Fair enough, I thought. Two government officials have accused him of being a crime chieftain, but everyone's entitled to a presumption of innocence.

A reporter named Sam Roberts (no relation to me) had the byline. Chan's $1,000 contribution to Ferraro's congressional race was mentioned in the middle of the article. John Buckley was cited as saying that he was checking to see if a contribution had been made to our campaign, but so far he had found no record of it. The article was void of anything about Chan's voter registration efforts for the Reagan-Bush campaign. Obviously, nobody on the campaign had volunteered any information about Chan's appointment as director of voter registration for Chinese-Americans for Reagan-Bush '84. The strategy was to sit on it unless asked a direct question. It was October 25 and there were now only 12 days left until the election.

In the article Chan's lawyer "vigorously denied" the allegations against his client but also couldn't say where his client was at the time. I didn't know how to interpret that. I wanted to believe Chan was on the run, but he also could have gone to ground while plotting his next move, which might involve revenge.

The *New York Post* also ran an article about Chan, portraying him as a Zaccaro tenant and crime boss who ran the Ghost Shadows criminal gang. The *Washington Post* featured an interview with Joan Mondale. She defended Ferraro against the negative attacks and the inference that her presence on the ticket had damaged the Mondale campaign.

Later in the day I heard from Ambrose. His team had put out feelers, but no one had any information on Chan's whereabouts. Buckley let me know that the campaign treasurer, Bay Buchanan, was returning a $1,000 contribution from Chan. He said he was about to tell the *New York Times* reporter.

"Where's she sending the check?" I said. "If Bay knows where Chan is, tell her to let me know!"

Of course, she was just returning it to the address he'd given on his contribution form. She had no better idea where to find Chan than anyone else.

I decided I didn't like our campaign's press strategy of sitting on the news that Eddie Chan was a minor official for Reagan-Bush '84. Sooner or later it would come out, and the later the worse it would be.

I preferred a technique I referred to as the "reverse spike." To spike a story meant to kill it. The phrase derived from the days when an editor would literally put stories the newspaper decided not to use on a wire spike. The reverse spike was a phenomenon I'd taken note of as a press spokesman. Sometimes you could kill an unflattering story in a major newspaper by giving it first to a less prestigious, lower-circulation rival. Once the rival ran the story the more prestigious paper wouldn't touch it.

I called the *New York Post* and gave Jeff Hawtin the full story about Eddie Chan's involvement with our campaign and his $1,000 contribution. The newspaper ran an article which gave prominence to Chan's contribution to Ferraro and mentioned his connection to Reagan-Bush '84. When the *New York Times* covered the same story, they barely gave it any space and buried it on the inside pages.

* * *

To me, the Chan episode showed that it was time for us to shift our operations into low gear. We'd had extraordinary luck. Leads we'd started investigating in July had materialized into a barrage of damaging publicity for the Mondale campaign. There were numerous official investigations underway into both Ferraro and Zaccaro's tangled affairs. The compartmented structure of our operation had withstood a leak to NBC and the campaign had emerged unscathed. Wirthlin's polls showed that Reagan was on his way to a reelection landslide.

There is a saying among political insiders that a week is a lifetime in politics. We had a little more than a week to go, and it didn't seem worth taking any major risks to dig up new information or tie up loose ends on Ferraro.

Yet the questions from the press persisted. On October 28, the *Philadelphia Inquirer* and *Boston Globe* ran articles in which Ferraro claimed she'd warned Walter Mondale that if he selected her as his running mate there would be news reports about Mafia connections. From the standpoint of a political strategist, I couldn't figure out why she thought this was to her advantage. For months she had denied that she was aware some of her associates and contributors were connected to criminal activity, and now she was acknowledging that she knew in advance these connections would come to light. She was not only validating the press scrutiny, she was invalidating her claim to innocence!

"She's getting tired," I told Art when I read the news. "This doesn't make sense."

"She's just doing what she's done all her life," Art replied. "She's laying the predicate. When the finger-pointing starts about why Mondale lost the election, she'll claim he knew what he was getting into when he chose her for vice president. That way it's not her fault for dragging the ticket down."

On October 29, the *Wall Street Journal* ran an in-depth report on the grand jury investigation into the Tieg Corporation case involving John Zaccaro. We were fairly confident that Zaccaro was going to be indicted but doubted it would happen before the election. The closer we came to Election

Day, the less likely it seemed that prosecutors would want to appear to be taking any action that could influence the outcome.

That same day, Ferraro made yet another rookie mistake. She banned reporters from the *Philadelphia Inquirer*, *New York Post*, and *Washington Times* from her campaign plane. Her emotion-driven action only created more news stories and made it appear that she had something to hide.

The *New York Times* ran an analytical piece on October 30 about the impact of the President's Commission on Organized Crime. It repeated the revelations regarding Eddie Chan and featured the way the commission had shielded the identity of many witnesses by placing them behind screens and disguising their voices with electronic scramblers. The thrust of the piece was that the security precautions were overly dramatic and perhaps intentionally so in order to draw attention to the hearings.

Roy Cohn, who had been a principal player in the McCarthy hearings, was interviewed for the article.

"I would say it's fantastic for a television series or a Hollywood movie," he opined, "but for something of the prestige of a presidential commission, if anything it defers to theatrics rather than substance."

I wondered whether Cohn really felt the hearings were too dramatic or if he just didn't like being upstaged.

It was getting harder to find the senior staff on the campaign. Many were out on the road, traveling with the president or vice president in the final week of campaigning. But I managed to track down Nofziger.

"I think we're done," I told Lyn. "Art and I have given it our best shot. If something falls into our laps in the next week, of course we'll use it. But we're going to back off on the digging."

"Johnny-boy, I think that calls for a drink!"

20

The Verdict

Before President Reagan could pay a Halloween morning visit to campaign headquarters, he had to make a hastily scheduled stop at the Indian embassy to sign a book of condolences. India's prime minister, Indira Gandhi, had just been assassinated that morning by two of her bodyguards as she walked from a bungalow at her official residence to an office building.

Her killing, at the hands of trusted insiders, was a nightmare scenario. It reminded me of the death of Egyptian president Anwar El-Sadat in 1981, early in Reagan's term, when he was reviewing a military parade. His assassins were led by an Egyptian army lieutenant. Following that attack the U.S. Secret Service became especially vigilant in making sure there were no loaded weapons in the hands of military personnel during presidential visits to military bases.

The Secret Service were jumpy at campaign headquarters. One fourth-floor aide was taken aside for questioning when a knife was discovered in his briefcase. He told the Secret Service that he lived in Washington, D.C., and kept it for self-defense. The agents didn't let him go until campaign manager Ed Rollins vouched for his character.

Despite the solemn events in India, there was a buzz of excitement throughout the building when Reagan arrived. The ostensible purpose of Reagan's visit to headquarters was to rally the campaign staff in the final week before the election. But like everything in politics, there was a dual purpose. The visit would result in a photo op and an event for television news coverage that night, showing prospective voters an upbeat Reagan and his troops on the verge of victory.

Earlier in the year, the White House was embarrassed when news reports came out that Reagan sometimes nodded off in Cabinet meetings. The age issue was behind him, but in true Reagan fashion, he couldn't resist making a joke of it as he addressed the staff.

"I know the long hours that many of you have put in, and some of you were up all night, I have found out, and working," he said. "I can only tell you that, if I could manage it, I would schedule a Cabinet meeting so we could all go over and take a nap together."

The laughter was sincere and appreciative.

I wasn't the only one pulling all-nighters late in the campaign. It was customary at this stage in a campaign to have the feeling that every ounce of effort might make the difference between winning and losing, and sleepless aides toiled during the final 150 hours of the presidential race. The only real effect of most of these last-hour marathons was to give the sleep-deprived a sense of satisfaction that when the votes were tallied, no matter what the outcome, they would know they'd given their all.

Reagan himself felt the pressure.

"Psychologically, I'm running one vote behind," he told the campaign staffers. "It feels better that way."

He wasn't behind at all. Gallup published a poll that morning showing Reagan beating Mondale 57 percent to 40 percent. Our own polling also showed a double-digit lead.

That afternoon Reagan unveiled a new postage stamp honoring Hispanic-Americans. The Rose Garden ceremony was covered by the press and coveted by the campaign strategists. For several years Reagan had courted Hispanic voters, and the stamp's unveiling was better than any campaign ad. To send the message home, Doug Watts' Tuesday Team advertising was also being broadcast in Spanish.

On November 1, Ronald and Nancy Reagan left the White House for their final campaign swing. The 14-city trip started in the Northeast and then worked its way westward. The plan was to wrap up Ronald Reagan's last campaign for public office in his home state of California. Stu Spencer and Senator Paul Laxalt travelled with the president and First Lady.

That same day, Aniello Dellacroce was arrested by IRS agents at the Ravenite Social Club on charges of tax evasion. The *New York Post* reported the arrest. An ambitious U.S. attorney named Rudy Giuliani had Dellacroce in his crosshairs. It was just the beginning of Dellacroce's legal troubles.

On November 3, the *Washington Post*/ABC poll showed Reagan with an 18-point lead over Mondale. The president was ahead in every state except Minnesota. During their stay in Little Rock, Arkansas, Spencer, Laxalt and Baker met with Reagan in his room at the Excelsior Hotel. Almost on a whim, Spencer suggested they make a stop in Minnesota on their way to St. Louis, Missouri.

On the morning of November 4, Air Force One touched down at Rochester, Minnesota. The event, hastily drawn together, consisted of brief remarks and questions and answers with the press at an airport. Asked by a reporter if

From left, Ronald Reagan, Jim Baker, Paul Laxalt and Stu Spencer at the Excelsior Hotel, Little Rock, Arkansas, November 3, 1984, during the final 14-city campaign swing with an impromptu stop in Mondale's home state of Minnesota (courtesy Ronald Reagan Presidential Library).

the Gipper would have tried to run up the score, Reagan responded: "I don't think of it as running up the score. The Gipper would never give up before the final whistle."

Another journalist asked why he didn't go to North Oaks and campaign in Mondale's home town.

"I didn't want to offend him," Reagan said. He became slightly wistful when asked what it felt like to be near the end of his last campaign.

"It's sort of like when coming up to your last football game of the season," he said, keeping up the sports analogy, "and knowing you weren't going to play football anymore."

In St. Louis, comedian Bob Hope gave Reagan an introduction that consisted of six minutes of one-liners. He started off by asking the crowd, "Are you all here on your way to the football game?"

The rally took place under the St. Louis Gateway arch. Hope said it reminded him of a "Texas croquet set."

Two years earlier, Hope had quipped: "You all know that Reagan is now our oldest chief executive…. Poli-Grip is now the official presidential seal."

Now he put his humor to work dispelling the age issue.

Telling the crowd that Reagan was in great shape, Hope said the president "stays in shape by getting up each morning and jogging three times around Tip O'Neill." The House Speaker, who put the rotund in the Capitol rotunda, had pushed Mondale to pick Gerry Ferraro as his running mate. I was glad to see Hope poking fun at O'Neill.

After lauding the economic growth and sense of prosperity that had returned to the country, Hope said, "And isn't it better to know that the hand in your pocket is your own?"

In his own left-handed way, the iconic comedian wrapped up by promising better things ahead in a second Reagan term.

"When Ronnie Reagan was making a picture," Hope said, "he was always better in the third reel than in the first."

The final day of campaigning was spent in California. Reagan spoke to packed rallies with crowds jacked up on the scent of victory and the adrenaline rush of an impending landslide. Back in Washington, Bill Greener, the Republican National Committee's communications director, took bets from the campaign's senior staff on the outcome of the election. The sums were nominal and Greener's pot was paltry, but the bragging rights for pegging the results correctly were substantial.

There were four categories: the popular vote percentage, the Electoral College total, and the House and Senate results. Whoever came closest to the correct tally in all four categories would win the pot. The top strategists from Atwater to Wirthlin were in on the betting.

I didn't plan to place a bet, but when Greener made a final round of "last chance" phone calls I gave it a shot and then got back to wrapping up the Ferraro files. By the end of November, I would be off the campaign payroll. I planned to have the entire operation shut down and the information we'd unearthed safely archived before I left.

On Election Day I cast my ballot at a moderately-crowded local precinct. It was a clear fall day with temps in the mid–60s, ideal for high voter turnout at the polls. Drive-time radio reports indicated that turnout was good up and down the East Coast.

At headquarters the telephone lines buzzed throughout the day. Everyone in politics has a network of people, and everyone in that network wants to be in the know. Calls flooded into and out of headquarters as people traded tidbits of information, trying to piece together what was happening across the country.

One caller would be ebullient, the next one anxious. Friendly reporters shared tips about their news organizations' exit polling. Inquisitive reporters called to see if we were hearing anything different than they were hearing. State campaign staff called from around the country with state and local updates.

Ashtrays filled up as the day wore on. An atmosphere of edgy anticipation settled over headquarters. I had to get out of the building for lunch. When

I got back not much had changed. No one had any reliable numbers, exit polls hadn't been published, and variations of the same inside information that had started circulating in the morning had now morphed into something almost unrecognizable after hours of the telephone game. I sometimes caught myself in the middle of a conversation questioning whether or not I'd heard something like this hours earlier. If I could have ignored the phone calls I would have, but it would have been extremely impolite, and I never knew whether the next call might hold some scintilla of news I didn't want to miss.

Around evening people began filtering out of headquarters toward the hotel where the Victory 84 celebration was being held in Washington. Art and I stayed at the office and watched the network news coverage. The day had passed without any major surprises, which was good news. Shortly after 8 p.m. EST, the three television networks projected that Reagan was the winner. The polls hadn't closed yet in 25 states, but the lead Reagan had in the exit polls seemed insurmountable.

Around 11 p.m. EST, Walter Mondale called Ronald Reagan at the Century Plaza Hotel in Los Angeles and conceded the election. When he heard Mondale's congratulations, Reagan gave a thumbs up to Nancy. A little after midnight Reagan capped off the Victory 84 celebration at the Century Plaza with a jubilant speech.

At the Century Plaza Hotel, Los Angeles, California, November 6, 1984, President Reagan gives Nancy the thumbs-up during phone call from Walter Mondale conceding the election (courtesy Ronald Reagan Presidential Library).

Doria Reagan, Nancy Reagan, and Ronald Reagan at the victory celebration at the Century Plaza Hotel, Los Angeles, California, November 6, 1984 (courtesy Ronald Reagan Presidential Library).

Reagan won every state except for Minnesota and the District of Columbia. He picked up 525 of the 538 Electoral College votes, the highest total for any president in history. He won 58.8 percent of the popular vote, picked up 16 seats in the House of Representatives, and Republicans kept control of the Senate despite the loss of two seats. At age 73, he was the oldest candidate to win a presidential election.

Demographically, his sweep was just as impressive. He won majorities in every age group of voters. Sixty-one percent of those between the ages of 18 and 24 voted for him. He led in every income group except those who made under $12,500 a year. He won the support of 34 percent of Hispanic voters and 58 percent of women voters. He even won a majority of Italian-American female voters.

Turnout was up in 1984. Five million more votes were cast in 1984 than in 1980 for a total of more than 90 million voters.

It took a little longer for the results to come in, but when we polled to see whether Ferraro had added anything to Mondale's vote total, we discovered that she had been a drag on the ticket. She cost him votes. Dick Wirthlin's nightmare scenario of a large gender gap and millions more female voters as a result of Geraldine Ferraro's selection as Mondale's running mate didn't materialize on Election Day.

There were many factors that gave Ronald Reagan such a decisive victory. Among them was our successful operation to neutralize the threat from Geraldine Ferraro's presence on the ticket.

The day after the election, Bill Greener called when I was in a meeting. There was a pink slip on my desk with the time and date and his name and phone number.

The message said: "You won $40."

Epilogue

About a week after the election, Ed Rollins asked me into his office. Angela Marie "Bay" Buchanan, the campaign treasurer, was sitting on the couch with a sheaf of invoices. I'd known Bay since 1979, when I interviewed with Nofziger at Citizens for the Republic. She'd been in the same role at CFTR as controller of Reagan's political action committee.

Bay asked me if an invoice for a private plane to West Point and back was a campaign expense. I said yes and gave a brief explanation. Then she asked if she should pay invoices from a law firm for the Zaccaro property record searches. I nodded and told her those records had paid for themselves many times over.

All political campaigns, from elections for country clerk all the way up to the presidency, involve scrutinizing the opposition for political vulnerabilities. The only exception to this rule is when a candidate runs unopposed. This is a feature of American elections that transcends bipartisanship. All candidates, Democrats and Republicans, Greens and Libertarians, even Independents, look for and exploit the weaknesses of opposing candidates. That is the nature of political competition in a democratic system of government.

Sometimes the vulnerabilities are unpopular policies or positions a candidate takes, but sometimes they are actions the candidate has taken that reveal unattractive aspects of their character or ethics. Either way, they've been part of American politics from the beginning and the 1984 Reagan campaign was no exception. No matter who Walter Mondale selected as his running mate, he or she would have received the same scrutiny we gave to Geraldine Ferraro.

Our investigation never had a formal budget. It wasn't a line item in the spreadsheets. If we needed to spend campaign funds, we did so and got approval later. Our authorization came from First Lady Nancy Reagan.

A month after the presidential election, the House Committee on Standards of Official Conduct issued its 795-page report titled "In the Matter of Representative Geraldine A. Ferraro." The committee found her in violation of the Ethics in Government Act of 1978. Her claims to exemption from disclosure requirements were rejected. Ten of the complaints against her concerning inadequate or improper financial disclosure were sustained. Interestingly, one of the inadequacies the committee cited concerned her failure to list rental income and a partial down-payment on 200 Lafayette Street, the building used as a warehouse for pornographic material. Because Ferraro was not returning to Congress after the end of the term, no disciplinary action (such as a reprimand or censure) was taken against her.

In January 1985, John Zaccaro entered a guilty plea in New York State supreme court in Manhattan to misdemeanor charges of submitting a false sales contract, an altered appraisal and a misleading net worth statement in order to fraudulently obtain bank financing for a real estate transaction in which he and his partners stood to make millions. Zaccaro told acting justice George F. Roberts (no relation to the author): "I have learned my lesson, Judge, the hard way." Before his sentencing, Geraldine Ferraro wrote a letter pleading for leniency on the grounds that her husband's legal troubles stemmed largely from her campaign. Saying it was highly unlikely that Zaccaro would repeat the offenses, the judge fined him $1,000 and sentenced Zaccaro to 150 hours of community service with youth groups and the homeless.

In October 1986, Zaccaro was indicted on felony charges for trying to extort a bribe from a cable television company seeking a franchise in Queens. A year later, a jury acquitted him after a key prosecution witness flip-flopped in his testimony about a phone conversation in which Zaccaro allegedly said a cable franchise could be obtained but it would cost a "substantial amount of money" and that he knew a guy who could take care of it. Initially, the witness characterized the phone call as a discussion of a bribe, but reversed himself and said Zaccaro could have been referring to "a corrupt process." Again, Gerry Ferraro blamed John's legal difficulties on her 1984 candidacy, saying no one would ever have scrutinized his business dealings if she had not run for vice president.

Ferraro flirted with running against incumbent Republican senator Alfonse D'Amato in the 1986 mid-term elections, but on December 11, 1985, she announced she'd decided against it because of an ongoing Justice Department investigation of the financing of her 1978 congressional campaign.

She ran for Senate in 1992. In its August 25, 1992, issue the *Village Voice* ran a front-page investigative story headlined "What You Don't Know About Ferraro and the Mob." The in-depth article was reported by Wayne Barrett and William Bastone.

"Ferraro has had a disturbing amount of contact with mob figures throughout much of her personal, political, and business life," it said. "A two-month *Voice* investigation establishes that mobsters helped underwrite her first congressional bid; have freely rented, bought, and borrowed from companies with which she was affiliated; and helped set her son up with a sweetheart commercial lease following his drug conviction."

In the eight years since the end of our investigations and Barrett and Bastone's article, new investigations and indictments had revealed additional Ferraro and Zaccaro associates with organized crime connections. The 1979 fundraiser chaired by Nick Sands for Ferraro included a dinner committee to help with ticket sales. Seven of the dinner committee members were either members of the Mafia or mob associates. One was later convicted of murder and another, Charles "One-Eyed Charlie" Martelli, went to prison for labor racketeering.

Robert DiBernardo, the pornography merchant who rented premises from John Zaccaro, was identified in the article as a Gambino crime family captain, or capo. During the 1984 presidential race, statements issued by Zaccaro's attorneys regarding the relationship between the landlord and his tenant created the impression that their dealings with one another were arm's length. In 1985, police surveillance picked up DiBernardo and John Zaccaro meeting on a street corner.

In total, the *Village Voice* article documented 24 organized crime ties with Ferraro and Zaccaro.

"Is this the sort of baggage," the *Voice* asked, "a U.S. senator should take to Washington, D.C.?"

Apparently the voters concluded the answer was no. Ferraro lost in the 1992 Democratic primary. She ran for the Senate again in 1998 and lost again in the primary. She never again held elective office.

*   *   *

P. Zaccaro Co., Inc.'s longtime tenant, Aniello Dellacroce, was indicted on tax evasion charges on November 1, 1984, by Rudy Giuliani, the U.S. attorney for the Southern District of New York. When he was booked, Dellacroce gave his address as 232 Mulberry Street but said he also lived on Staten Island.

The U.S. Attorney's Office went on high alert after Dellacroce's arrest. Police sources picked up rumors that Italian Mafiosi planned to disrupt the Justice Department's vendetta against the "five families" who controlled most organized crime in the United States. Three Sicilians armed with a rifle with telescopic sights were arrested trying to cross the border between Canada and the United States. Authorities feared they were a Mafia hit team out to kill prosecutors, agents and witnesses.

On February 26, 1985, Giuliani announced indictments of the bosses and top lieutenants of the Mafia's five crime families: the Bonannos, Colombos, Gambinos, Genoveses, and Luccheses. Paul Castellano, the head of the Gambinos, was charged with racketeering and extortion, along with his underboss, Aniello Dellacroce. The indictments were part of a nationwide crackdown on organized crime that the Justice Department had launched in August of 1983.

The undercover investigations coincided with the public work of the President's Commission on Organized Crime, and together they spelled what Giuliani called "a great day for law enforcement" but "a bad day for the Mafia." In March 1985, Dellacroce was separately indicted for murder, loan-sharking, gambling and hijacking. He died of cancer in December of 1985 before his case came to trial. In November 1986 Gambino boss Paul Castellano was found guilty on all 151 counts in the indictment. Two months later he was sentenced to 100 years in prison.

*   *   *

Edward Tse Chiu Chan, a.k.a. Eddie Chan, never complied with the subpoena to appear before the President's Commission on Organized Crime. As rumors spread through New York's Chinatown that Chan was going to be arrested, hundreds of depositors thronged to the Chatham and Mott Street branches of the United Orient Bank to withdraw their money. Some waited in line for as long as four hours. Between November 5 and November 7 (the bank was closed on November 6, Election Day) more than $3 million in deposits were withdrawn. A few days later, Eddie Chan resigned his position as vice chairman of the United Orient Bank. He fled the country and has disappeared from public view. According to the 1992 *Village Voice* article, an FBI document on Edward Tse Chiu Chan's associates lists Geraldine Ferraro as an "acquaintance" and describes Eddie Chan himself as "a murder contractor and narcotics dealer."

He has reportedly been sighted in China and Vietnam.

*   *   *

Ronald Reagan signed the Executive Order bringing the President's Commission on Organized Crime into existence. When he authorized it, Reagan said he hoped the commission would create "the kind of public support that is vital" for eliminating organized crime. The work Art Teele and I carried out under Stu Spencer's direction generated months of news stories, heightening public awareness of the seedy intersection between politics and organized crime.

The real credit for raising public awareness belongs to Nancy Reagan. Her directive to scrutinize Ferraro's background and expose any Mafia connections did more to draw public attention to organized crime during the final 100 days of the 1984 campaign than the commission accomplished in the three years of its existence.

As the prosecution and jailings of Mafia chiefs mounted after the 1984 campaign, I began to wonder whether thwarting Reagan's drive against organized crime might have motivated the Mafia's five families to try and prevent his reelection. Perhaps it was just a coincidence that a vice-presidential candidate with so many mob links and so little political experience was chosen as Walter Mondale's running mate. It's open to speculation whether a Mondale-Ferraro presidency would have pursued organized crime with the same zeal and determination as the Reagan Administration did in the second term.

* * *

By the end of November, most of us were off the campaign payroll.

Stu Spencer returned to his consulting firm, splitting his time between his home in Newport Beach, California, and his Washington office. Stu kept inviting me to the annual Wheelspinner's party, a gathering of Southern California political types, but unfortunately the timing was never right for me to attend. When the Iran-Contra scandal broke in 1986, Stu returned to Washington and took a job in the White House to guide the Reagans through the crisis.

* * *

Lyn Nofziger returned to his consulting firm, Nofziger & Bragg. We stayed in close touch. During the TWA 847 hostage crisis in Beirut, I was speaking with Lyn on the phone about the president's options for gaining the hostages' release when the line suddenly went dead. I called Lyn back and suggested we meet for lunch at Mo & Joe's Café and talk face to face. We both presumed the line had been cut by the National Security Agency because of the sensitivity of the matter. Neither of us guessed that this latest hostage crisis would be the germination of the Iran-Contra affair, in which the Administration was accused of trading military weapons for hostages and using profits from the weapons sales to arm the Nicaraguan contras.

In early 1987, Special Counsel John McKay opened an investigation into Lyn's contacts with Elizabeth Dole and Ed Meese on behalf of Wedtech, a scandal-embroiled defense contractor. That summer Lyn was indicted on six counts of violating the Ethics in Government Act. Meant to curb the use of undue influence, the law prohibited federal employees from lobbying their prior places of employment for two years following their departure from a government job.

Lyn had scrupulously avoided contacting the Office of Political Affairs, which he headed in Reagan's first term, but thought he was following the law when he contacted White House officials in places where he had not worked. Not long before, Michael Deaver, who also left the White House to lobby, was indicted for giving false testimony to a congressional committee and grand jury investigating violations of the Ethics in Government Act.

Harry Truman reportedly said that if you want a friend in Washington, get a dog. In fact, he probably never said anything like it. He didn't particularly like dogs and definitely didn't want one in the White House. But the quip illustrates Washington's nature. It's a town where power provides popularity, but where the powerless are quickly abandoned by the sycophants and opportunists who gravitate toward the powerful. Even friends can be afraid to associate openly with someone under the shadow of a scandal. Some are simply afraid that it will tarnish their reputation, while others dread they might fall under the investigators' scrutiny.

Lyn had warned me during my first week at the White House not to be fooled by the sudden burst of popularity among acquaintances, contacts, and would-be friends.

"The same people who wouldn't return your calls before you got this job," he said, "won't return them after you leave. Always remember that."

I continued to meet Lyn at Mo & Joe's, usually for breakfast, throughout the investigation and subsequent trial. Lyn was generally upbeat, even though his business was losing clients and his legal fees were mounting.

In December 1987, Deaver was convicted on three counts of perjury and sentenced to three years in prison, a $100,000 fine, and 1,500 hours of community service. The prison sentence was later converted to three years of probation.

Despite Deaver's poor fortune, Lyn remained optimistic. In January 1988, his trial started. The prosecutor, Lovida H. Coleman, Jr., accused him of having "cashed in" on his connections to Reagan. In March, Lyn was convicted on three felony counts of illegal lobbying.

He wore his trademark Mickey Mouse tie to his sentencing. Lyn told the judge he wasn't remorseful because he was convinced he was innocent. The judge gave him 90 days in prison and a $30,000 fine. Lyn appealed, and in late 1988 the U.S. Court of Appeals overturned his conviction. Coleman took the case to the Supreme Court in an effort to put Lyn in jail, but the Supreme Court refused to reinstate the conviction.

Lyn's legal fees topped $1.5 million. A legal defense fund set up in his name helped defray some of the costs, but his consulting business never recovered. He wrote four western novels and a memoir and dabbled in politics. In 2006, he died of cancer.

In a tribute to Lyn, Nancy attested to his standing among Reagan's advisors.

"Lyn was with us from the gubernatorial campaign in 1965 through the early White House days," she said, "and Ronnie valued his advice and good humor as much as anyone's."

*   *   *

Lee Atwater went into the consulting business the day after the 1984 campaign as a senior partner of the Virginia-based firm of Black, Manafort, Stone & Kelly. Three of his partners—Charlie Black, Paul Manafort and Roger Stone—had built their reputations as regional directors of the 1980 and 1984 Reagan campaigns. Atwater started driving a new Mercedes 190E and told me he'd reached the point in life "where it's time to start accumulatin' a little something."

In 1986, he headed the Fund for Victory, Vice President George Bush's political action committee, and later managed Bush's presidential campaign until Jim Baker took over in the summer of 1988. Atwater became chairman of the Republican National Committee after the campaign. In March 1990 he was diagnosed with an astrocytoma, an aggressive brain tumor.

During his illness, Lee apologized to many of his political rivals and claimed to have found solace in the Bible. Jim Pinkerton encouraged me to visit him in the hospital, but I never went. I didn't want to be part of Atwater's attempts to bargain with fate through a death-bed spiritual conversion.

When Ed Rollins was interviewed for a 2008 documentary about Lee called *Boogie Man: The Lee Atwater Story*, he told the following anecdote: "[Atwater] was telling this story about how a Living Bible was what was giving him faith and I said to Mary Matalin, 'I really, sincerely hope that he found peace.' She said, 'Ed, when we were cleaning up his things afterwards, the Bible was still wrapped in the cellophane and had never been taken out of the package,' which just told you everything there was. He was spinning right to the end."

Atwater died in 1991. His run inside the Beltway lasted about 10 years, two decades shy of the 30 years he thought he'd be in the game when we talked about loyalty early in the 1984 campaign.

*   *   *

In 1986, President Reagan appointed Congressman Barber Conable as president of the World Bank. Conable was the first career politician to hold the post as well as the first World Bank president without Wall Street experience. His expertise was budgetary, and Conable introduced a number of reforms before leaving the bank in 1991.

He and Reagan both liked to doodle during meetings. When Reagan heard about Conable's habit, he asked for some of the drawings. Conable sent several, and Reagan reciprocated by sending a few of his own on White House stationery.

"Barber," he penned on the page, "these are just doodles. Yours are art."

After his tenure at the World Bank, Conable left Washington, D.C., to return home to the small-town virtues of Batavia, New York. According to a local professor who became friends with him, Yanek Mieczkowski, Conable believed staying in Washington as a lobbyist or influence-peddler would have been "mercenary" and a misuse of the power his constituents had entrusted to him.

* * *

Mike Sotirhos, the campaign official who enlisted Eddie Chan as director of voter registration for Chinese-Americans for Reagan-Bush '84, was appointed U.S. ambassador to Jamaica. The government of Jamaica awarded him its "Order of Distinction" and gave him the honorary rank of commander. In 1989, President Bush made him U.S. ambassador to Greece, making him the first Greek-American to ever hold that position.

* * *

Myles Ambrose, who was instrumental in uncovering the organized crime figures orbiting around Geraldine Ferraro, wanted to be U.S. ambassador to Ireland. When the post opened up in 1985 I made a push for Ambrose, but the plum job went instead to Peggy Heckler. As secretary of Health and Human Services, Heckler had failed to impress Don Regan, the president's new chief of staff. Regan wanted Reagan to fire Heckler, but the compromise was to give her the ambassadorship. Ambrose was disappointed but understanding.

I was less so. One of the hazards of anonymity and unsung accomplishments is that they often go unrewarded, at least in politics. In intelligence agencies, there are secret award ceremonies and medals conferred. Often the medals remain locked in a government safe until the end of an intelligence officer's career. But the honor is at least bestowed.

In politics, secrets have to be guarded even more closely than the CIA does with its classified material. To disclose why someone deserves consideration for a plum job like an ambassadorship is to reveal the secret, and in politics, as in espionage, secrets are a form of currency. They are fungible. They can be used to blackmail or to sabotage. One of the reasons the many worthy volunteers who helped us investigate Ferraro rarely got more than a thank you in return is that we kept our secrets for decades, even within the inner circles of the Reagan presidency.

Ronald Reagan had a plaque on his desk in the Oval Office inscribed with the words: "There is no limit to what a man can do or where he can go if he does not mind who gets the credit."

It applied perfectly to the work of our investigative teams in 1984.

* * *

For Art Teele and me, it wasn't goodbye after the 1984 campaign—it was "¡Hasta luego!" We started out the campaign never having met each other, but by the time it ended we were close buddies. If our friendship had matchmakers, they were Geraldine Ferraro and Nancy Reagan. The bond between us was forged by pressure-filled adventures born with good humor and grace.

Art returned to his home state of Florida to practice law. One of his clients was NASCAR founder Bill France. Over the years Art invited me to meet him at Daytona for the races, but unfortunately the timing never worked out.

Public service was what really motivated Art, so he put law on the back-burner and ran for a seat on the Metro-Dade County Commission in Miami. By 1996, he had become chairman of the Board of County Commissioners and set his sights on becoming executive mayor. He called me that spring and asked me to work on his campaign. I signed on and commuted between Washington and Miami. There were five candidates in the race, and after the first balloting it narrowed to a run-off between Art and Alex Penelas, a Cuban-American. Penelas won the mayoral run-off.

Art didn't let the defeat keep him down for long. He ran for Miami city commissioner and won.

Art threw his energy into development of the Overtown district he represented and became head of the Community Redevelopment Agency (CRA). He was particularly interested in fostering the creation of an arts and entertainment district, without displacing local businesses. The minutes of board meetings show frequent tension between Teele and developers eager to use CRA funds and power. Contracts for construction of parking garages fell under scrutiny after an auditor claimed there were irregularities in the books, and state attorney Katherine Fernandez Rundle began to investigate. She hired Richard Scruggs, a prosecutor who had worked for U.S. attorney general Janet Reno in the Clinton Administration and had experience with public corruption cases.

The Miami-Dade County Police assigned a surveillance team of six undercover detectives called Task Force Five to follow Art from dawn to dusk, looking for evidence of pay-offs or bribes. It was August 2004 when Detective Jorge Plasencia decided to follow Art's wife, Stephanie, when she left work at Miami International Airport. Plasencia had no authority to follow her. Stephanie Teele wasn't under investigation, and his orders did not include tailing her. For reasons that only he can explain, Plasencia acted alone, without any other police officers with him and without informing his superiors of his plans.

Stephanie Teele noticed the light-colored sports utility vehicle that was constantly behind her. When she got home and parked, she locked her car and waited until other people were nearby before getting out. That night she told Art someone was stalking her.

It was Detective Plasencia's unauthorized surveillance that led Art to intervene on August 24 when he saw a white SUV with dark tinted windows following his wife's car. He drove alongside the SUV and tried to get it to pull over. When the driver kept going, Art called 911 and kept pace with the SUV until he was able to pull in front and bring it to a halt. He challenged the people following Stephanie to identify themselves. The police initially refused to do so. The ensuing confrontation resulted in Art being charged on September 15, 2004, with threatening police officers and trying to interfere with an investigation. At trial, he was convicted.

Florida's Third Circuit Court of Appeals overturned his conviction on April 17, 2007. In a stinging rebuke to police and prosecutors, Judge Dennis J. Murphy found that there were "simply no facts" to support the charges against Teele. The evidence on the 911 tapes flatly refuted the prosecutor's allegations.

"It is evident from the record that Teele never saw Detective Bullard's badge and was never provided his name," Judge Murphy wrote in his opinion. "Teele asked to see the identification repeatedly, a completely lawful request given that Teele saw Detective Bullard in street clothes and an unmarked car, following his wife. At the time of this discussion the officers had no warrant, had not announced a lawful purpose for following Mrs. Teele but instead denied that they had followed her or that they intended to arrest Teele."

The judge ordered the trial court to enter a verdict of acquittal.

Art had been dead for almost two years.

Scruggs and Rundle suffered another high-profile setback when they went after African American county commissioner Michele Spence-Jones on corruption charges similar to those alleged against Art. Judge Rosa Rodriguez said during the trial that she was "finding it difficult to understand the state's theory" of the alleged crimes. The jury apparently agreed. It took them 90 minutes to acquit Spence-Jones on all charges.

Richard Scruggs resigned from the State Attorney's Office not long after the failed prosecution of Michele Spence-Jones. I can't help wondering if the not guilty verdict would have been the same if Art had gone to trial.

A year after Art's death, Miami mayor Manny Diaz presided over the dedication of the new Grand Promenade Entertainment District in Overtown. The backdrop included the official seal of the City of Miami and the American and Florida state flags. The press turned out to cover the event.

"Today is the first of many celebrations of the legacy of Art Teele in Miami," Mayor Diaz proclaimed at the ribbon-cutting.

Frank Rollason, the executive director of the Community Redevelopment Agency, gave a speech crediting Art for redevelopment of the downtown area. Art had fought for the old railroad right of way to be turned into a pedestrian promenade. Developments that investigators considered fraud-ridden, like parking garages, turned out to be key in bringing people to the revitalized arts district. The same contracts that had generated corruption probes were now lauded.

In 12 months, Arthur Earle Teele, Jr., went from pariah to visionary. The exoneration and adulation came too late for Art, but it was sweet for those who never believed the worst about him.

Michael Lacey, the founder of the chain of New Times newspapers that ran "Tales of Teele: Sleaze Stories," acknowledged that the Miami New Times should never have printed the article.

"You can't publish unsubstantiated police reports," he told New York Magazine in a 2005 interview. "We were irresponsible."

In 2012 Lacey sold his newspaper holdings to concentrate on a lucrative new website, Backpage, which featured adult advertising. In 2014 Backpage generated $135 million in advertising revenue. A year later the business was valued at $600 million.

In 2017 the U.S. Senate's Permanent Subcommittee on Investigations held hearings on allegations that Backpage fostered prostitution and human trafficking. Lacey and a partner were called to testify but refused to coop-erate. They pleaded the Fifth Amendment and invoked their right against self-incrimination.

On April 6, 2018, the FBI raided Lacey's residence in Paradise Valley, Arizona, just as he was about to hold a party to celebrate his wedding vows after a recent remarriage. FBI agents told Lacey he was under arrest on federal charges of "money laundering and prostitution." On the same day, Backpage was seized by federal authorities and shut down.

Lacey is awaiting trial as of the date of this writing. The Miami New Times is still publishing—under new management and a new editor.

In 2014, the CRA sold the promenade to two separate bidders for a total of $10.16 million. One of the new owners is the Miami Worldcenter, a high-density development project covering 30 acres of the old downtown. Another downtown property that was razed for the Worldcenter develop-ment was the Miami Herald building.

One of my favorite fiction writers is John D. MacDonald, whose mys-tery novels feature a character named Travis McGee, a crime solver who calls himself a "salvage consultant." MacDonald's books are set in Florida, and real estate developers are often at the root of his plots. Personally, I'm persuaded that there is a lot more to be revealed about my friend Art Teele, and there is something plausible to his belief that he was being persecuted because he'd made powerful enemies. I've read too many Travis McGee mys-teries to think that anything connected to real estate in Florida ever has a simple explanation.

*   *   *

After the 1984 campaign, I had interest from Ash Green, an editor at Al-fred A. Knopf, in publishing my story about the Reagan campaign. I seriously pursued it until Stu Spencer and Ed Rollins asked me not to write the book. Spencer worried that it would embarrass the Reagans, especially Nancy, so I decided to pass on the opportunity. I took a brief consulting job at the U.S. Department of Education with my former boss, Anne Graham, and then re-joined the staff of the Office of Planning and Evaluation at the White House.

Shortly thereafter there was a White House reshuffle. Chief of Staff Jim Baker traded jobs with Treasury Secretary Don Regan. Ed Meese departed for the post of attorney general. When Regan folded the Office of Planning and Evaluation into the Office of Policy Development, my boss, Bruce Chapman, was appointed ambassador to the United Nations Organizations in Vienna.

Ed Rollins, who worked briefly for Stu Spencer's consulting firm, Spencer-Roberts (no relation to the author), returned to the White House to head an-other merged entity created by the Regan team, the Office of Political and Governmental Affairs. Ed asked me to join as special assistant to the president, and I agreed. The Regan team had other ideas, and never approved Ed's orga-nization chart that included the special assistant slot, so I made do with my old title of associate director of the Office of Political and Governmental Affairs. My new office was in the West Wing instead of the Old Executive Office Build-ing, which was a step up in the ultra-hierarchical world of the White House.

Throughout 1985 I worked on projects as varied as dealing with high-profile political appointments to how the president should respond to the terrorist hijacking of TWA 847 and subsequent hostage incidents to building legislative support for congressional funding of the MX missile program. One of the areas I became involved in was aid to the Nicaraguan Contras, the anti–Sandinista rebel forces supported by the CIA.

Toward the end of 1985 Ed Rollins left the White House to join a politi-cal campaign consulting firm headed by Doug Watts and Sal Russo, a former Reagan aide and California political strategist. The new firm was Russo, Watts & Rollins. I was asked to join as vice president for international business and said yes.

My work as an international political consultant was fun and stimulat-ing, sometimes too much so. In Argentina I was caught up in a military coup attempt that for two nervous days could have gone either way. During an emergency session of a provincial legislature, I led a group in declaring our support on live television for Argentina's fledgling democracy and warned of serious consequences from Washington if the military units still on the fence supported the coup. When the danger finally passed, I went back to Buenos Aires just in time for anti-coup protests to turn into a small riot and ended up ducking into a cafeteria just before windows started shattering and trash bins were set on fire.

I was working with Nawaz Sharif, at the time chief minister of the Punjab, when the riots over novelist Salman Rushdie's perceived blasphemy broke out in Pakistan. My work took me throughout South America and as far as South Africa and Sri Lanka. When I wasn't handling client work, I volunteered with the State Department, National Endowment for Democracy and International Republican Institute on democracy-building and public diplomacy projects in Eastern Europe and the former U.S.S.R. At a democracy conference in Kyrgyzstan, several Uighurs and Chinese political activists crossed the border to attend.

Lyn Nofziger wasn't the only Reagan-Bush '84 veteran being investigated in the 1980s. After the Iran-Contra scandal broke, I was questioned about my role by the FBI, the investigative staff of the House Select Committee to Investigate Covert Arms Transactions with Iran and the Senate Select Committee on Secret Military Assistance to Iran and the Nicaraguan Opposition, *and* lawyers on the staff of Independent Counsel Lawrence Walsh. When I worked at the White House in 1985, I introduced a conservative fundraiser named Carl Russell "Spitz" Channell to Richard Miller. Money they raised was used to purchase weapons for the Contras in violation of a congressional prohibition known as the Boland Amendment. Independent Counsel Walsh's investigation dragged on for seven years.

Aside from some volunteer work on the 1988 Bush presidential campaign, where I headed a team of former CIA employees in assessing George H.W. Bush's vulnerabilities and ways in which the Democrats might attack him or the Bush family, I tried to stay out of domestic politics. In 1992, when Ross Perot announced his candidacy for president, Ed Rollins asked me to be deputy campaign manager. Perot's platform appealed to me and the challenge of electing an Independent was alluring, but I declined. Howard Bane had worked with Perot during the CIA's planning for the rescue of the U.S. embassy hostages in Iran and knew Perot's traits. He cautioned me against taking the job. Perot, Howard said, had a habit of changing his mind suddenly. Not long after I declined Ed's offer Perot pulled out of the race, only to re-enter it months later. I was grateful to Howard for sparing me the roller-coaster ride. When the Bush campaign found out I might join Perot, they called me and offered "anything you want." I turned them down too. There was only one president I ever wanted to work for, and that was Ronald Reagan.

I did become an advisor to the Ukrainian equivalent of the White House and was deeply involved in the negotiations over dismantling Ukraine's strategic missiles and the return of their nuclear warheads to Russia. In 1993 a top Ukrainian White House official asked me to a private meeting to discuss how to bind Crimea to Kiev. We helped the Ukrainian Academy of Sciences conduct the first Western-style public opinion poll in the country, and I was invited to lecture at the Foreign Ministry and other forums.

A client proposed a project to build a nuclear fuel plant for Ukraine and to modernize its nuclear power reactors. The plant would have eliminated Ukraine's reliance on Russian nuclear plant fuel. These were major undertakings that attracted the attention of Russian intelligence and, because of the millions of dollars involved, corrupt Ukrainian officials. In 1994, when a senior Ukrainian official demanded payments that were illegal under U.S. law, I decided to end my work as an international political consultant.

Starting in 1986, I consulted part-time for John McLaughlin on his weekly television shows, *The McLaughlin Group* and *John McLaughlin's One-on-One*. McLaughlin was a Jesuit priest before he went into politics and then broadcasting. He was a White House speechwriter for Richard Nixon and a candidate for U.S. Senate in Rhode Island. When the Watergate tape recordings revealed Nixon's vulgarity and use of profanity, the country was shocked. John McLaughlin gave a learned disquisition from the White House press podium justifying why presidents sometimes use profanity. The press lampooned him as "Nixon's Padre." A political cartoon bearing that title was the first time I heard about John McLaughlin, back in the early '70s.

His background was truly ecumenical. He was charming, gregarious, and brilliant, but he could also be acerbic, peremptory, and obstinate. We were a good match.

"I know I can be a bastard," he often said to me, drawing out the second "r" with an exaggerated New England accent that made the word come out "bahstawd."

I worked with McLaughlin for 31 years, starting as a consultant and becoming a senior producer. During much of that time *The McLaughlin Group* was the top-rated political talk show in the country. McLaughlin became a celebrity, and the show was often a news leader. The angles McLaughlin probed over the weekend would become front-page news throughout the following week.

Sometimes I would come straight from the airport after an overseas trip to meet with John at his production offices or at his home. We went over the shows together, with McLaughlin asking my opinion on every latest news development and wanting the inside "skinny" on what was happening behind the scenes. He had his own sources but always wanted more information, and we would talk right up to the minute when he went on set to tape the shows. Over the years the arrangement evolved into a deep friendship. We were literally co-creators of each broadcast, even if we sometimes spent more time laughing at each other's jokes than focusing on the work.

In August 1993, Independent Counsel Lawrence Walsh's report on the Iran-Contra affair was released. Walsh concluded that I played a "minor role" in the affair by introducing Spitz Channell and Rich Miller. They were the first two co-conspirators to be indicted by Walsh. Years later, when the probe's background documents were available on the Internet, I read many of the depositions taken by Walsh's team. I was stunned to see how many times my name came up as the prosecutors asked about my role and tried to tie me to their case.

In 1996 I needed to get a copy of a presidential commission report as soon as it was available. The standard procedure was to contract a courier and then call the White House to have a copy set aside for immediate pick up. When I made my request, the voice on the other end of the phone asked if I had access to the "World Wide Web."

"If you do," she said, "you can get the report right now online."

The following year, I left Washington along with my new wife Elizabeth and moved to Lake Tahoe, California. I kept up my contacts by telephone and email and made regular trips back to Washington to see friends and stay in touch. Thanks to communications technology, the Internet and airlines, I kept working with McLaughlin. As my perspective expanded beyond the Washington Beltway, the challenge of producing two weekly television shows became even more satisfying. My journalistic work expanded into feature writing and investigative pieces for magazines like John F. Kennedy Jr.'s *George, The American Spectator*, and *Reader's Digest*. I wrote a book on the role of First Ladies in presidential politics and co-authored a book, with Elizabeth, on the history of Tibet's struggle for independence from China. I am now a full-time writer and artist.

* * *

A myth of inevitability about Reagan's 1984 reelection victory arose and solidified over the years, like layers of sediment turning to stone. Incumbency and the economy's strong comeback were credited for making Reagan an all-but-invincible candidate. But there was nothing inevitable about it. It took hard work, luck, daring, and risk to get Ronald Reagan reelected in 1984.

Before Reagan, America had three failed presidencies in a row. Richard Nixon left office in disgrace; incumbent president Gerald Ford beat Reagan for the 1976 GOP nomination but then went on to lose the general election; and incumbent president Jimmy Carter lost office after only one term. Incumbency is only an advantage if people like your policies and character; otherwise it's an albatross around your neck.

If the economic recovery alone were enough to make Reagan's reelection inevitable, it wasn't apparent in the polls in late 1983 and early 1984. Voters preferred former astronaut and U.S. senator John Glenn over Ronald Reagan in those match-ups. If Glenn had won the Democratic nomination, history might be different. If Mondale had chosen Glenn or Gary Hart as his running mate, he might have been more competitive against Reagan and Bush. If Geraldine Ferraro's background had been blemish-free, she might have attracted more support to the ticket.

The magnitude of Reagan's popular vote and Electoral College victory over Mondale and Ferraro has obscured the many turning points in the 1984 presidential contest in which events might have gone the other way. The age issue had the potential to alter the election if Reagan had stumbled as badly in the second debate as he did in the first.

In September of 1984, the CIA issued a report through the President's Foreign Intelligence Advisory Board (PFIAB) on the state of the Soviet Union. It painted a bleak picture of the Soviet economy's inability to sustain growth, its widening ethnic and nationality divisions, declining Russian population growth, and its overall economic decline. CIA Director Bill Casey worked closely with PFIAB on the report, which represented his belief about the eventual demise of the USSR. It was a belief Reagan shared.

Some of Ronald Reagan's greatest achievements—arms reduction agreements with the Soviets, seizing the opportunity created by Mikhail Gorbachev's era of glasnost, the historic trip to Moscow—were turning points that marked the beginning of the end of the decades-long Cold War.

Without a second term in office, none of these things would have happened as they did.

But the second term also featured the Iran-Contra affair, turmoil in the White House with the firing of Chief of Staff Don Regan, a sharp dip in the president's approval ratings, and a domestic agenda consumed by the imperative of political survival. After passage of the 1986 tax reform bill, Reagan's was largely a caretaker presidency in terms of domestic policy.

In the fall of 1988, when Reagan was campaigning for Vice President George Bush, I was asked to help the presidential advance team plan an open-air political rally in Cherry Hill, New Jersey. At the time, I was working on a presidential campaign in Costa Rica, but I agreed to do one last trip for the Gipper.

We pulled out all the stops. For the event's climax we had skydivers holding flares with red, white and blue plumes of smoke, fireworks, a giant American flag seeming to rise effortlessly into the sky, and a large brass band. The audience went nuts at the extravaganza, and Reagan grinned with delight.

Chief of Staff Ken Duberstein came over to me while Reagan watched the parachutists.

"Whoa, that was almost over the top," he said, smiling like a kid at the circus, "or maybe it was over the top."

All of us on the team knew it was going to be the last time we created a campaign event for President Ronald Reagan. There's nothing inevitable about a dynamite political rally. We gave it the same energy and meticulous planning we would have if he were running for a third term.

Index

Page numbers in **bold italics** indicate pages with illustrations

A and B Team 77
ABC 18, 142, 159
Abdul Enterprises, Inc. 116
ABSCAM 116
Adams, John Quincy 2
advertising: adult 230; campaign 20–22, 27, 45; negative 65; television 21–22, 92, 115
African American 8–10, 46, 95, 102–103, 124, 186, 229
age issue 22, 142, 165, 175–176, 179–180, 195–196, 215, 235
Ahearn, Rick 38
Ailes, Roger E. 21, 124, 194–195
Air America 207
Air Force One 28, **45, 163**, 172, 177, 179–180, 185, 214
Air Force Two 187
Air National Guard 166
Albosta, Don 103, 105
Alexander, Don 69–71, 81–82, 125–126, 128, 131, 135, 155
Alexandria, Virginia 38, 110
Alfred A. Knopf 1, 231
Allison, Ed 115–117, 127
Ally & Gargano 20
Alvarado, Francisco 9
Ambrose, Myles 74, 100, 123, 128, 135–136, 140, 149–150, 152, 169–170, 203, 205, 210, 227
American Battle Monuments Commission 26
American Enterprise Institute 104
American Military Cemetery 22, 25, 37–**40**
The American Spectator 234
Andrews Air Force Base 27, 172
anonymous tipsters 4, 74
anti-abortion protestors 139, 156
Apalachin, New York 147
Apalachin Conference 147, 199
appointments, political 62
approval ratings 58, 78–79, 235
AR-15 148
Argentina 149, 231
Arkansas 46, 214–215
Arlington, Virginia 16
arrest records 168

Arthur Young & Co., Inc. 80
arts and entertainment district 228–229
Asbury Park, New Jersey 148
Asher, James 194
Asian crime syndicates 152, 198–210
assassination 33, 38, 153, 174, 195, 200, 213
assault 153
Associated Press 75, 123, 187, 194
Atlanta, Georgia 206
Atlanta Associates, Inc. 206
Atlanta Constitution 194
Attack Meeting 16, 44, 51, 58, 64, 94, 99, 112, 115–116, 129, 138–139, 188
attack on Reagan's religious convictions 52, 56
"attacks on the rights of blacks and other minorities" 173
attorney-client privilege 60
Atwater, Lee Harvey 16, **45**–47, 54, 61, 63, 78, 80, 82–84, 105–106, 108–109, 114, 134–136, 138–139, 141–145, 156, 162, 179, 190, 200, 203, 216, 226; "a spy" 115
au pair 136–137
Australia 64, 208–209
Austria 231
Axis powers 24
Ayatollah Khomeini 65

B-17 "Flying Fortress" bomber 24–25, 30, 33
B-Grade movie actor 17
Bacharach, Judy 52–53
Backpage 230
Bakaly, Charles II 29–30
Baker, Howard 112
Baker, James A. III **15**–16, 39, 63, 65, 81–82, 104, 108, 112, 117, 136, 139–140, 144, 159–**160**, 161, 163–165, 179, 194–195, 214–**215**, 226
Baldrige, Malcolm 113, 115
Baltimore Sun 195
Bane, Anita 73
Bane, Howard 73–74, 121, 174, 232
Barber, Cliff 129, 157–158, 165–170, 176, 190–191, 203, 205
Barlett, Don 95–97, 146, 155–156, 158
Baroody, Mike 112

Barr, William 3
Barrett, Wayne 221–222
Barris, George 149
"basket of deplorables" 1
Bastone, William 221–222
Batavia, New York 226
Battle of Corregidor 66
Bauman, Arnold 193
Baxter, Terry 185
Bayard Street 199
Bayer, Michael 54, 67–68, 129, 134, 146
Bayeux, France 25
Le Bayeux hotel 25, 27, 34
Bayeux tapestry 31
BBDO 20
"Bear" 21–22, 27
Bear Stearns 85
Beck Is Back 81
Beijing 47, 204
Beirut, Lebanon 26, 140, 142, 182, 224
Belgian 117
Beltway 46, 143, 175, 226, 234
Bible 226
"biggest busts in history" 68
The Birdcage 64
Black, Charles 108, 226
Black, Manafort, Stone & Kelly 226
Black ministers 9
Black Panthers 124
blackmail 149, 227
Blacks for Reagan-Bush '80 7, 55, 103
Blankley, Anthony 14, 159
Bloody Mary 135
BO-NA-TE Distributors 193
Board of County Commissioners 228
"body broker" 154
Boland Amendment 232
Bolton, Roger 112
Bombay gin 88
Bonanno crime syndicate 222–223
Bonavena, Oscar 148–149
Boogie Man: The Lee Atwater Story 226
Boston, Massachusetts 192
Boston Globe 211
Bowery and Spring Realty Corporation 147
Bradenton Herald 194
Bradley, Bill 46
Brady, James 38, 174
Breslin, Jimmy 122
Breslin, Rosemary 122
bribes 131, 151
Broder, David 46, 176, 195–196
Bronx 147, 151
Bronze Star 8, 25, 70
Brooks Brothers 110
brothel 148–149
Brymer, Willard Ross 148–149
Bucchianieri, Virgil 148–149
Buchanan, Angela Marie "Bay" 210, 220
Buckingham Palace 22

Buckley, John 48–49, 112–113, 210
Bucky the Wonder Horse 187
Buenos Aires, Argentina 231
building code violations 121
bullet-proof jackets 200
bullion depository 166
Bumpers, Dale 46
burlesque club 167
Bury St. Edmunds, England 24
Bush, Barbara 187–188
Bush, George H.W. 61, 84, *86*, 112, 115, 125, 165, 176, 177, 187–188, 226, 232, 235
Bush, Jeb 8
Business Roundtable 113
Butler Aviation 165
BuzzFeed 3

The Cabin in the Sky 148
Cabinet 13, 64, 88, 102, 105, 112–113, 115, 162, 213–214
Cabinet Room 85
Caen, France 35
La Cage aux Folles 64
California 10, 13, 20, 42–43, 53, 56–57, 65, 124, 142, 214, 216–218, 224
California Democratic Primary 22
Callahan, Bill 75, 135, 203
calvados 35
Camp David 159–*160*, 162
Camp Lejeune, North Carolina 26–27, 182
campaign: advertising 26–22, 27, 45; contributors 74, 95, 128–129, 131, 152, 169, 199, 206; negative campaigning 1–2
Canada 153
"cancer closet" 123
Cannon House Office Building 118
Canton, China 204
Capitol Hill 38, 69, 94, 110, 112, 116–118, 126, 129, 174, 207
"capo di tutti capi" 51, 147
car bomb 66
Caribbean 119
Carpenters Union 152
Carter, Amy 18
Carter, Jimmy 15, 17–18, 65, 103–105, 117, 166, 234
Casey, Bill 104, 209, 235
Castellano, Paul 222
Catalano, Michael 154
Catholic bishops 139–140, 143
Catholic faith 52
Catholic voters 58, 60
Caucasians 124
CBS 26–27, 29–31, 37–40, 90, 93–94, 142
CBS Evening News 33
Central America 195, 207
Central Intelligence Agency (CIA) 3, 53, 61, 73–74, 77, 104, 195, 207, 209, 227, 231–232, 235
Century Plaza Hotel *217–218*

Chan, Edward Tse Chiu 152–153, 198–208, 210–212, 223, 227
Channell, Carl Russell "Spitz" 232, 233
Chapman, Bruce 15, 231
character witness 147
Charles de Gaulle Airport 24, 40
Charlotte Observer 194
Charrow, Bob 81, 117
Chatham Street 223
Cheney, Richard 94
Chennault, Anna 202, 207–208
Chennault, Claire 207–208
Chernenko, Andrei 19
Cherry Hill, New Jersey 235
Chicago, Illinois 65, 153, 199–200
Chin, Peter 151
China 47, 61, 204, 223, 234
"China Lobby" 207
China-Mott Associates 206
China Royal 204
Chinese Americans 152, 201–203, 227
Chinese Help in National Affairs 204
Chinese political activists 232
Chinese secret service 205
Chinese Welfare Council 202, 204
Chrysler K-Car 106–107
Church, Misty 162
Churchill, Winston 171
Cincinnati Enquirer 194
Citizens for the Republic (CFTR) 12–13, 42, 85, 157, 200
Civil Air Transport 207
Clarey, Don 171
Cleveland, Ohio 116
Cleveland Place 86, 152, 193
Cline, Ray 104
Clinton, Hillary 1, 3
Clinton administration 228
CNN 49
cocaine 200
Cockney Pearly Kings 84
cocktail hour 88, 107
CODEL 166
Cody, Wyoming 42
Coelho, Tony 142–143, 176
Cohn, Roy 49–*51*, 52–53, 58, 60, 65–66, *72*, 75–76, 85–86, *87*, 93, 152, 169, 190, 192–193, 203, 212
Cold War 19, 25, 235
Coleman, Lovida H., Jr. 225
Colgate, Lisa 78, 124–125, 131–132
Colleville-sur-Mer, France 24
Colombo crime syndicate 148, 206, 222–223
Coloni, Dominick 190
Colored Town 8
Columbia University 129
Columbus Day 165, 187
Committee on Standards of Official Conduct of the United States House of Representatives 113

Committee to Reelect the President (CREEP) 90, 142
Communism 171
Community Redevelopment Agency (CRA) 8, 228–229
Conable, Barber 114–120, 126, 129, 141, 226–227
confederacy of pirates 55
"confidence coefficient" 17
Conforte, Joe 148–149
Conforte, Sally 148
Congress 48, 54, 70, 88, 103, 161, 191, 221
Congressional Black Caucus 117
congressional campaigns 74–75, 131, 193, 199, 210, 221
congressional investigation 103
Congressional Record 54
conservatorships 95, 121, 131, 141, 143, 157
SS *Constitution* 151
Continental King Lung Group 200
Contras 19, 195, 207, 224, 231–232
Cooksey, Sherrie 82
Copley News 13, 58
corruption 66, 95–96, 122, 149, 228–230, 233
Costa Rica 235
countdown meeting 28, 30, 173–174, 177
cowboys 96, 113, 156
Coyle, Tim 28–29, 31–34, 39
Crimea 232
criminal history 137
criminal probe 2, 8–10, 127
criminal youth gang 153
Crippen, Robert 180
Cronkite, Walter 33–34
Crossfire Hurricane 3
Cuban Americans 10, 228
Cuban Missile Crisis 18, 25, 104, 195
Cuero, Texas 66
Cunningham, Larry 37–40
Cuomo, Mario 46
cut-outs 66

D-Day 22–41
Dallas, Texas 81–82, 114, 152, 193, 207
Dallas Times Herald 194
D'Amato, Alfonse 100, 202, 221
Damm, Helene Von 57
Darman, Richard G. 22–23, 45, 112, 159–*160*, 161–165, 179, 194–195
Davis, Fredrick 9
Davis, Loyal 57
Davis, Michele 48–50, 64, 101
The Day After 18
Dayton, Ohio 173, 179–181, 185–186
Dayton Arcade 175
Daytona, Florida 228
DC 101 110
Deacon, Richard 205
Deane, Deborah 78–79
death threats 157–158, 168–169

Deaver, Michael K. *15*–16, 20, 27, 39–40,
58, 60, 81, 108, 161–164, 172, 179, 184–186,
224–225; theory of presidential events 22–23
debate, vice-presidential 100, 125, 145, 165,
176–177, 187
"Debategate" 103–104
debates, presidential 18, 65, 103, 105, 159–160,
162–167, 171–172, 175–176, 190–191, 194–196,
235; briefing books 103, 105; strategy 163
Decision Making Information (DMI) 14, 78
DeFede, Jim 8–10
Delahanty, Thomas 38, 174
Del Carlo, Bob 148
Della Femina Traviano 20–21
Dellacroce, Aniello 85–87, 154, 193, 214, 222
DelliBovi, Al 74, 100, 102, 143
DeLutro, Anthony 154
Democratic coalition 44
Democratic Congressional Campaign
Committee (DCCC) 142
Democratic National Committee (DNC) 1
Democratic National Convention 56, 65, 188
Democratic Party 89, 142, 155, 168, 220
Democratic Primaries 22, 36, 48
Democratic voters, women 60, 78–79
Department of Education 85, 159, 161, 231
Department of Health and Human Services
(HHS) 227
Department of Housing and Urban
Development (HUD) 102, 106–107
Department of Health, Education and Welfare
(HEW) 17
Department of Justice (DOJ) 3, 67, 74, 103,
149–150, 222–223
Department of State 103, 232
Department of Transportation (DOT) 7, 54, 56
Department of the Treasury 74
Deshler, Ohio 177, 184
Detroit, Michigan *50*
Deukmejian, George 20
DeVasto, Frannie 168, 189
DeVasto, Michael 167–168, 189
"Dewey Beats Truman" 171
DeWine, Mike 179
dial-up modem 48, 101
Diaz, Manny 229
DiBernardo, Robert 222
"dirty tricks" 90, 140, 142, 144, 146, 155–156,
190
"divide black and white, rich and poor,
Christian and Jew" 17
Dole, Elizabeth 224
Dole, Robert 84, 11–113, 115
Domenici, Pete 115
Donatelli, Frank *15*
Doubleday 103
Drug Enforcement Administration 200
Duberstein, Ken 112, 235
The Dubliner 207
Ducks, Tony 131

Duggin, Thelma 103
Dulles Airport 24
dumpster divers 65, 103
Durham, John 2–3
Dusenberry, Phil 20

East Coast 189, 216
Eastern Europe 171, 232
Eastwood, Clint 149
economic recovery 65
Edinburgh, Duke of 26
1800 M Street 125
18th Airborne 7
8th Army Air Force Bomber Command 24
Eisenhower, Dwight 196
Election Day 2, 21, 66, 79, 98, 114, 116, 135–136,
162, 191, 197, 211–212, 216–219, 223
Electoral College 21, 44, 162, 176, 216, 218,
235
Electronics Industry Association 28
Elizabeth II, Queen 26
Elmets, Doug 42
Elmore, Minnesota 52
embassy hostages, Iran 65, 104–105, 166, 232
enforcers 154, 200, 205
England 13, 22, 25, 31
English Channel 25, 35, 38
English pub 207
Equal Rights Amendment 173
Eskew, Tucker 138–139, 200
Ethics in Government Act of 1978 1, 76, 80, 82,
92, 119, 220–221, 224
Ethnic Voters Division 200
Eureka College Scholarship Program *51*
Europe 18, 22, 110, 127–128, 151, 172
Evans & Novak 87
Excelsior Hotel 214–*215*
ex-detectives 74
Executive branch 102, 149–150
Executive Order 198, 223
exit polls 216–217
explosives 140, 172, 182
extortion 153, 199, 222

F Street 207
Farrell, Harold 197
"Father O'Neill" 86
Federal Bureau of Investigation (FBI) 3, 98,
114, 116, 149, 223, 230, 232
Federal Election Commission (FEC) 4, 62, 68,
74–75, 129
Federal Hall, Manhattan 198
Feehan, John 200
Feinstein, Diane 36
felony charges 221
female voters, backlash from 66
feminism 71, 122
Ferber, Jack 99–100
Ferdinand Magellan train car 171–172, 180–186
Ferraro, Antonetta 151, 167–170, 189–190

Ferraro, Dominic 151–152, 167–170, 189–190
Ferraro, Geraldine *49–50, 97*
Ferraro, Nicholas 123
Ferraro: My Story 5
"Ferraro's Press Strategy" 80
Fielding, Fred 82
Fifth Amendment 230
financial disclosure forms 75–76, 80–83, 88, 93, 114, 116–120, 128–130, 139, 143
financial irregularities 114, 119–120, 126, 131, 133, 134, 141, 156–157
Fineman, Howard 89–90, 143
Finkelstein, Art 100
First Amendment 173
First Lady's Council on Drug Abuse Education 59
Fischer, Dave 39, 179
"Five Dragons" era 199
Flint, Michigan *50, 97*
Florida 171, 228–230
Florida Third Circuit Court of Appeals 229
Flying Tigers 207
focus groups 10
foot soldiers 67
Ford, Gerald 15, 113, 234
Ford Administration 38
Ford factory 179
Fordham University School of Law 151
Foreign Intelligence Surveillance Act (FISA) 3
foreign interference in elections 2, 18–19
foreign policy 194
Foreign Service 12–15
Forest Hill 122
Fort Bragg, North Carolina 7
Fort Knox 166
Fort Lauderdale, Florida 171
Fossedal, Gregory 85, 95
Fox, Charles 179
Fox, Sharon 179
Frajo Associates Inc. (FRAJO) 86, 153, 193, 204, 206
France 24–41
France, Bill 228
Francke, Linda Bird 5
Fratianno, Jimmy "The Weasel" 149
Freedom of Information Act 102, 150
"Fritzbusters" 140
Fuller, Craig 113
Fulton, Missouri 171
Fund for Victory 226
Funzi 131
Fusion GPS 1, 3

G-7 23
Galante, Carmine 51
Gallup 214
Gambino, Carlo 154, 205
Gambino crime syndicate 51, 67, 85–87, 130–131, 152, 154–155, 193, 201, 205–206, 222–223
Gambino-Triad drug connection 205, 209

gambling illegal, 86, 153–154, 167–168, 199, 203
Gambling with History 103
Gandhi, Indira 213
Gangel, Jamie 138, 140–144, 155–156, 200
Garden of the Missing 26, 29
Garrick, Robert 105
Gartland, John 173–174, 177–178
gay bar 64
gender 56, 61
Gender Gap 58–59, 79, 218
Genovese crime syndicate 51, 154, 206, 222–223
George 234
George Washington Parkway, Virginia 14
George Washington University Hospital 175
Georgia 206
Gergen, David 104
German 110
Germany 24–25, 166
Gerry: A Woman Making History 122
Ghost Shadows 153–154, 199–201, 203–206, 210
Ghostbusters 140
Gin Beck restaurant 153
The Gipper 215, 235
Giuliani, Rudy 214, 222–223
glasnost 235
Glenn, John 15, 234
Gold, Vic 46, 188
Gold Coast Railroad Museum 171
Golden Triangle 205, 207
Goldfinger 199
Gorbachev, Mikhail 235
Graham, Anne 58–59, 161, 231
Grand Fortune restaurant 204
grand jury investigation 130–131, 148, 155, 157, 197, 211
Grand Promenade Entertainment District 229
Graux, Nancy 117–118
Graux, Yves 117–118
Gray, Alfred M., Jr. 27
Greece 56, 227
Green, Asa 95–97
Green, Ash 1, 231
Green, Bill 201–202
Greener, Bill 46, 54, 67–68, 71, 74, 101, 106, 113, 135, 216, 219
Greensboro Daily News 194
Grenada 27
Groomes, Karen 172
ground-launched cruise missiles 18
Grubert, Arthur 74
Guest, Achille 124–125, 129, 153–154, 203
"Guinea Chasers" 74, 121, 128, 203
gumshoes 136
guns 74, 133, 147–148, 152–153, 167, 199, 222

Hackman, Larry 121
"Hail to the Chief" 179–180

Haiphong harbor, Vietnam 88
Hair of Capitol Hill 117
Haldeman, H.R. 114
Halloween 213
Halper, Stefan 104
Hammer, Joshua 122
Hannaford, Peter 105
Hanoi, Vietnam 88
Harnisch, Robert 156–157
Harp lager 207–208
Hart, Gary 17, 22, 36, 44, 46, 48, 234
Hart, Steve 28, 33–34, 173, 179–180, 184
Harvard University 70
Hatch Act 67, 102
Hawtin, Guy 86–87, 169–170, 188–189, 191–192, 211
"Heartland Express" 177, 179–186
The Heartland Special 171, *181*, 185
Heckler, Peggy 227
hecklers 140, 142, 144
Hemings, Sally 2
Henkel, Bill 39, 172, 179, 184
heroin 199–201, 205
Hicks, Christopher 112
high crimes and misdemeanors 103
Highway 87 169
hijacking 223, 231
Hinckley, John, Jr. 38, 174
Hispanic Americans 214, 218
Hogan, Frank 71, 122–123, 129, 134, 150–151, 156, 203
Hollywood 31, 50, 161, 212
Hong, Alfred 201–202, 204
Hong Kong 152–153, 198–200
"hooked up to jumper cables" 61
Hooley, James 172, 179, 184
Hope, Bob 215–216
Hopkins, Keven 42, 112, 115
Horowitz, Michael 3
hostage incidents 231
Hotel Washington 92–93
House Ethics Committee 76, 81, 83, 88–89, 94, 113–117, 125, 128–130, 132–133, 220–221
House Judiciary Committee 198
House of Representatives 75, 89, 103, 218
House Post Office and Civil Service Subcommittee 103
House Select Committee to Investigate Covert Arms Transactions with Iran 232
House Un-American Activities Committee 50
Houston Post 194
Hudson River 166, 189
Huffy Corporation 179
Human Events 161–162
Hume, James 23
Hunan Gardens 204
Hunt, Terence 187
Hyatt Hotel, Washington, D.C. 16, 107
Hyatt Regency Hotel, Louisville, Kentucky 163

Iacocca, Lee 106
IBM Selectric typewriter 48, 94, 181
"icy stare" 59
Illinois 44, 46
immigrant success story 72
impeachment 103
"In the Matter of Representative Geraldine A. Ferraro" 220–221
inauguration, presidential 99
incumbency 234
Independent Counsel 140, 224, 232
Independents 220; women voters 60
India 213
Indian embassy 213
Inspector General's report 3
intelligence community 104
intelligence operation 104
Internal Revenue Service 70, 76, 127, 214
International Brotherhood of Teamsters 98
International Longshoreman's Association 187
International Republican Institute 232
investigative assets 75, 121–122
Iran 33, 105, 166
Iran-Contra affair 224, 232–235
Ireland 22, 125
Irish pub 207
"Iron Curtain" speech 171–172
Italian Americans 58, 60, 76, 133, 218
"It's morning in America" 21, 92
Iwo Jima 114

Jackson, Andrew 2
Jackson, Jesse 46–47
Jackson, Rachel 2
Jackson Memorial Medical Center 10
Jacobs, Haskell 206
Jacobson, Mark 204–205, 208
Jamaica 227
Jaroslavsky, Rich 142
Jefferson, Thomas 1
Jefferson Memorial 14
Jesuit priest 233
Jesus 57
"Jewel of the Sierra" 56
Jim Crow 8
Johnson, James 142–143
Jones, Dan 104
journalistic integrity 155
Juskovitz, Jeannette 206
J.W. Marriott 95

Kabuki Theater 34
Kalb, Marvin 142
Kansas 194
Kansas City, Kansas 194
Kassof, Edwin 95
Kaufman, Irving 193, 198–199
Keble College 155
Kennedy, John Fitzgerald 33, 147, 176, 195
Kennedy, John Fitzgerald, Jr. 234

Kennedy, Robert F. 147
Kennedy, Ted 161
Kennedy Center 62
Kennedy International Airport 85
Kentucky 159, 163
Kentucky Center for the Arts 159
Kerner, Gabriela 110
Khachigian, Ken 42–44, 46–47, 101, 112, 179, 181–*182*, 183
kickbacks 131, 150–151
Kiev, Ukraine 232
King, Martin Luther, Jr. 33
Kohl, Helmut 31
Korean War 25
Kraft, Joseph 176
Ku Klux Klan 17
Kuhn, Jim 28, 38–40
Kuomintang 204, 207–208
Kwitny, Jonathan 130, 134
Kyrgyzstan 232
Kyrillos, Joe 125

Labor Day 112
Lacey, Michael 230
Lafayette Street 193, 221
LaForte, Joseph "Joe the Cat," Sr. 86–87, 130–131, 152, 154–155, 193
Lake, Jim 46–48, 101, 112, 124, 141, 164
Lake Tahoe, California 56–57
landslide 145, 162, 211
Lanusse, Alejandro 149
LaRosa, Michael "Mike the Baker" 95–97, 131
Latin America 128
Latinos 124
Latona, Lawrence J. 86, 130, 154–155
Laviano, Dominick 189
law enforcement 149
Lawndale, California 53
Laxalt, Carol 56
Laxalt, Paul 56–57, 115, 164, 214–*215*
LBJ Bar and Grill 16
"Leadership 80" 103
leaks 11, 81–82, 141–145, 155, 168, 203, 211
Lebanon 27, 182
Lexington Herald-Leader 194
Libertarians 220
Library of Congress 67
Lima, Ohio 177, 181–182
Lincoln Mark IV Bugazzi 149
Lincoln Town Car 74
Lithgow, John 18
"Little Italy" 147, 193
Little Rock, Arkansas 214–*215*
loan sharking 223
loans, illegal 75, 119, 156
lobbying, illegal 225
Loews-Anataole Hotel 81, 84
London, England 12, 64, 84, 128, 175, 200, 208
Longfellow Avenue 151
Los Angeles, California 12–13, 44, 56

Los Angeles Herald-Examiner 194
Los Angeles Times 197
Louie, Nicky 153–154, 199–200, 205, 208
Louisville, Kentucky 159, 163, 172
loyalty 108
Lucchese crime syndicate 222–223
Luciano, Charles "Lucky" 189
Luftwaffe 33

Maalox 57
MacDonald, John D. 230
machine gun 33, 36
Mad Max 110
Madison Avenue 20
Madrid, Spain 128, 175
Mafia 11, 51, 60, 66–68, 74, 85–87, 89–90, 93, 96–98, 122–123, 130–131, 134, 140, 146–155, 166, 168, 189–194, 196–197, 199, 211, 221–224; Mafia hit team 222
Magruder, Jeb 90
Mahe, Eddie 46–47
The Mall 111
Maloney, Gary 54
Manafort, Paul 108, 226
Manhattan 131, 134, 156, 197–198, 221
manslaughter 149
Maranzano, Salvatore 147
Marine Corps 27
Marine One 26, 36, 180
Marlboro 13, 49, 81, 101, 111, 123, 145, 179, 192, 201
Marlette Lake, Nevada 56
Martelli, Charles "One-Eyed Charlie" 222
Marx Brothers 161
Marxist influence 50
Maryland 73, 153
Marymount Academy 151
Marymount Manhattan College 151
Matalin, Mary 226
McCarthy, Joseph 50, 212
McCarthy, Timothy 38, 174
McCormack, Dave 121
McEwen, Bob 179
McEwen, Elizabeth 179
McGee, Travis 230
McKay, John 224
McLaughlin, John 88, 233–234
The McLaughlin Group 88, 233
McLaughlin's One on One 233
McManus, Michael A. 20–21, 49–50, 60, 82
Meese, Edwin III 16, 140, 224, 231
Meet the Press 142
Memorial Bridge 110
Mercedes 190E 29, 32, 226
Messerschmitt fighters 24
Messner, Tom 20
Metro–Dade County Commission 228
Miami, Florida 7–11, 44, 127, 141, 228–230
Miami–Dade County Police 228–230
Miami–Dade State Attorney 8, 228–229

Miami Herald 7–10, 194, 230
Miami International Airport 228
Miami New Times 9–10, 230
Miami Worldcenter 230
The Michael Douglas Show 21
Michigan 49–50, 103, 159
Mickenberg, Murray 206
Mickey Mouse 225
Mieczkowski, Yanek 226
military coup 231
Mill Street 189
Miller, Richard 232–233
Milwaukee Journal 194
Minnesota 47, 52, 162, 214–215, 218
Minuteman missile 25
Mirra, Anthony 154
misdemeanor charges 221
Mission District 124
Mission Rebels in Action 124
Missouri 171, 191, 214
Mitchell, Andrea 69
Mitterand, Francois 25–26, 29, 39
Mo & Joe's 225
"mobbed up" 53
mobsters 60, 65–66, 85–87, 90, 122, 129,
    130–131, 189, 192, 221–224
moles 104, 109
Mondale, Joan 210
Mondale, Walter 17, 22, 42–44, 47–48, 52, 65,
    79, 96, 112, 115, 129, 140, 142, 162, 194–195,
    196, 211, 217, 220, 235
money laundering 153, 230
Montgomery County, Maryland 153
Mont-Saint-Michel, France 32–34
moon landing 33
Moral Majority 64
Morgan, Lewis & Bocktius 69
Morgenthau, Robert 156–157
Morris, Dan 46
Moscow, USSR 235
motorcade, presidential 178–179, 184
Mott Street 152–154, 199, 204, 222
Mudd, Roger 142
Mulberry Street 86, 93, 130, 154–155, 193, 222
Municipal Auditorium, Kansas City 194–196
Murat, Princess Caroline 125
murder 153, 222–223
Murdoch, Rupert *72*, 190–191
Murphy, Dennis T. 229
Mustang II 107, 111, 150
Mustang Ranch 148–149
MX missile 231
My Name Is Geraldine Ferraro 123
myth of inevitability 234

Napoleon's axiom 47
narcotics 154
NASCAR 228
National Aeronautics and Space Administra-
    tion (NASA) 180

National Airport 81, 165, 170, 186
National Archaeological Museum 118
National Association of Counties Building
    (NACO) 16, 208
National Chairman of Chinese Americans for
    Reagan-Bush 202
National Commission on Excellence in
    Education 159
National Director of Chinese-American voter
    registration 200, 202–203, 210, 227
National Endowment for Democracy 232
National Geographic 31
National Organization for Women 44
National Security Agency (NSA) 224
National Security Council (NSC) 104, 179
Native American artifacts 118–119
Nazco, Felix 10
NBC 69, 78, 134–144, 146, 155, 203, 211
NBC Nightly News 140
negative-to-positive ratio 61, 79, 132
Nena 110
net worth 85
Nevada 12, 56, 127, 148–149
New England 233
New Jersey 44, 99, 148, 185, 235
New York 61, 71, 75, 97, 107, 143, 198–199, 201,
    205, 222, 226
New York City 44, 71, 74–75, 85, 99, 129, 134,
    152, 166, 203–204; Chinatown 152–153, 204,
    208, 210, 223
New York City Real Estate Bureau 150–151
New York County District Attorney 71,
    122–123
New York Daily News 122
New York Department of State 141
New York Magazine 85–86, 93
New York Ninth Congressional District 100
New York Police Department 74, 147, 153,
    155, 199
New York Post 72, 143, 169–170, 176, 188–191,
    197, 210–212, 214
New York Republican Party 203
New York Republican Party's Heritage Groups
    Council 201
New York State Supreme Court 221
New York Times 75, 95, 104, 129, 135, 142–143,
    150, 156, 175–176, 187, 197, 210–212
New York Tribune 76
New York University 85
Newburgh, New York 71, 147, 151, 166–169,
    188–190
Newport Beach, California 42
news conference 68, 85, 163–164
Newsday 75, 191, 194
Newsweek 89
Ng Fook Funeral, Inc. 204
Nicaragua 19, 207
nickel-and-dime store 71, 151–152, 167
911 tapes 229
"99 Luftballons" 110

"99 Red Balloons" 110
Nixon, Richard 70, 88, 90, 113–114, 174,
  233–234
Nixon White House 43, 88
"Nixon's Padre" 233
Nofziger, Bonnie 35–36
Nofziger, Franklyn C. vi, 12–*15*, 17–*20*, 35–36,
  44, 48, 58–59, 74, 88, 90, 101, 103, 112–113,
  115–116, 135–136, 138–140, 142, 144, 174, 188,
  200–201, 212, 224–225, 232
Nofziger & Bragg 224
Normandy, France 22–41, 47–48, 65, 111, 173
Normandy advance team 28
North Atlantic Treaty Organization
  (NATO) 18–19
North Carolina 26–27, 182
North Oaks, Minnesota 215
Northrop, Stuart 179
nostalgia 17, 22
Novak, Robert 87–89, 95, 143
nuclear arms control 19, 235
Nuclear Freeze Movement 18–19, 100
nuclear fuel 233
nuclear weapons 18–19, 22–23, 100, 173, 231,
  232–233

Ocean City, Maryland 73
"October Surprise" 65, 103–105
Office of Strategic Services (OSS) 104, 125
Ohio 44, 116, 171–173, 177, 179–186
Ohr, Bruce 3
Ohr, Nellie 3
Old Executive Office Building 12, 21, 88, 104,
  231
Old Montgomery County Courthouse 173, 179
Olympics 18–19, 44, 56
Omaha Beach 22–41
Omaha World Herald 194
On Leong Tong 198–199, 202–205
one-minute speeches 94
O'Neill, Hugh 38
O'Neill, Tip 36, 48, 116–118, 161, 176, 192, 216
operational security 108
opium 207
opposition research 1–5, 7, 17, 43, 48, 54, 101,
  105–106, 121, 146
Orange County, California 12
"Order of Distinction" 227
Oregon 78
organized crime 1, 11, 5, 66–68, 71, 74–76,
  85–87, 89–90, 93, 95, 128–129, 130–131,
  133–134, 146–155, 169, 189–194, 196–201,
  203–212, 221–224, 227
Organized Crime and Illicit Narcotics Report
  154
Osborne, Kathy 179
Ottawa, Ohio 182–183
Oval Office *43, 54, 72*, 79, 140, 227
Overtown, Miami 8, 228–230
Oxford University 12, 23–24, 73, 156, 205

P. Zacarro Company, Inc. 71, 85, 130–131, 147,
  151, 154–155, 222
Pacific Coast Highway 13
Page, Carter 3
The Palm 126
Panama 127
Paradise Valley, Arizona 230
Paris, France 24, 40
Parisi, Camillo 152
Parisi, Carmine 152
Pasadena Star-News 194
payments, illegal 233
Penelas, Alex 7, 228
Pennsylvania Avenue 16, 93, 167
Perot, Ross 232
Perrysburg, Ohio 177, 184–185
Pershing II missiles 18
persona non grata 38
Petrillo, Dominick "The Gap" 189
Phelan, Alice 95, 141, 157
pheromones 124
Philadelphia Civic Center 176
Philadelphia Inquirer 94–97, 121–122, 128–129,
  131, 133, 136, 140–143, 146, 150, 155–158,
  167–170, 176, 190, 193–194, 197, 211–212
Philip, Prince 26
Philippines 66
philosophy, politics and economics (PPE) 56
photo opportunity 80, 181–185
Pierce, Samuel, Jr. 102, 107
Pinkerton, Jim 45, 108, 135, 226
Pitts, Milton 117
Pittsburgh Post-Gazette 194
Plachy, Sylvia 204
Plasencia, Jorge 228
P.L.S. Clothing Manufacturing Company 147
Poindexter, John 179
Pointe du Hoc, France 26, 30
polarization, racial and ethnic 10
Poli-Grip 215
polls 10, 13–15, 18, 33, 43, 47–48, 53, 60–63,
  78–79, 132, 161–162, 164, 167, 176, 188, 195,
  211, 214, 218, 232
popular vote 176, 218, 235
pornography 51, 76, 186, 193, 221–222
Port Authority of New York and New Jersey
  156, 197
Portland, Oregon 78
Potowmack Landing 14
POW 66
Powell, Edlow 124
Prado Museum 118
presidential advance team 183, 235
President's Commission on Organized
  Crime 66–67, 197–121, 203, 212, 223
President's Foreign Intelligence Advisory
  Board (PFIAB) 235
press advance 28
press coverage 22
"the Prince of Darkness" 87

prison 131
pro-choice position 52
probate papers 62
Profaci, Joseph 130, 133, 147–148, 151, 193
Profaci, Salvatore 131, 133, 147–148, 151, 193
Prohibition 189
prostitution 230
"protection" 153
protestors 142–144, 156, 173–174, 177, 231–231
"Prouder, Stronger, Better" 21
public right to know 96, 192
Pulitzer prize 96
Punjab 232
Purple Heart 8

Queens, New York 61, 221
Queens County District Attorney 123
"Quixote" 64
Quotes and Votes project 54, 67

racism accusations 17–18
racketeering 95, 222
"Rally Against Reagan" 173
R&R Partners 21
rape 153
Rating the First Ladies: The Women Who
    Influenced the Presidency 2
ratings: negative 79, 84, 132; positive 79, 132
Ravenite Social Club 154–155, 214
Rawhide 39
Reader's Digest 234
Reagan, Doria 218
Reagan, Nancy 1, 20, 22, 25–26, 29, 37–40, 48,
    50, 51–53, 55–57, 59–60, 66, 69, 76, 81, 83,
    93, 108, 160, 163–165, 182, 188, 214, 217–218,
    220, 223, 225, 228, 231
Reagan, Ronald 15, 22, 25–26, 29, 37–40, 43,
    50, 51, 54, 56, 72, 86, 108, 139–140, 159–160,
    163, 164–165, 179–180, 181–182, 186, 194,
    196, 214–216, 215, 216, 217–218, 226–227,
    231, 234–235; Achilles' heel 59; Christianity
    40, 52, 57, 68–69, 77; education initiative
    161–162; humor 19–20, 68, 184–185, 195, 214
Reagan-Bush '80 campaign 28, 42, 50, 52–53,
    65, 99, 103–105, 128, 142
Reagan-Bush '84 campaign 1, 4, 12, 54, 101,
    128, 130, 140, 144, 190, 201, 210–211, 232;
    headquarters 16, 23, 42, 48, 67, 73–74, 92,
    121, 133, 138, 146, 159, 213
"Reaganomics" 65
The Reagans: A Political Portrait 105
real estate developers 79
recusal 117–118
"Red Scare" 50
reelection: results 218, 234; strategy 42–47, 53,
    58, 69, 75
Regan, Don 112, 227, 231, 235
Republic of China Air Force 207
Republican National Committee 13, 54,
    67–68, 74, 101–102, 146, 216, 226

Republican National Convention 12, 69,
    78–80, 84–91, 86–87, 95, 132
Republican Party 66, 115, 166, 220
Reuters 132
"reverse spike" 210
Rhode Island 233
Rhodes, James 179
Riney, Hal 20–21
riots 232
Rivers, Phil 26, 37, 39
Robards, Jason 18
Roberts, Benjamin 15, 73, 123–124, 136, 187
Roberts, George F. 221
Roberts, John 55, 87, 163
Roberts, Patricia Harris 17
Roberts, Robert 24–25
Roberts, Sam 210
Robertson, Ron 77, 82, 117–118, 176
Rochester, Minnesota 214–215
Rockwell, Norman 52
Rodino, Peter 198
Rodriguez, Rosa 229
Rogers, John F.W. 179
Rogich, Sig 21
Rolex 199
Rollason, Frank 229
Rolling Stone 48
Rollins, Edward J., Jr 1, 12, 48–52, 64–65,
    68–69, 74, 80, 82–84, 87–90, 96, 106, 135–
    136, 138–144, 162, 179, 200, 213, 220, 226, 231
Rolodex 72
Roosevelt, Franklin Delano 171
Roosevelt, Theodore, Jr. 26, 37–39
Roosevelt Room 85
Rose Garden strategy 17, 22, 42, 45, 47
Rosenker, Mark 28, 35–36
Rothwell, Bruce 72, 86
The Roxy 167, 189
"Ruffles and Flourishes" 179–180
Ruge, Daniel 39
Rund, Chuck 4, 60–62, 78–79, 145
Rundle, Katherine F. 8, 228–229
Rushdie, Salman 232
Russia 1–4, 19
Russian intelligence 233
Russo, Sal 231
Russo, Watts & Rollins 231
Ryskind, Allan 161–162
Ryskind, Morrie 161

sabotage 227
Sadat, Anwar 213
Safire, William 175
St. Croix 119
St. John's Hospital 193
St. Louis, Missouri 214–215
St. Louis Globe-Democrat 194
St. Paul, Minnesota 47
Salerno, Anthony "Fat Tony" 51
Samoan 124

San Diego State University 32
San Francisco, California 12, 124
San Jose Mercury News 194
Sandinistas 231
Sands, Nicholas Mario 74, 75, 128, 152, 193–194, 196–197, 222
Sandy, Sherrie 124
Santa Monica, California 12–13
Santiago, Dominic 74, 152, 193–194, 196–197
Saperstein, Mike 85
Saturday radio address 162–163
Schackne, Bob 90, 92–94, 143
Schedule C 102
Schmorr, Roger 185
Screen Actors Guild 50
Scruggs, Richard 228–229
Scully's bar 167, 169
Seattle Times 194
Second Marine Division 27
second term 113, 128, 216, 224, 235
Secret Service 27–28, 30, 37–40, 172–175, 183, 213
Senate 218
Senate Government Operations Committee 154
Senate Judiciary Committee 128, 198
Senate organized crime reports 130
Senate Permanent Subcommittee on Investigations 50, 230
Senate Select Committee on Secret Military Assistance to Iran and the Nicaraguan Opposition 232
senatorial campaigns 221–222
sexism 71, 122, 151
Sharif, Nawaz 232
Shawnee Mission High School 163
Shelby, Rick 124
Shields, Mark 162
shooting, gangland-style 152
Shribman, David 142
Sidney, Ohio 177, 180–181
Sig Sauer 10
Singapore 200
Sino-Soviet split 104
Sixty Minutes 92
Smith, William French 199
"smoking gun" 114
snipers 172
Snyder, Mitch 16
social conservatives 64
Social Security 115
Soo Yuen Benevolent Association 153
Sotirhos, Michael 200–203, 207, 227
South Africa 232
South America 232
South Carolina 61, 114, 138
South Lawn 163
Southern District of New York 222
Soviet diplomats 19
Soviet Union (USSR) 2, 18–19, 207, 232, 235

Space Shuttle *Challenger* 180
Space Shuttle *Columbia* 180
Spaghetti Western 149
Spain 14, 25, 118, 127
Speakes, Larry 39, 179
Special Service Staff 70
speeches, presidential 23
Spence, Floyd 61, 114, 128–129
Spence-Jone, Michele 229
Spencer, Stuart K. 1, 42–*43*, *45*, 52–53, 55, 65–66, 71, 73–74, 78, 81–84, 90, 92–94, 96, 101, 103–104, 106, 114, 118–122, 135–136, 140–141, 143–146, 155, 159–*160*, 169, 190–191, 201, 209, 214–*215*, 223–224, 231
Sperling Breakfast 68
Sri Lanka 232
Star Distributors 76
Stars of David 25
State Department 12, 15
State of the Union addresses 163
Staten Island, New York 222
Steele, Christopher 1–2
Steele dossier 1, 3–4
Stein, Alice Louise 32
Stein, Jacob 140
Steinem, Gloria 122
Steinthal, Eric 190
Stevenson, Adlai 196
sting operation 116
Stirling, Penny 124
Stockman, David 112, 159, 161, 164–165, 194
Stokes, Louis 116–117
Stone, Roger 50, 99–102, 108, 143, 157, 170, 181, 203
Storey County, Nevada 148–149
Strategic Defense Initiative (SDI) 19–20
strategy conference call 46–47, 115
Stromberg, Lotta 136
Strother, Candace 67
Studdert, Steve 161, 171–172
stump speech 181–182
subpoena 66
Sung Sing Theater 204
Supreme Court 175, 225
surrogates 17, 56, 58, 61, 78, 94, 103, 139
"the Swill Hole" 54, 101

Taittinger Blanc de Blanc champagne 40
Taiwan 204, 207
Task Force Five 228
tax evasion 214
tax experts 69, 119–120
tax returns 69–71, 76–83, 88, 92, 119–120, 143
Teele, Arthur E., Jr. 7, 52–*54*, 55–56, 59–71, 73, 77–78, 80, 82–83, 88–91, 94–97, 100, 103, 105–109, 114, 116–120, 122–123, 125–128, 133–136, 139–143, 146, 149, 155, 157–158, 165–170, 175–176, 190–192, 200–201, 203–204, 209, 211, 217, 223, 227–230; acquittal 229
Teele, Stephanie 10, 228–229

Teeley, Pete 188
Teeter, Robert M. 21, 42, 44–45, 63
television ads 21–22, 92, 115
terrorism 140, 182, 231
Terry, Grey 35–36
Texas 44, 66, 81–91
"Texas croquet set" 215
Thatcher, Margaret 43
Thayer Hotel 157, 166–167, 190
thirteen, unlucky 77, 130, 186
Thomas, Helen 68
Thurmond, Strom 198
Tibet 234
Tieg Corporation 211
Time magazine 35–36
tipsters 53, 59–60, 62, 64, 74, 76, 96–97, 126, 131, 150, 190, 203
Today Show 78
Toledo Express Airport 185
toothpaste commercials 111–112
Towery, Ken 66–67
tradecraft 2, 205
Trewhitt, Henry 195
Triads 152, 198–200, 205, 208–209
"trip photo" 22, 40
Trivial Pursuit 135
"troika" 16
SS troopers 35
Truman, Harry 171–172, 225
Trump, Donald J. 1, 3–4
"Tuesday Team" 21, 92, 124, 214
Turnipseed, Tom 61
Tutwiler, Margaret DeBardeleben 82, 104, 139, 179
TWA 24
TWA hostage crisis 224, 231
Twin Towers 166

Uighurs 232
Ukraine 232–233
Ukrainian Academy of Sciences 232
Ukrainian Foreign Ministry 232
Ukranian White House 232
"umbrella theme" 44
underboss 67, 85
Union City, New Jersey 99
Union Station 180
United Nations General Assembly 44
United Orient Bank 199, 203–204, 208, 223
United Press International (UPI) 68, 75, 123, 140
United States 22–24, 166, 207–209, 222
U.S. Ambassador to Ireland 227
U.S. Ambassador to Jamaica 227
U.S. Ambassador to United Nations Organizations 231
U.S. attorney 74, 221
U.S. Car One 171, 180–181, 183
U.S. Chamber of Commerce 113
U.S. Court of Appeals 225

Unitel 75, 136, 140, 152, 203
University of California, Irvine 32
Updike, John 81
Urban Mass Transit Administration (UMTA) 7, 54, 56, 100
urban renewal 175
Uricolb, Eugene 154
Utah 54
Utah Beach 26

Vacca, Rosina 153
Valis, Wayne 103–104
Vancouver, Canada 200
Vatican 47
vice-president, selection 44, 47–48, 50, 220, 224
Victory '84 celebration 217–218
Vienna, Austria 231
Vietnam 223
Vietnam veterans 25
Vietnam War 7–8, 25, 88
Vietnam War Memorial 25
Village Voice 48, 204–205, 208, 221–222
VIPs 185
Virginia 187
Virginia City, Nevada 148
Voices for Victory 49, 101
volunteers 74–75, 202, 227
voter registration 202
voter turnout 61, 78–79, 216–217

Wall Street 104, 226
Wall Street Journal 75, 85, 95, 130, 133, 142–143, 176, 211
Walsh, Erin 99, 101
Walsh, Lawrence 232–234
Walters, Barbara 159
war-monger, Reagan's image as 17
Warsaw Pact 18
Washington, Martha 1
Washington, D.C. 24, 42, 49, 69, 73, 92, 108, 110–111, 126–127, 133, 142, 157, 166, 198, 201, 205, 216, 224–226, 231, 234
Washington Hilton 38, 174
Washington Legal Foundation 76, 81, 83, 114, 116–117, 128, 130
Washington Monument 14
Washington Post 46, 76, 94–95, 132, 169, 187, 195, 214
Washington press corps 46
Washington Times 176, 212
Watergate 67, 114, 233
Waterside Plaza 204
Watson, Steve 118, 121
Watts, Doug 20–22, 124, 214, 231
Wedtech 224
Weinstein, Jon 121
Wells, Jeff 169, 188–189, 191–192
West Basement 172
West Parmenter Street 189

West Point 157, 165–166, 169, 220
West Wing 231
West Wing barbershop 117
Westminster College 171
"What You Don't Know About Ferraro and the Mob" 221–222
Wheaton College 123
Wheelspinners party 224
whistle stop tour 171–172, 175–186
whistleblower 126
White House 13–*15*, *20*–21, *51*, *55*, 68, 90, 93, 101, 108, 111, 117, 137, 159, 163, 166, 171–172, 174, 185, 208, 224–226, 231–232, 233–235
White House Communications Agency (WHCA) 28, 172
White House Counsel's Office 82
White House Office of Management and Budget(OMB) 112, 159
White House Office of Planning and Evaluation (OPE) 12–13, 16, 26, 231
White House Office of Policy Development 231
White House Office of Political Affairs 82, 224
White House Office of Political and Governmental Affairs 231
White House Office of Presidential Advance 22, 35, 37, 161, 171–172
White House Office of Presidential Speechwriting 13, 42, 111, 161–162
White House Press Office 33
White House press pool 173–174

White House staff 27–28, 112, 139, 162, 173, 175
white papers 94, 109, 114
White Tigers 154
Wicker, Tom 162
William the Conqueror 31
Williams, David 198–200
Williams, JoBeth 18
Williams, Robin 64
Wirthlin, Richard B. 14–15, 21, 46–47, 54, 60, 69, 76, 111–112, 211, 216, 218
Wirthlin's strategic dilemma 62–63, 78, 84
woman for vice president 36, 44, 48
women voters 60, 66, 78–79, 145, 218
Womens Army Corps 35
Wong, David 154
World Bank 226
World War II 24, 31, 33, 35, 61, 66, 114, 124, 207
"World Wide Web" 234
Wright Patterson Air Force Base 172
Wyoming 42, 94

Zacarro, Frank 150–151, 206
Zacarro, John 4, 51, 64–65, 68, 76, 102, 119, 126, 130–131, 150–152, 154–157, 193–194, 197, 204, 206, 211, 222 guilty plea 221–222
Zaccaro, Philip 130, 133, 147, 150, 154, 193–194, 199, 206
Zaccaro, Rose 153
Zippo 111
Zirinsky, Susan 26–27, 94